POPULAR CULTURE AND PERFORMANCE IN THE VICTORIAN CITY

This lively and highly innovative book reconstructs the texture and meaning of popular pleasure in the Victorian entertainment industry. Integrating theories of language and social action with close reading of contemporary sources, Peter Bailey provides a richly detailed study of the pub, music-hall, theatre and comic newspaper. Analysis of the interplay between entrepreneurs, performers, social critics and audience reveals distinctive codes of humour, sociability and glamour that constituted a new populist ideology of consumerism and the good time. Bailey shows how the new leisure world offered a repertoire of roles that enabled its audience to negotiate the unsettling encounters of urban life. The book offers challenging interpretations of respectability, sexuality, and the cultural politics of class and gender in a distinctive, personal voice.

POPULAR CULTURE AND PERFORMANCE IN THE VICTORIAN CITY

PETER BAILEY

CAMBRIDGE
UNIVERSITY PRESS

PUBLISHED BY THE PRESS SYNDICATE OF THE UNIVERSITY OF CAMBRIDGE
The Pitt Building, Trumpington Street, Cambridge, United Kingdom

CAMBRIDGE UNIVERSITY PRESS
The Edinburgh Building, Cambridge CB2 2RU, UK   http://www.cup.cam.ac.uk
40 West 20th Street, New York, NY 10011–4211, USA   http://www.cup.org
10 Stamford Road, Oakleigh, Melbourne 3166, Australia
Ruiz de Alarcón 13, 28014 Madrid, Spain

First published 1998
Reprinted 2000

Printed in the United Kingdom at the University Press, Cambridge

Typeset in Baskerville 11/12.5 pt [VN]

A catalogue record for this book is available from the British Library

ISBN 0 521 57417 x hardback

For Bonnie and Steve

Contents

Illustrations

Acknowledgments

Paradoxically, writing is both a solitary endeavour and one undertaken in the numerous company of that disembodied audience which crowds the mental gallery above the scholar's desk – friends, enemies, rival authorities, great names, maybe a favourite aunt or two – variously murmuring encouragement, sneering dissent or frowning in incomprehension. Happily a number of these imagined voices have taken on a more personal presence, materialising as friends and collaborators whom I am pleased to thank for their help in several ways in the production and accumulation of the essays in this book. Since my graduate days at the University of British Columbia I have enjoyed the warm support of James Winter and James Hammerton (*les deux jims*). At the University of Manitoba, the Department of History has proved a most congenial and supportive body of colleagues, tolerant of my frequent absences and chronic Winniphobia. Among the students I thank the 'Bailey Boys' (of both sexes) for enlivening my seminars. The Victorian Studies Association of Western Canada has provided a stimulating audience for the debut of several pieces in this collection as papers at its annual conferences. Among others from this agreeable collective I am particularly grateful to Chris Kent, UM colleagues Bob O'Kell and Arlene Young, Avril Torrance, Ian Dyck and my former student Chris Hosgood for their interest and encouragement over the years. Elsewhere I have learned a lot in the friendly company of a younger generation of historians, notably Chris Waters (a fellow cultural schizophrenic), Judith Allen, Rohan McWilliam, and James Vernon, who volunteered helpful comments on the Introduction. I thank John Earl and David Cheshire for generous instruction on music halls. Joel Kaplan, Sheila Stowell, and Jackie Bratton in particular have been ever-ready friends and collaborators in theatre history, and David Kunzle has shared my enthusiasm for Ally Sloper. Working on the margins (in more than one sense) I have been greatly encouraged by the

positive interest of Don Gray, Leonore Davidoff, Patrick Joyce, and
Judith Walkowitz. Among other supporters, knowing or otherwise, I
thank Ken Hughes, Ruth Richardson and Brian Hurwitz, Dagmar and
Roy Kift, Tony and Wendy Brennan. I must also record my appreciation of the company at Dave's Deli and University College who have
greatly enriched my excursions into vulgar culture. For secretarial help I
am grateful to Debra Kirby and, a most amiable and efficient conspirator, Helen Osman. It has also been a pleasure to work with Victoria
Cooper, my editor at Cambridge University Press. Finally I am much
beholden to the Social Sciences and Humanities Research Council of
Canada for their generous financial support over the years: thank you
indeed.

With the exception of the Introduction, the chapters in this book have
previously appeared as articles or essays and I am grateful for permission to reprint them. Chapter 1 appeared in *Victorian Studies* 21
(Autumn 1977, Indiana University Press); chapter 2 in *Journal of Social
History* 12 (Spring 1979); chapter 3 in *History Workshop Journal* 16 (Autumn
1983, Oxford University Press); chapter 4 in Peter Bailey (ed.), *Music
Hall: The Business of Pleasure*, (Open University Press, 1986); chapter 5 in J.
S. Bratton (ed.), *Music Hall: Performance and Style*, (Open University Press),
1986; chapter 6 in *Past and Present* 144 (August 1994) World Copyright:
The Past and Present Society, 175 Banbury Road, Oxford, England;
chapter 7 in *Gender and History* 2 (Summer 1990); chapter 8 in Michael
Booth and Joel Kaplan (eds.), *The Edwardian Theatre: Essays on Performance
and the Stage*, (Cambridge University Press, 1996); chapter 9 in *Body and
Society* 2 (June 1996).

The illustrations on pp. 78 and 135 are reproduced by permission of
the Royal Photographic Society and the British Library respectively.

Introduction
Social history, cultural studies and the cad

It gives me great pleasure (as the music-hall chairman would have said) to introduce this collection of essays. Written over some twenty years they represent an enthusiastic if occasionally bemused journey along the shifting frontiers of social history; sometimes, it pleases me to think, in touch with the vanguard, at other times mopping up or consolidating with the second wave. Metaphors of the journey and a frontier landscape come readily to someone who has spent his career in geographical isolation on the Canadian prairies, those of skirmish and embattlement are appropriate for anyone traversing the contested terrain of British social history. To give more specific context to this collection and its author I begin with a brief overview of this terrain, a familiar enough story to many, but one that bears retelling from a personal perspective.

Social history, we are now advised, is in crisis, a chronic state of affairs compared to the heady days of the 1960s when I first enlisted.[1] Having shed its previous largely inferior status as a merely residual category, social history was then confidently addressing a new and more demanding agenda, together with a new and more demanding methodology. Hitherto neglected but significant groups, notably working people, were to be the proper subjects of full historical recovery, an exercise facilitated by closer engagement with the other social sciences. An earnest native empiricism was to be leavened with interdisciplinary insights and directed at the great swathe of historical experience ignored by establishment history with its narrow formal emphasis on politics and economics. Prominent in the new expeditionary corps of seekers of 'the social' was a cadre from the New Left inspired by the youngish Old Bustard, E. P. Thompson. The project was a radical challenge to orthodoxy with a totalising vision of how a new social history could grasp the workings of a whole society.

An important concern in this redefined social history was culture. This too was a redefined category expanded beyond the elitist confines of 'the best that has been thought and said' to embrace the ordinary and the popular. It was from this more anthropological perspective that Raymond Williams as literary critic urged the study of culture as 'a whole way of life' in terms of 'its structures of thought and feeling'. Both Williams and Thompson invested culture and its human subjects with a significant measure of power or agency, limited but by no means superseded by the economic or material constraints of society and its dominant class. This new cultural materialism encouraged historians to reconstruct popular or working-class culture as a vital force in the making of class identity and its political expression, a process most directly understood by connecting with the lived experience of its participants. Williams and Thompson were also inspirational figures in the formation of the complementary new field of cultural studies. A pioneer institution, the Birmingham Centre for Contemporary Cultural Studies, was founded by another literary scholar, Richard Hoggart, whose sympathetic readings of working-class culture were also important for social historians. Insistently interdisciplinary, cultural studies in general gave critical priority to the popular culture of the day and became more aggressively theorised and political. For those on the left, culture was the pursuit of the political by other means.[2]

Cultural studies in the seventies became a major conduit for continental theory in the form of various 'structuralisms' that generated intense debate on the left and soon impinged on mainstream academia. The structures discernible to writers like Althusser and Foucault were more insidious and oppressive than those of Williams' earlier rather hazy humanist 'structures of feeling'. The first and ultimate structure was language, a predetermined force shaped by the dominant ideology and 'always, already' there. 'Language speaks us' – rather than the other way round – was the most forbidding proposition of the new theory. Other work on the primacy of language contributed to the so-called 'linguistic turn' which had a strong impact on conceptions of culture. Thus culture was further redefined as signifying practice, such that all its phenomena could now be read on the model of language as so many coded texts constructed from a repertoire of signs in particular structures of meanings. These structures could also take the form of discourse or a deployment of language identified by Foucault as an expert 'knowledge' that defined the power of special interest groups. Barthes demonstrated how the linguistic or semiotic model of culture could be extended beyond the written and the verbal to decode the meaning of a wrestling match or steak and chips.

At the same time as the structuralist incursion, in tandem yet in conflict, came the eruption of critical feminism. In social history as elsewhere, more or less comfortably angry young men were assailed by much angrier women protesting against the languages and practices that had constructed them as subordinates in the academy as throughout history. The voices and vocabularies of vanguard scholarship continued in ferment – 'Keep it complex!' was one slogan from Birmingham. By the eighties Derrida and other literary-cum-psychological theorists of both genders were being saluted (or reviled) as 'post-structuralists' engaged in the yet more challenging practice of 'deconstruction'. The very concept of structure was attacked as too rigidly ordered to comprehend the endless fluidity of all signs and meanings. If all the world was now a text, it was a text without a centre. Another radical critical mode was that of post-colonialism which questioned ethnic and national identities and emphasised the otherness of post-imperial peoples. The fragmentation of meaning and the blurring of categories emphasised by the post structuralists is now taken to be typical of our present day 'post-modern' world such that the two terms are becoming interchangeable. Indeed, all the theories and developments outlined above – the discovery of culture, the linguistic turn, the brawling clutch of structuralisms, critical feminism – are likely to be badged indiscriminately as post-modernism.

Social historians' engagement with the new learning has been contentious and incomplete. Thompson, who had opened up the study of culture and alerted historians to the significance of language in his own distinctive manner, vigorously resisted continental theory. There were heated confrontations between those like himself, the 'culturalists', who read culture as an oppositional medium, and structuralists who took a bleaker, more determinist view. Gramsci's theories found considerable favour, since his model of hegemony posited an uneasy and recomposing process of cultural articulation in which the dynamics of resistance and domination were in continual negotiation. By the early eighties, Stedman Jones, one of the most prominent of post-Thompsonian historians in nineteenth-century British studies, was urging a fuller engagement with language as the beginning of the social chain, exemplified in his reconsideration of class in discursive rather than sociological terms.[3]

More recently Patrick Joyce has taken up the van with his promotion of a new post-modern social history. Struggling like a latterday Laocoon to divest himself of the received wisdom on class and class consciousness, he has argued for the existence of other powerful collective social identities discernible in the several populist discourses that constructed meanings in the lives of nineteenth-century working people. In a further restless questioning of social history practice Joyce has moved on to deconstruct collective identities through an investigation of subjectivity, or the making of the individual self whose identity is mutually determined in interaction with 'the social' or the collectivity of selves. For Joyce, identity, individual and collective, is primarily a cultural construct constituted by language as deployed in symbolic narratives, of which class is only one among the many told by and to ourselves. Storied language rather than the material 'facts' of social being is what structures experience. This experience is reconceived more circumspectly as another form of representation rather than the voice of an authentic reality. The determinist note is redeemed by an insistence on the creative act of language which can enable the historical actor – and ourselves – to remake meaning. If language is a prison, as some maintain, we can nonetheless flex the bars – or change prisons. Thus agency lives, though with difficulty. The message of post-modernist thought, according to Joyce, 'is immensely liberating, but immensely troubling'.[4]

Within the profession there are many who are neither liberated, threatened, nor likely to think in these terms, as the post-modern intrusion is met with either disdain or indifference. History has in general been among the more conservative disciplines in its response to radical new thinking, and social history in Britain, for all it was born in dissent, has long since established its own comfortable protocols, not that very different from previous practice.[5] It attends to neglected areas, it tries to make connections and realise a sense of the whole; but it is still stolidly empirical, minimally reflexive, wary of theorising, and only timidly engaged with other disciplines. Problems of epistemology scarcely intrude. Historians, it is maintained, have always approached texts with scepticism, are well-schooled in close reading, and have always been alert to sub-texts or reading between the lines. They may not be as sublimely confident as Lord Acton of resolving all historical questions, but they know their job and they get on with it in largely unproblematical fact-rich production. They might add that much of the language of the new linguistically alert scholarship is impenetrable, a mix of the abstruse and the banal. At one end of the scale reified categories like 'the social' and 'the popular' march numbingly across the page, while at the other end particularist studies become so involuted in the mining of meaning that they disappear up their own text.

Yet what amounts to a new politics of knowledge is hardly likely to go away, not least in its critique of the issue that has dominated the agenda of modern social history in Britain – the social and material reality of class. Sapped by gender and race, class now seems about to collapse into mere difference, a master (*sic*) category on its last legs. Social identity, we are now told, starts with the self, a multiple subject constructed by language, culture and the symbolic system, a self for whom class may be one narrative thread among many, for whom work and material exist-ence may be less significant than consumption and life style. Class is an imagined community competing with other collective identities for the allegiance of an overdetermined subject.[6]

Class is a strong theme in many of the essays collected here, over-stated no doubt in the earlier ones, but still a plausible enough proposi-tion where its operations are situated in specific positions and exchanges among social actors. If class is largely an imagined or invented phenom-enon then it must still be imagined or invented out of some thing or things which include material being or experience, however represen-ted. In the later essays I have taken more account of gender and recomposing fractional identities in the crowd, but the mark of class sticks like a burr in nineteenth-century society and remains among the more potent vectors of difference, however indeterminate or relativised. Even so, the reconception of class as an imaginary or discursive con-struct is richly suggestive, not least when applied to historians as well as history.

Social history since the sixties, I would argue, has been preoccupied with class because it is itself the product of class. The project recruited heavily from the first generations of beneficiaries of the 1944 Education Act, for whom a university education and the prospect of university or polytechnic employment was unprecedented in the experience of their (pardon me) class. Uneasily and incompletely embourgeoised they took up social history and its privileging of the working class from a mix of retrospective political commitment, class guilt, and various other inse-curities – social, masculine and professional. Thompson's writings of-fered an epic model whose many replications in tone provided a purpos-ive and moralised narrative for lesser class crusaders. In pursuit of class truths, social history became a comradely endeavour; gentlemanly in-itials (preferably three) were superseded by so many Geoffs and Daves. Either lacking or suspicious of established forms of cultural capital, the lumpenpolytechnic, as it was unkindly badged, found its own voice. Stirring and fruitful though it was, this fundamentally redemptive exercise inevitably overloaded the class reading of history. If social history is now in crisis, it is a mid-life crisis among a generation of petit bourgeois males for whom an explanation, a vindication of self through the surrogate and collective identity of class has been ambushed by gender, confounded by Thatcher, and sapped by a new intellectual scepticism. The search for the true self turns inward, displaced into a new history and a new language, its personal imperatives still mostly under wraps. The fall of class is a fall from class, though nostalgia for the old categories still shows and old insecurities still surface – one champion of the new learning confides wryly that he feels more secondary modern than post-modern.

This collection is informed by its own personal narrative, in uneasy dialogue with the larger generational story. Brought up in the 1950s in a respectable working-class family, I was converted into a petty bourgeois at grammar school. 'Bailey is a gentleman', wrote the headmaster in his letter of reference for Oxford, conferring both accolade and curse that have proved difficult to live down or up to. Intimidated yet entranced by Oxford's savoir faire I pursued the authentic self in two opposite directions at once. With no very sound credentials I played the unreconstructed prole – 'What a dull life', observed a Wykhamist, 'drinking beer, throwing darts and saying fuck.' At the same time I learned how to tie a bowtie and give plausible impersonations of the true bourgeois gentilhomme. I was, of course, no more than a vulgar pretender, a descendant of that despicable Victorian type, the cad, though as yet a cad without the courage of his (lack of) convictions. Drink eased the perplexities of the immature self, perplexities more than anger, for its disablements seemed a consequence of personal deficiency as much as of cultural dislocation. An uncertain revenge was exacted in small ways – a yobbish campaign to disestablish the college beagle pack, desultory vandalism, throwing up on an old Etonian. Temperamentally averse to formal politics and guilty for not having been truly oppressed, I assumed an heroic class alias in history, a safely distanced role reinforced by geography as I left England for Canada, less the organic intellectual than a petit bourgeois place seeker masquerading as academic flaneur.

Distance also gave me space to find my own voice in history and scholarship. In graduate study at the University of British Columbia, I moved away from the heavily inhabited terrains of work and politics to a personally more congenial field of experience, leisure (chapter 1, below). And I fell into bad company. There was indeed plenty of class conflict in Victorian leisure, but its working-class combatants often seemed to me more wily and opportunist than Fabian respectables or the forthright ideologues of Thompsonian descent. Bill Banks (chapter 2) suggested the readiness with which working men could turn the tables on their betters by the calculated performance of different roles that exploited the fragmented milieu of big city life. On this model I recast stolid English workers as a shifty lot, 'playing the system and winning back small but relishable gains in a class war gone underground.'[7] There was of course a good deal of personal projection in this but in Canada (teaching at the University of Manitoba) I was also benefiting from the perspective of a more detached middle ground, alert to the echoes of neo-Marxist debates from the homeland while exposed to American urban sociology and symbolic interactionism from across the border. Thus I was discovering what in Gramscian terms was a war of position rather than a war of movement by borrowing from Goffman to reconstruct the micro-politics of personal encounter, mediating between theories of class consciousness and the situational specifics of a more mobile modern consciousness. This early application of behavioural models of modernity (anticipating today's fashionable interest by nearly twenty years) did however put me at odds with the orthodoxies of the new social history in Britain for whom transatlantic sociology was then highly suspect, its liberal norms and language of 'modernisation' derided as another form of American imperialism. Bill Banks was turned down by the newest British journal in the field, whose pinched response belied its public call for enterprising scholarship; he was warmly welcomed in North America.

Looking back now it is plain that not only was Bill Banks the first of a sequence of cultural anti-heroes (and alter egos) but that he and they are complicit with another anti-hero, the modern city, though this too was to depart from the accepted perceptions of British historians. Homegrown social history still represents the rapidly expanding nineteenth-century city as proving ground for the native popular genius in maintaining community in a seeming social wasteland.[8] While there is undoubtedly evidence for this, it neglects the extensive dislocations of urban life as part of the more general onset of modernity where this is understood not only as the rationalising agenda of government and industry but as a fluid behavioural field and particular quality of experience. By this reading (as much continental European as transatlantic) the security of the putative 'urban village' dissolves into what Judith Walkowitz, the American historian of 1880s London, calls 'a cityscape of strangers and secrets'. This is the city as heterotopia, where cads of both sexes can flourish, a world bristling with others that generates both opportunity and anxiety.9

There were certainly other less than sterling chaps exploiting the modern city and its new sites as a stage on which to play out bravura presentations of self, notably the impressively crapulous cartoon marauder Ally Sloper (chapter 3) and the first music-hall superstar, George Leybourne as Champagne Charlie (chapter 5). This work was increasingly influenced by a burgeoning interpretive literature in cultural studies and what amounted to a new cultural history with a particular investment in anthropology and the study of mentalities (chapter 4). I was encouraged by the eclectic enthusiasms of Raphael Samuel and History Workshop and was excited by the sophisticated primers published by the Open University to accompany its course in popular culture OU 203. From these and other sources I learned more about the multiple meanings of popular forms and everyday life, how to take apart the taken for granted, the significance of style and surface, processes of appropriation and exchange between cultural fractions, the reach of power and ideology, the function of discourse and interpellation – and modern subjectivity. Thus I was further initiated into 'theory', though this is being rather pretentious since it was a matter of fitful and oblique engagement rather than full frontal embrace. How much time and intellectual energy should be invested in a frequently, often literally alien literature in competition with the historian's hallowed duty to his sources? Direct invocation of new gods was tentative, witness an early allusion to Barthes (chapter 5) revealing my own facetious English disdain for extravagant 'foreign' ideas.

In the same piece I was still trying to reconcile my tricksters and anti-heroes with conventional categories as I strove to prove Leybourne's Champagne Charlie 'authentically' working-class, a conclusion at odds with the hybrid persona I had just been deconstructing. For all Leybourne's egregious appropriations of the apparatus of the gentleman (what had his headmaster said to him?) I was less confident in an unequivocally oppositional reading of music hall and the agency of its actors and audiences. As a laboratory of style whose patrons went there to learn how to conduct themselves as competent moderns, music hall validated the extended metaphor of the city as theatre; in the audience as well as on stage its social actors assumed and switched roles in the psychic and performative traffic of alternative identities – a kind of cultural cross-dressing. While such improvisations offered sometimes critical alternatives to ascribed social roles they suggested too the anxieties and ambiguities that undercut the performance of identity. The 'knowingness' that informed music-hall humour (chapter 6) offered a language of competence that might give a worldly gloss to the (re)presentation of self and subvert official prescriptions of respectability, yet its confident tropes could also be unstable and self-deceiving. While appropriately dramatic, the sociological model of role-playing used in reading Bill Banks now seems too tidy in its functionalist assumptions of an inherent equilibrium and a singular core self with which all role performances are reconcilable. As modern subjects the social actors of this milieu are better understood as the transient tenants of various and competing subject positions, each a multiple-self unevenly defined in collusive antithesis with the dominant cultural order.

Enter gender and sexuality, or 'Champagne Charlie Meets the Barmaid'. Though much more disturbing elements in the formation of individual and collective identities, these factors had been marginalised or ignored in social history while earnest blokes like myself worried away at class. Feminist scholarship provoked sustained attention to the differences of gender, turning the tables on the male as the more problematical other. The study of the barmaid (chapter 7) tackles the question of gendered identities in popular culture, demonstrating with the aid of visual texts how the spatial and visual dynamics of the modernised Victorian pub were so managed to create a new mode of profitable yet licit sexuality that I term 'parasexuality'. If this was manifestly a male positioning of the woman it also reveals the male hunger for emotional recognition from the woman that new capitalist regimes of pleasure both served and frustrated. These structures of stimulation and containment have a particular personal resonance to a survivor of a 1950s adolescence who is still working to understand and expunge strongly residual Victorian sexual norms. For me, the firm injunction that 'Nice girls don't' (though barmaids might) always carried the corollary that 'Nice boys shouldn't', setting up a powerful internal struggle between the prig and the cad. Similar tensions informed the brokered sexuality that underlay the otherwise sanitised narratives of musical comedy (chapter 8), a richly suggestive new middlebrow genre of the 1890s with ambiguous representations of the woman as 'girl' – the girl who was 'naughty but nice'.

More than one of the pieces in this collection registers in passing a persistent but mostly unexamined property and, indeed, resource of popular culture – noise. One should not have to listen too hard to recognise that noise was not merely incidental but central to the pleasure or displeasure of contemporaries, to whom it also served as a metaphor for the modern city in all its pullulating density. The concluding chapter attempts to open up the study of the cultural phenomenon of sound with a brief history of (Victorian) noise. While at one level this offers an entirely proper corrective to historians for overprivileging seeing and looking to the neglect of hearing and listening, it might also be heard as a parting shot at the pious keepers of the professional tone who still patrol British academic life. Historians as well as history should be noisier.

'Know thyself' is an ancient injunction with which most of us would concur, while adding the hasty rider 'but keep it to thyself'. Objective knowledge and professional good manners demand the erasure of any explicit self. Yet the selves are surfacing. For feminists the often painful release of the personal has been a crucial exercise in staking out identity and recovering the history of an oppressed sex. But for men also, however privileged in gender power, there is a need to reconcile or oppose the troubled self and its histories with received accounts and their approved historical others. There is precedent too in the important function of autobiography for Thompson and other male 'founders' of cultural studies. The prospect of a rush of middle-aged scholarly flashers is unsettling, but as social history seeks to conflate the social and the psychic and reconstruct collectivities through a fuller understanding of the subject, some form of self-witnessing seems to be a necessary instruction and a likely resource for its practitioners.[10]

The pieces that follow appear mostly in their original published form. Though each can be read separately, some minor additions have been made to assist continuity plus some small changes from the original sequence of production to provide greater thematic coherence. References have been updated. Overall, the collection moves from an initial concern with the more formal perceptions and prescriptions attending the formation of the Victorians' new leisure world to questions of popular practice and meaning.

Popular culture is conceived of here as a sprawling hybrid, a generically eclectic ensemble or repertoire of texts, sites and practices that constitute a widely shared social and symbolic resource. In the nineteenth century it is increasingly colonised by emergent culture industries, a rogue branch of liberal capitalism whose operations may at one and the same time match or surpass the Fordist or Taylorist aspirations of manufacturing industry, while retaining a populist address akin to the pseudo-gemeinschaft of the publican and the prostitute. These industries – the new pub, the music hall, the theatre, and the popular press –

compete with each other, territorially and rhetorically, as also with the state and other respectable fractions of the social order. The constituency for popular culture fluctuates and recomposes; while not coterminous with any single class it is broadly democratic, answering both to the ritual promptings of an indigenous custom, old and newly forged, and the slicker formulations of mass or middlebrow commercial confection. It generates its own initiatives while readily appropriating from other sources, including 'high' or elite culture. Its materials are put to specific and selective use by its consumers, who variously embrace, modify or resist its meanings under the particular conditions and relationships of its reception.

The culture of working people at the core of popular culture has, largely on the sample of the industrial town or proletarian ghetto, been characterised as 'a culture of control', exercising, in Hoggart's words, 'a certain gripping wholeness'. But there were clearly other more dynamic dimensions to popular experience, typified by De Certeau's compelling metaphor of modern life as lived out in 'the ciphered river of the streets', to which we should add other urban sites and situations in which the membrane of custom and community dissolves and meanings are much less certainly known.[11] From an interactive perspective that allows for a more volatile mix of players, real and imaginary, than those of the self-enclosed working-class neighbourhood, nineteenth-century popular culture can be understood as a performance culture no less than those of early modern or 'traditional' societies that have more readily qualified for the term among historians and cultural anthropologists. Compared to the latter's more formally ritualised and communal occasions, its social dramas are, however, more often situational, improvisatory and individualised. This is a culture that trades in carnivalesque echoes of excess and inversion, grand utopian conceits of a permanent democracy of pleasure and the emotionalised myths of melodrama in which the good and the true prevail. But in less extravagant or formalised terms it also deals extensively in the tactics of the diurnal, in the micro-politics and implicit knowledges of everyday life, their rehearsal and critique. Its meanings, like its satisfactions, are ambiguous and far from always benign, mixing the reactionary and conservative with the potentially subversive.

Attention to language and the imaginary offers one route to a fuller understanding of the dynamics of popular culture and their implications for politics and power in the broader sense, though this exercise needs that careful grounding in the specific and the contextual – rigour without rigor mortis – which is still the necessary and distinctive contribution of the historian. This is uncharacteristically earnest talk from a cad, but in its crisis social history has become exciting again, suggesting a new history from the inside as well as from below, with the prospect of a more intimate understanding of its actors, and of ourselves.

CHAPTER I

The Victorian middle class and the problem of leisure

'Let us then consent to a little unharnessing from the go-carts of life.' By 1864, when this appeal was made in a progressive periodical addressing itself to 'The Philosophy of Amusement', such concern for the place of recreation in modern life was less a protest against some begrudging spirit of the times, than a recognition of the greatly expanded world of middle-class leisure.[1] The vigorous growth of this new leisure world impressed itself on contemporaries from the mid-century, forcing acknowledgment from the gravest of witnesses. Commenting on 'modern amusements' on 20 June 1876, a lead article in *The Times* remarked:

The space we ourselves are from time to time compelled to surrender to this class of subject is in itself not the least proof of the importance they have attained . . . a mingled mass of perfectly legitimate pleasures ever thrusting themselves forward in a variety of shapes, some known, some unknown, to our more easily contented ancestors, and all together making continually increasing demands upon our time, upon our money, and not least, upon our strength and powers of endurance.

While the querulous tone was part of the house style on such matters, the note of discomfiture was echoed in numerous other writings, and it is clear that the advent of modern leisure had a disturbing impact on middle-class sensibilities, particularly in the mid-Victorian years upon which this essay is focused. It has been well said that the problem of leisure for most commentators is the problem of other people's leisure, and historically this issue has been debated with almost exclusive reference to its manifestations in the life of the working class.[2] This perspective ignores the fact that the first and most substantial modern beneficiaries of the hitherto aristocratic privilege of leisure were the middle classes. It was their uneasy initiation into its new freedoms (and constraints) that did much to define Western society's perceptions of leisure as a problem and to colour the prescriptive discussion of its proper role in the life of others.

I

Leisure and its enjoyments were hardly a mid-Victorian invention, but contemporaries were frequently moved to draw a contrast between the more abundant leisure of their own day and the meagre commons of previous decades. In the eighteenth century the middle classes in London and the older provincial centres of England had enjoyed a cultural life of considerable vigour and sociability, and many of its institutions, if not its original élan, had survived into the early-Victorian period.[3] In the new towns too, middle-class life had not been all jejune: a Bolton lawyer who took articles in the 1830s recalled that hard work had taken its reward in leisure hours enlivened by a constant round of amateur dramatics, discussion clubs, much dancing, singing, and athletic exercise, together with the relaxations of fireside and garden.[4] Such a life-style could not have been unique to John Taylor, but the more general recollection of middle and late Victorians was of an immediate past that was grey and joyless. 'We must remember,' wrote the novelist Walter Besant, 'how very little play went on even among the comfortable and opulent classes in those days . . . dullness and a serious view of life seemed inseparable.' In response to the pressures of the Industrial and French Revolutions, utilitarian and evangelical disciplines had severely restricted the gratifications of leisure; as Eric Hobsbawm has remarked, the Victorian bourgeoisie had had their own 'Bleak Age' to endure.[5]

Relief came with greater economic security and the time and services that it could buy. By the 1850s the disquieting fluctuations that had characterised the economy of previous decades had levelled out; men who had weathered the exigencies of those years could afford to rest awhile on a comfortable plateau of prosperity, accompanied by wives whose domestic duties were taken care of by a growing army of servants. Constant attention to business was no longer necessary for the successful; contentious major political issues no longer bit into their time, and a mellowing process suffused their lives. We may take the Ashworth brothers of Bolton as an example. In the 1840s they had struggled through a period of uncertain profits and imperilled their business by their preoccupation with the Anti-Corn Law League; in the fifties they felt secure enough to delegate the running of their mill to subordinates and to allow themselves a series of travelling holidays.[6]

As the mid-Victorian period unfolded, the pursuit of leisure won an increasing number of devotees, for it was not only master manufacturers who enjoyed the new bounty, but the lesser lights in a middle class that was becoming both more numerous and more prosperous. Henry Mayhew sought to represent a new middle-class type in his account of Cockayne, a very minor captain of industry, but one whose thirty-five years in command of a soap factory in Clapham had earned him a trip to Paris.[7] This was in the 1860s, by which time the diffusion of leisure among the middle classes was plain to all. Its reach continued to widen throughout the period, as T. H. S. Escott observed some twenty years later:

A social movement quite as remarkable as that which has been going forward among the better portion of the English middle class, has been taking place, and is now steadily progressing on a lower social stratum. This class would once have been called the small shopkeeper class, and its present condition is almost the growth of yesterday . . . Only the commercial prosperity of England could have generated the new order from which the chief patrons of theatres and outdoor amusements are drawn.[8]

There were always new recruits for the single-minded pursuit of money, but the second or later generations of successful business and professional families were less disposed to answer its exclusive imperatives. The younger Gurneys of Norwich were 'rather more inclined to stand before the fire with their hands in the fronts of very good riding breeches' than to attend daily at the bank.[9] The *Saturday Review* remarked in the sixties how rapidly the 'habit of enjoyment' had spread among the young. 'It is,' the journal maintained, 'an axiom with many young people that they have a right to be always amused, or to be always going to be amused.'[10] Certainly the middle-class young (of whom more were surviving into early adulthood) enjoyed more free time than their elders had done. The increasing emphasis upon public school and, to a lesser extent, university education as indispensable requirements for middle-class gentility meant a prolonged freedom from the immediate pressures of earning a living. Eventually put to work in the family firm, but advised to defer marriage until he achieved an independent competence, the son and heir often continued to exploit the generosity of the paterfamilias – 'stretching his legs under the governor's mahogany', as the popular phrase had it – and apply himself more to play than business. This much is clear from a lively debate on the young man of the day in the correspondence columns of the *Daily Telegraph* in the late sixties.[11] Though her options were much more limited, the young unmarried woman also had more leisure time at her disposal.

The 'habit of enjoyment' flourished most conspicuously in the metropolis, yet in varying degrees the expansion of leisure appears to have enlivened middle-class society across the country.[12] The diffusion and encouragement of the new appetite was greatly assisted by major improvements in communications. By the early fifties the major lines in the British rail system were completed or under construction, and rail travel both stimulated a general public curiosity and helped to break down regional insularities of mind and practice. Of equal importance in dissipating the tedium of England's Coketowns and Dulboroughs was the growth of the cheap press and the increase in newspaper advertising. Escott recorded the effects thus: 'The cheap press . . . has transformed the severely domesticated Briton of both sexes, of all ages, who belonged to a bygone generation, into an eager, actively enquiring, socially omniscient citizen of the world, ever on the outlook for new excitements, habitually demanding social pleasure in fresh forms.'[13]

The forms that this new social pleasure took have been made familiar enough to us, and there is no need here to offer a detailed inventory.[14] Certainly a great deal took place within the ambit of the home and family, though public amenities and amusements were also expanding. Recreation out-of-doors revealed a growing predilection for physical exercise, and the strainings of amateur athletes and part-time soldiers in turn generated new leisure festivals for the whole family. The railway excursion offered fresh opportunities for recreational travel and increased the range of the family vacation at a time when the annual holiday was becoming a permanent feature of middle-class leisure expectations.

II

The new leisure did not, however, afford its practitioners complete and unalloyed delight. Analysing the palsied progress of a middle-class dinner party, Anthony Trollope concluded that the pursuit of leisure in England was as laborious, affected, and dull as most foreign observers had persistently made it out to be, and Jean Froissart's ancient tag – 'They take their pleasures sadly, after their fashion' – became a frequently paraded cliché among the other numerous contemporary critics of the English at play.[15] Yet the same commentaries also reveal that the Victorians were suffering from something more than some vague congenital Gothic melancholia, for their problem of leisure was a many-sided one, which reflected the new and complex patterns of a modern society.

In the first place, the Victorians were discovering that recreation in the railway age meant planning and preparation; timetables – Bradshaw's was first published in 1839, with monthly supplements from 1841 – meant an increasing preoccupation with time budgeting and the coordination of people and services. Some members of society, it is true, refused to be intimidated by such constraints. There is, for example, the pleasing if apocryphal story of a young sprig of the nobility bent upon catching a train to Manchester, who arrived at the London terminal to be informed by the stationmaster that the Manchester train had in fact just left. 'Well,' said his lordship, unmoved, 'Bwing me another!' A further exercise in the grand manner is attributed to Richard Burton, the explorer: reading in his London home of some exotic tribe or people who had escaped his attention, he would, so one of his modern biographers tells us, depart immediately for the new terra incognita, pausing only to shout to his hapless wife, 'Pay, pack and follow!'[16] For the majority of heads of households, however, mobilising the family and its impedimenta for an excursion or annual vacation must have been a great deal less expeditious. In another of its frequent moments of disenchantment with the modern 'holyday', *The Times* emphasised the tension this involved: 'It is work, and it is tiring work . . . it entails a perpetual attention to time, and all the anxieties and irritations of that responsibility'.[17]

Men were not freed of such anxieties and irritations when they arrived at the haven of a holiday or other place or occasion for legitimate ease, for as creatures of an industrial society they continued to be governed by its insistence on the precise and purposive ordering of time. Leisure was haunted by the imperatives of a rigid work discipline, as the *Saturday Review* pointed out:

The results of the man's whole mode of life, the almost instinctive disposition to proceed methodically in the laying out of one's time . . . may prove fatal to the enjoyment of leisure. People trained to habits of order and punctuality, and to the most scrupulous employment of every moment are not fitted for the easy careless attitude of the holidaymaker.

Herein lay a considerable constraint upon relaxation or spontaneity – 'There is', maintained the *Saturday Review*, 'a sort of mechanical style in our joys.'[18]

A further major tension derived from the endemic status anxiety of the middle classes, for leisure represented a new and relatively unstructured area in the life-space where social distinctions were particularly vulnerable. The infiltration of social undesirables into the leisure circle at home could be controlled by the increasingly sophisticated access rituals surrounding the calling card, but greater dangers lay abroad.[19] Contemplating the progress of modern leisure, *The Times*, 30 August 1860, discerned the makings of 'a great revolution . . . great displacement of masses, momentous changes of level'. In an article written in the sixties on the prospective 'plebification of art', the journalist Matthew Browne remarked that 'social boundary lines are not so sharply drawn as they used to be . . . In other words the old cordon sanitaires have snapped under the pressure of the multitudes, and we have not yet succeeded in twisting new ones'.[20] Encroachment on the select territory of bourgeois leisure from below became an offensive physical reality when the working man left his urban ghetto and trespassed on the privacy of his betters. After four weeks at an East Coast resort, wrote James Ewing Ritchie, 'I began to tremble at the very sight of an excursionist'. Such reports emphasised the drunken rowdiness and contumely of excursion crowds and shared a common imagery and tone expressive of the repugnance of the middle-class witness to the holiday invasions of the masses. Thus, the human cargo of the cheap excursion train was never simply deposited at the station, it was 'vomited forth', and proceeded everywhere in 'drunken swarms'.[21] This then was Matthew Arnold's populace: '. . . that vast portion . . . of the working class which, raw and half-developed, has long lain half-hidden amidst its poverty and squalor, and is now issuing from its hiding-place to assert an Englishman's heaven-born privilege of doing as he likes, meeting where it likes, bawling what it likes, breaking what it likes'.[22] It is clear that the new mobility and independence of the urban crowd left the normal bourgeois defences of residential segregation and presumptions of plebeian deference badly dented.

The advance of the multitudes was rendered even more threatening with their accession to allegedly extensive new bounties of time and money. There was a long-standing conviction that workers enjoyed more free time than their superiors, but this putative advantage seems to have gone unresented until the seventies. Then, as economic recession threatened a contraction in middle-class living standards, the evidence of the improved earnings which accompanied the shorter hours won by industrial workers provoked much exasperated comment.[23] *The Times* remarked tetchily in 1873 how more wages and idle time furnish 'this abundant leisure [which] is, indeed, the . . . luxury of the so-called working class'[24] and a periodical writer, J. Keningale Cook, outlined the implications of this development in telling fashion: 'From being machines, fit only for machine work or inert quiescence, the masses are given the liberty of being men – gentlemen indeed, if in that term be applied the possession of leisure, the power of being 'at large' – a coveted attribute of gentility.'[25] The message was not lost on the middle classes, as Walter Besant noted. 'They have', he wrote, 'perceived that their amusements – also, which seems the last straw, their vices – can be enjoyed by the base mechanical sort, insomuch that, if this kind of thing goes on, there must in the end follow an effacement of all classes.'[26] The bourgeois pursuit of leisure was, therefore, attended by constant vigilance in defence of the social frontiers of class.

Harassed by time and preoccupied with status, the Victorian middle classes had a more central problem to contend with in the matter of choice in leisure. As a class whose root traditions had been determined by the imperatives of work, they had only an attenuated leisure culture to draw upon, so that the new social space that opened before them was something of an embarrassment – as the sociologist Nels Anderson has put it, Western society created leisure without intending to and was unprepared for this by-product of work.[27] Historically, of course, leisure had been a suspect quantity in bourgeois ideology. Traditionally, leisure dispensed its own licence, and it was its abuse which had imprinted itself most deeply on middle-class consciousness; in a work-oriented value system it represented an invitation to indolence and prodigality – the weakness of an ill-disciplined and animalistic working class, the badge of a vicious and unduly privileged aristocracy.[28] Despite the still considerable fascination with the aristocratic model, some lordly pleasures continued to be stigmatised in the mid-Victorian period as the corrupt diversions of an unreformed nobility.[29] By much the same process, certain traditional convivialities had now become inadmissible, yet the question of their appropriate replacement was not easily answered, as the *Saturday Review* explained in an article on 'Evening Amusements' on 4 January 1862:

It is a very fine thing to have cured ourselves of the boosing [*sic*] habits of our ancestors; but there is no doubt that the moral conquest has left a formidable void in our social existence . . . the gentlemen used to be drunk, and are now sober; and the mistress of the house, who got rid of them in the drinking days, has to bear the burden of their reformation, and find amusements to beguile the weary hours of sobriety.

The void had to be filled, but each of the components in this necessarily ad hoc creation had to meet demanding standards of probity to conform with the middle classes' self-image as the moral arbiters of society.

The problem of moral legitimation was compounded by the fundamentally new position which leisure occupied in modern life.[30] In ideal
typology, pre-industrial life consisted of a continuum of integrated
activities sited in the stable milieu of compact local communities of
residence and kinship, occupation and faith. Social life was predominantly gregarious, public, and proportioned on a human scale. Work
and leisure were intermingled, and both great and small exercises in
sociability were governed by the prescriptive ties of a heavily ritualised
communal custom. The combined process of industrialisation and urbanisation effectively compressed and concentrated leisure and separated it out as a discrete new sector in an increasingly compartmentalised
life-space. The new pattern and priorities of a modern society were well
established in mid-nineteenth-century Britain, as the magazine *Leisure
Hour*, 1 January 1852, made clear: 'Let there be no intermingling of work
and play; keep the head clear and the hand busy until the bell rings for
repose.' For the middle classes, moreover, the division between work
and leisure had become not only temporal but spatial, for the lure of
suburbia obliged them to commute between city workplace and suburban home. The general expansion of urban population in terms of
numbers and occupational diversity as well as space increasingly fragmented and diluted social interaction, a development much assisted in
middle-class life by the bourgeois taste for privacy. Thus was leisure
severed from its traditional moorings in work, community, and common custom. In its new location in the life-space it took on a new and
disturbing character – in the words of one wryly perceptive Victorian
churchman, leisure now constituted 'a sort of neutral ground which we
may fairly call our own'.[31] Here then was a fluid and open territory
which offered a freedom that outstripped the reach of traditional social
controls. To middle-class sensibilities, leisure represented a normative
as well as a cultural void and placed alarming new responsibilities upon
the individual's capacity for self-direction.

This posed a serious dilemma for liberal values. A society based on a
paramount belief in the benevolent operation of free will had in theory
to concede the right of the individual to pursue his own choice in leisure
– according to a common contemporary analogy, 'Free trade, free
religion, free art and free self-culture are all bound up in the same
bundle and stand or fall together' (Browne, p. 253). Yet the various
discontinuities of modern life gave a man at his leisure a mobility and
anonymity which removed him from that supervision by his fellows
which was still regarded as a desirable if formally unacknowledged

constraint upon individual conduct. George Dawson, the prominent Birmingham nonconformist minister, drew attention to this in a sermon on the morals of travelling.[32] 'It was', he maintained, 'not *what* we do, but whether it will be known, that we fear'. For him, the dereliction that came with escape from such controls was exemplified in holiday misconduct abroad – 'the doing of a thing that is wrong in another country which you would be ashamed to do here among your neighbours'. Given the fragmented nature of the social landscape in modern city life, one could move outside the vision of society's moral vigilantes within a much shorter compass than that of foreign travel, as Ritchie noted in the example of the businessmen who drank heavily in the City, but passed as models of respectability in their home neighbourhoods – the Jekylls and Hydes of suburbia.[33] The temptation to delinquency was thought to be most acute for the young, particularly among the army of rootless young office workers in the great urban centres (the modern variant of that medieval anathema, *les gens sans aveu*). 'The immense size and total unlocalisation of life,' wrote a correspondent to the *Daily Telegraph*, 12 January 1869, 'tends to make the career of a young man excessively individual . . . he loses the fear of censure which is the guiding idea of much life in smaller places.' The structural displacement of leisure had unbalanced the liberal formula for reconciling individual initiative with the needs of social conformity.

Leisure constituted a threat to the discipline and cohesion of the bourgeois world not only by virtue of its unprecedented abundance, but because of its new place in the pattern of life. Thus we may understand why contemporary debate on this issue among a ruling class raised on a classical education afforded few acknowledgments of leisure as a modern equivalent of the *otium cum dignitate* of antiquity or a fundamental component of the Good Life of the future. To the Victorian middle class, leisure was less the bountiful land in which to site Utopia, than some dangerous frontier zone which outran the writ of established law and order. If the middle class nonetheless found the call to leisure irresistible, they were in urgent need of a new apologia or rationale which offered a satisfactory redefinition of its morally acceptable constituents. For guidance they looked to their churches and other leaders of opinion.

III

'What amusements are lawful to persons who wish to live a religious life' was, according to another Birmingham preacher of national repute,

Robert W. Dale, 'the question by which many good people are sorely perplexed.' It was, in particular, noted another minister, a question most frequently raised by the young.[34] Answering it could be a prickly business to judge from the trepidation with which clergymen first ventured upon its public debate. In a sermon at Sheffield in 1860, the Reverend Greville J. Chester maintained that: 'The subject of amusement is of such importance and involves such tremendous interests that I might well shrink from bringing it before you.'[35] This was no imaginary fear, for another Sheffield Anglican minister, Samuel Earnshaw, came close to losing his living after his sermon on the subject in the same year. Chester had moved gingerly, but Earnshaw pressed a bold attack against the evangelical proscriptions on games, sports, and other public amusements, claiming that there was no scriptural justification for such a stance. It was, he argued, in any case 'unnatural to resist the call of nature for exercise in honouring what were simply the commandments of mere men.' Earnshaw appealed for a more charitable attitude towards the theatre and other public amusements, endorsing the example of the Royal Family who, he said, 'openly do the very things which the arbiters of religious opinions and models of Christian practice have pronounced irreconcilable with a religious state of mind'. In all, Earnshaw was trying to reconcile the Church with what he obviously considered to be the tolerable peccadilloes of a modern society. 'Is anything,' he asked, 'permanently gained by increasing the burdens and restraints of a religious life?'[36]

Other churchmen remained more cautious in address, but the willingness to relax some of the religious restraints on the new appetite for leisure clearly grew. Reviewing the issue in 1867, John Morley felt able to report that 'even within the most contracted limits, the range of allowable recreations is being extended.'[37] Dale's position is instructive here, for the Congregational Union, of which he was chairman, held two symposia in an attempt to argue out a revised catalogue of permissible leisure pursuits.[38] Dale was anxious to redeem the old evangelical strictures from charges of casuistry and to explain them in terms of common sense rather than scriptural sanction. The proscribed amusements had, he maintained, been rightly condemned because of 'the accessories with which they had been associated'. Thus, he explained, racing had been excoriated because of the gambling which was so much a part of it; billiards had been condemned because the expensive equipment it required would usually only have been provided in a public house. As circumstances changed, so certain amusements might well be rehabilitated: racing was still beyond the pale, but billiards, where it was sited in the home and thus subsumed under the new category of 'domestic athletics', was returning to respectability. Dale acknowledged that there were some honourable exceptions in a sea of otherwise perverse popular fiction and condoned dancing provided it was not excessive or tainted by 'unsavoury social intercourse'. The majority of his colleagues still found dancing inadmissible and the veto on the theatre remained unanimous; all the speakers at the symposia stressed the desirability of keeping amusements within the home. Clearly a good many activities were still disallowed, but Dale did offer some general advice whose modern sounding relativism is an indication of the growing flexibility of churchmen on this question. He emphasised that 'each generation must examine recreation anew' and also urged a more charitable attitude towards the recreations of one's neighbours. 'That may be safe to them,' he argued, 'which is perilous to us.'

The principal test of conscience or moral propriety for any amusement, according to many clergymen, was its efficacy as an adjunct or complement to work. In this context, the Victorians preferred to talk of recreation rather than leisure. 'Glov'd and essenced leisure,' as Archbishop Thomson of York referred to it,[39] was too debased and soft-centred a word to invest with a sense of purpose sufficient to anchor its activities firmly in the existing value system. Recreation sounded a brisker note, and the literal implications of the word were driven home time after time. 'Recreation,' echoed the Reverend John E. Clarke, 'is the re-creation, the creation anew of fresh strength for tomorrow's work.' 'Unless recreation leaves us ready and willing to begin work again,' warned another clergyman, 'there has been something wrong in its use.'[40] Pleasure seekers were also reminded that Christianity had a high sense of the value of time and that duty to others should find a place in recreation.[41]

If the margin of tolerance grew, the churches' attitude toward leisure remained nonetheless deeply ambivalent throughout the mid-Victorian period. Halting dispensations on the range of permissible recreations contributed to the general erosion of the churches' pastoral presence in the life of Victorian society for, unless they controlled them, the churches were thereby endorsing counter attractions to the religious life and most likely also assisting in the dilution of the Sabbath.[42] Moreover, the spectacle of an increasing public addiction to pleasure suggested how readily tolerance could be abused, so that concessions were set amid a daunting panoply of admonitory advice. Thus the prominent Broad

Churchman, Henry Haweis, though occupying the middle ground on
the leisure question and conceding its place in modern life, could not
suppress the rhetoric of apocalypse; 'Our streets are reeking with the
abuse of pleasure; our society is rotten with it; our social fabric is
crumbling beneath it; our best institutions are being shaken and para-
lysed by it.'[43] Pleasure, he allowed, was 'a legitimate incident of life, but
not a legitimate end,' and he impressed upon his audience the need to
subject its blandishments to the strictest tests of conscience. It was, he
charged, a weighty matter, of a piece with the great questions of biblical
warranty and evolution.[44] According to another clerical injunction,
infinite issues were involved in the smallest acts of recreation (Jones, p.
49).

Contributors to the periodical press frequently offered secular coun-
sel on the proper conduct of leisure, and a seasonable piece on holidays
from the *Cornhill Magazine* in 1867 provides us with a representative
article of this type.[45] After the usual breezy bon voyage to the vacationer, the author, Peter W. Clayden, proceeded to consider the nature,
method, and purpose of recreation – 'A subject only now beginning to
be understood.' He emphasised how modes of life had been transformed
by industrial progress, and how, in response to the demands of modern
civilisation, Englishmen had developed 'magnificent nervous organisations' which gave them an expanded capacity for work. This enabled
them to continue to exploit the opportunities of the nineteenth-century
world, but the cost of the new regimen was high: 'Our great grand-
fathers ambled along with an almost restful movement; we rush along at
high pressure, with fearful wear and noise. Their work was almost play
compared with ours . . . A kind of necessity is upon us, even at home,
much more in our spheres of duty or activity, and all continuous
necessity is a strain'.

Readers could, therefore, rest assured that holidays and recreation
were deserved and necessary, as relief from this strain; they allowed 'the
rebound of an elastic nature from the repression and constraint of
civilised life'. The rebound was best absorbed in recreation which
afforded a total change of pace, direction, and environment, for 'work
and play, like day and night, are opposites, and the widest unlikeness
between them is the truest completeness of each'. 'Renewal and recreation', argued Clayden, 'proceeds on the principle of antithesis.' According to this prescription, men were encouraged to seek recreations
that provided the greatest contrast to their normal occupation, and the
writer sought to free the holidaymaker from the oppressive fears of

ridicule that too often confounded this stratagem. Clayden was, in fact, unusually sensitive to the potential of leisure for the intellectual and cultural enrichment of the individual, but this humanistic evaluation was subordinated to the primary validation of recreation as an adjunct to work. Work and play were antithetical in form only; in purpose they were part of a single natural process in which work was sovereign. Work disciplines had to be projected into play, not vice versa. What Clayden in effect was saying was that play was change of work, as much as change from work. Many other writers were in accord with him on this point, and the sentiment became a commonplace under the imprimatur of William Gladstone, who maintained that recreation was nought but change of employment, exemplifying the ideal in his retreat from the toils of office to the arduous pleasures of tree felling on his estate at Hawarden.[46] Thus was the principle of antithesis made conditional upon that of utility.

There was some comfort to be had from these deliberations. Recreation was judged necessary for the responsible citizen, for it fortified him against the debilities of modern city life and maintained his efficiency at work; in short, it was represented as a duty.[47] Given the proper setting and the proper company – provided most naturally within the home and family – leisure was a legitimate exercise, in moderation. Where the individual was thought mature enough to have internalised the new rationale, he might justifiably devote at least some of his leisure to self-improvement. Yet, misgivings clearly persisted, and the obligation to refer all recreations to a moral calculus continued to impair the satisfactions of leisure, as Clayden noted: 'We do not proscribe amusement as previous generations have done, nor do we go heartily into them, as Paganism did and the Latin races do; but we indulge in them and apologise for them. We take some of our more pleasant and more needful recreations with a half suspicion that they are only half right' (p. 318). Moreover, the legitimation of leisure as a vital auxiliary to work and the caveats against unproductive recreations obliged the novitiate to demonstrate the purpose and utility of his leisure. The new rationale was made to bristle with the highest of intentions.

To judge from the volume of attention devoted to this question in the press and pulpit, the English bourgeoisie, as a class, felt the difficulties of adjustment to leisure most keenly in the 1860s and 1870s. From exiguous beginnings, leisure had become an established component in middle-class life-styles and expectations. At this point it was too familiar and acceptable to be relinquished, yet still too worldly and sybaritic in association to be easily accommodated within the value system of a class whose self-image and public face were defined by a salient moral rectitude. Increasing leisure and the purchase or maintenance of commodities and services to enliven its passing were part of a broader pattern of increased consumption; middle-class incomes had risen considerably since the mid-century, prices had held steady or decreased, and improved techniques of distribution and retailing made the market place more seductive. Thus, the concern to reconcile material and moral worlds in the matter of leisure was part of a more general process of cultural reconstruction in these years, part of an attempt, in the words of a recent student of the Victorian middle-class family, 'to build a world in which civilised man kept moral pace with his comforts' (Frankle, p. 294). In addition to the tensions of this operation came the apprehensions of the seventies that class and status differentials were being eroded by the leisure gains of the masses, whose life was now caricatured in the middle-class press as one long August bank holiday.[48] These fears seem far fetched to us perhaps, but they were real enough to contemporaries, especially when the economic security of the middle classes seemed jeopardised by a business depression. Pertinent here too, it seems, was the extension of the franchise in 1867. In an article entitled 'Social Barriers', the *Saturday Review* for 26 April 1873 claimed that it was the implications of this measure in particular which had heightened bourgeois concern for the more effective demarcation of class territory in leisure – 'The destruction of a political privilege,' the journal observed, 'is tacitly compensated by an increase of social exclusiveness.'

IV

In these same years, however, the evidence of growing satisfaction from leisure runs in persistent counterpoint to the evidence of anxiety and unease. Towards the end of the seventies the *Saturday Review*, which had shown itself to be particularly sensitive to the changing mores of the new leisure world, felt able to register 'a growth in the capacity of disposing of leisure pleasantly' among the middle class, observing that 'the sum total of felicity derived . . . is greater than a review of its limitations at first suggests'.[49] While devising a new rationale for leisure in this period, the Victorian middle class was also busy endowing its practice with an appropriate form and substance.

Accordingly, some of the problems seemed to be yielding to solution. The irritations of organising leisure to a precise schedule no doubt remained in large part, but specialised travel services took some of the strain off the vacationer, and the redoubtable hotels built for the first-class railway tourist protected him and his family from contact with undesirables. These social fortresses with their regimented staff and castellated architecture formed part of the culture capsule constructed by a burgeoning tourist industry to provide a continuum of comfort and security for the middle-class traveller at rest or on the move.[50] The middle class, or their agents, also proved resourceful in devising 'rational' recreations that combined with the more respectable or modified of older pastimes to fill the leisure void and swell the number of 'perfectly legitimate pleasures'. Particularly prominent were the new model athletic sports spawned by the reformed public schools. Here the tests of antithesis and utility were squarely met: playing the game not only fulfilled a prime need for physical recreation among a sedentary urban middle class, but further recommended itself as a patriotic exercise and an important agent of moral and social discipline. Thus at the same time as the excesses of pigeon shooting at the Hurlingham provoked ritual denunciations of a dissolute nobility, the new middle-class enthusiasm for the pristine elitist virtues of physical prowess advertised a revived predilection for the aristocratic life style – provided, of course, that it admitted the kind of restraints represented by the humane and rational code that disciplined the manliness of the new athleticism. The rehabilitation of the aristocratic model, which Escott dated to the seventies, gave a new cachet to the fashions of the 'upper ten thousand' and helped to dissolve some of the old bourgeois resistance to modish as well as lordly pleasures.[51] Within another decade the increasing use of photography in the fashionable press developed a sense of visual gregariousness in its readers which further served to advertise and endorse the appeals of leisure among the well-to-do.[52]

The pattern of organisation of the new model sports alerts us to the important role of the voluntary association in the formalisation of leisure. Semi-private clubs and societies provided an institutionalised focus for many local communities of interest, not only in sports, but also in a wide range of activities which in varying degrees provided elements of sociability and recreation. Formal association spread the costs of providing amenities and served to extend the social protection of the home by its checks upon admission. It also acted as a moral umbrella beyond the home by providing a certain degree of publicity, that is, according to contemporary usage, the condition or fact of being open to public observation or knowledge. The relatively intimate ambience of the club restored something of the normative bond of mutual vigilance amid the anonymity and discontinuities of a big city. Moreover, association reinforced the awareness of a collective class participation, which helped to make middle-class leisure self-validating.[53]

By the turn of the century the growth and practice of leisure had become more luxuriant and assured. The apparatus of leisure was now more extensive, visible, and technically sophisticated, and public amenities – with effective price differentials and other access controls – multiplied. Evident in all of this was the quickening pulse of commercial enterprise which did much to enlarge and glamorise leisure, while taking care to demonstrate an appropriate degree of respectability.[54] This expanding leisure world was shared by all levels of society, but its bounty was most generous for the middle classes, particularly for the proliferating group of rentiers, the coupon clippers, the budding Schlegels, for whom leisure was now a way of life.[55] Though initially beset by formlessness and uncertainty, the Victorian bourgeoisie had created a viable leisure culture which successfully assimilated the priorities of a modern industrial society to the sensibilities of an often tender class conscience. For the most part, the onset of leisure had proven neither apocalyptic nor besotting, and the middle classes had shown themselves capable of exploiting its dynamic properties to reinforce class identity and build a new sense of community in a cellular suburban society.

Discussions of leisure and its proper place in middle-class life continued in the late-Victorian period, but the tone was generally more liberal and relaxed. Clerical misgivings remained, but were now mostly disregarded – the question of recreation, as the Dean of Manchester admitted to the Church Congress in 1886, had passed under the jurisdiction of a 'non-Christian humanitarianism'.[56] Progressive opinion in the nineties proclaimed the rise of a new hedonism which championed self-development over self-sacrifice; the motto of the new era, according to Grant Allen, had changed from 'Be virtuous and you will be happy' to 'Be happy and you will be virtuous.'[57] Yet it would be ingenuous to suppose that the tensions and ambiguities which had accompanied that earlier efflorescence of leisure had been completely dispelled. Echoes of the old moral rigour were still strong and certain defensive habits of conformity died hard – at the turn of the century, for example, the historian William Lecky commented that 'young men who are really idle pretend to be busy.'[58] Previous evidence suggests that the young were often less ready to connive and were foremost in exploiting leisure to test the elasticity of class mores; we may wonder, therefore, how far the vexing question of free choice, far from having been resolved, had in fact been localised within the private family as one of the issues in the intergenerational and sexual conflicts of the nineties. One anxiety, it is plain, had not been exercised – the bourgeois fear of the vulgarisation of leisure. Despite its many defences, the middle classes were still fearful for their leisure status, and when Charles Masterman updated Matthew Arnold for the Edwardians, the image he used to represent the break-through of the 'Multitudes' was that of a bank holiday crowd invading a private garden.[59]

This essay has had a limited objective, namely to show how the Victorian middle classes perceived the advent of modern leisure and to suggest how they adapted to some of its challenges. It has obviously presented a very generalised and impressionistic picture of the middle-class response. I have imagined my constituency as mostly outside the rarefied world of high society, but have otherwise done little to differen-tiate in terms of age, gender, income level, type of work, religious affiliation, geography, and degree of contiguity with other social groups. A consideration of these variables – which might best be done in local studies – is clearly necessary if the patterns of middle-class adaptation are to be fully elucidated.[60] It is important that the middle classes not be left neglected in the growing research into the history of leisure in the nineteenth century, for they did much to determine the moral and ideological climate of its growth. The fact of their own increasingly unabashed pursuit of leisure served ultimately to legitimise it for the rest of society and to secure it as a right rather than a privilege of modern life. Yet, the anxieties that beset the middle class during their initiation into the new leisure world of industrial society were never completely extirpated, but were rather displaced onto the working class. Central to the discomfiture of the Victorian bourgeoisie had been the realisation that modern leisure threatened the ties that bound men and women to society. As a new kind of freedom, leisure demanded a new kind of social discipline, which seemed to place a heavy and largely unprecedented responsibility upon the will of the individual and the isolated family. If the proper exercise of this responsibility had tested the moral resources of the middle class, how then could it be safely entrusted to untutored working people? For as long as this question met with no very confident answer from those in authority, the dominant culture would continue to identify leisure as a problem.

CHAPTER 2

A role analysis of working-class respectability

'*Will the real Bill Banks please stand up?*'

Respectability is again respectable. Long employed as a convenient and unfocused shorthand for all that was taken to be typical of social correctness among the Victorian middle and lower-middle class, the term has recently been invested with a new consequence and complexity. Historians now identify respectability as a highly specific value system of considerable normative power, whose most important consequence was to incorporate a minor but significant sector of the working class into the social consensus that assured mid-Victorian society in particular its overall cohesion and stability, and it is in the precise manner and degree of this incorporation that they discern a complexity unassociated with the previous simple portmanteau sense of the term. Published work on this phenomenon has already significantly expanded our understanding of cultural differentiation within the working class and raised important questions about the mechanisms of social control and cultural hegemony, but this chapter argues that we still underestimate the dynamic properties in working-class respectability and have yet properly to relate its operation to the human geography of the modern city and the behaviour patterns of the modern city dweller. In the case made here, the latter is represented as a predominantly male figure. The inflections of respectability specific to women abroad in the city are examined in later chapters.

Let us first look more closely at the recent reassessments of respectability. Geoffrey Best, in his impressive text on the mid-Victorian period, claims that respectability exerted 'a socially soothing tendency, by assimilating the most widely separated groups (separated socially or geographically) to a common cult'. 'Here,' he maintains, 'was the sharpest of all lines of social division, between those who were and those who were not respectable; a sharper line by far than that between rich and poor, employer and employee, or capitalist and proletarian.'[1] This is brisk and conclusive in tone, and indeed Best claims to find nothing new or complicated about it, but in his discussion of respectability he does give some weight to its variations and ambiguities, particularly in working-class life, and it is these features of its operation rather than its unequivocal conformities that have impressed other students of the period. Whatever its net effect as a social emollient, it is plain from other work that respectability could be subtly, even abruptly differentiated in terms of class. Brian Harrison in his study of Victorian temperance interests shows how these coalesced into a pan-class movement which captured many working men for respectability, but argues that the movement's proletarian converts were far from deferential rubber-stamps for its predominantly middle-class values – rather they generated their own independent convictions that gave them confidence to criticise the existing social order on other issues.[2] The same phenomenon is more fully discovered in Trygve Tholfsen's suggestive examination of working-class radicalism in the period, which identifies a cadre of workingmen who subscribed to the new consensual ideology of 'mid-Victorianism' with its seductively orchestrated rhetoric of progress and self-culture, yet at the same time sustained an independent radical critique of capital and its values.[3]

More particularised local studies of the labour aristocracy (the stratum long held to be most susceptible to some form of embourgeoisement) demonstrate how artisan elites evolved sub-cultures of respectability as class-specific responses to the social reality of their own world and the coercive structure of mid-Victorian capitalism.[4] Thus working people reformulated the official values of respectability and preserved a distinct and irreducible class identity in its practice. Clearly the integration of the skilled worker was a far from even or finite process, and the social peace of the period is increasingly represented as the product of continual negotiation between capital and labour in a muted, yet highly charged, sub-dialectic operating across the long and convoluted cultural frontier between the classes. Working-class respectability was, in a sense, a sublimation of the overt class hostility of the Chartist era, but it carried within it the tensions of unresolved social conflict.[5] The new studies are coloured by a variety of historiographical and ideological persuasions – liberal empirical or neo-Whig, idealist-functional, New Left Gramscian – but together they present us with a suggestive picture of the respectable working man (both individually and collectively) as a complex and autonomous social actor; however considerable the imprint of bourgeois values, clearly not all working men so touched were its passive recipients.

So far this is convincing enough but it may well be that respectability was still more polyvalent than any or all of these interpretations allow: for notwithstanding their authors' sensitivity to the particular texture of working-class life, the respectable working man that they present us with is often too stolidly predictable and earnestly cerebral a social type to be readily believable. In the first instance, working-class respectability, whether primarily emulative or indigenous, is implicitly represented as a cultural absolute: once a respectable, always a respectable (with the corollary holding true for the non-respectables or roughs). Secondly, the working-class respectable is invariably cast as a ideologue: his respectability is primarily an intellectual construct, a systematic body of values and beliefs thought through beyond the level of common sense or a merely ad hoc response to a particular social exigency. Thus have historians tended to reinforce the stereotype of a basic and exclusive duality in working-class culture while simultaneously fastening the working-class respectable into a characterological straitjacket. Such emphases seem to stem in large part from a situation of some piquancy, namely, that in response to their evidence, today's historians can still be governed by the most pristine of Victorian reflexes: for in this case, they appear to have unwittingly adopted nineteenth-century presumptions of behavioural consistency that ignore the changes wrought in patterns of personal conduct and social interaction by the new circumstances of modern city life. In consequence, they have scarcely taken into account the likelihood that respectability was practised in a more limited and situational sense than that of a lived ideal or permanent code of values, and thus have passed over the potentially fruitful proposition that respectability was assumed as a role (or cluster of roles) as much as it was espoused as an ideology.

I

There can, of course, be no doubt that respectability was a clearly recognised and much exalted contemporary ideal. Indeed it was considered a principal prerequisite for true citizenship. 'To be respectable,' declared the *Cornhill Magazine*, 'is . . . to come up to that most real, though very indefinite standard of goodness, the attainment of which is exacted of everyone as a condition of being allowed to associate upon terms of ostensible equality with the rest of the human race.'[6] Respectability primarily enjoined moral rectitude, but in addition, it also demanded economic continence and self-sufficiency. Though its possession was a badge of conformity, its attainment was a matter of independent individual achievement through an ongoing process of self-discipline and self-improvement. Essentially a distillation of evangelical disciplines, it represented a secular version of election – minus the uncertainties – and in so far as it demanded an appropriate faith and conduct, it both incorporated an ideology and defined a life-style.

By the tests of respectability observers identified two discrete and exclusive constituencies in working-class life. Thus respectables and non-respectables were clearly distinguished in the reform strategy of Henry Solly – the middle-class founder of the working men's club movement – who appealed to 'the more prudent, worthier members of the working class' to seek refuge in the clubs, away from 'their reckless, drinking, cowardly, or dishonest neighbours.'[7] This characterisation of the dichotomy in more abrupt and emotively judgmental terms than those of respectable and non-respectable was common: other commentators also discriminated between respectables and 'roughs', 'thinkers and drinkers', or 'virtuous and vicious'. To the Victorian bourgeois there was no confusion as to the elect and non-elect in working-class life.

What evidence lent support to this formulation? For contemporaries there were several indicators of the firm establishment of respectability in working-class life. There were the heartening if anonymous statistics recording the accumulative deposits of small investors in the Post Office Savings Bank. On the evidence of the good behaviour on shilling days at the Great Exhibition, lower-class public manners had much improved – an impression reinforced locally by the views from the platform when middle-class visitors attended temperance soirées or other set pieces of rational recreation and charitable schemes of improvement. The behaviour of the Lancashire operatives during the cotton famine provided striking proof of a new self-control and moral forbearance among workers, and the industrial north in general seemed to Victorian commentators to offer further convincing evidence of working-class progress on the approved model. The concentration of such improvement among an artisan elite was central to the reform case in the formulating of the Reform bill of 1867.[8] Certainly the establishment of such bridgeheads of respectability among the working classes was thrown into relief by the great wash of the non-respectable poor whose number and contumacy were both impressively offensive. In Bolton, a correspondent wrote to the local paper complaining of 'crowds of men and boys' loafing on the street corners, 'for the most part all in their deshabillé . . . applying the expression "bloody" to almost every person and thing that came their way'. The offence was compounded when working people made their mass break-out from the urban ghetto and thrust themselves in upon the privacy of their betters: after four weeks in Southend, to quote the journalist Ewing Ritchie again, 'I began to tremble at the sight of an excursionist'. Good manners were no defence against the boorishness of the non-elect, as seen in a Charles Keen cartoon of the period which records an exchange between a genteel tourist and a 'powerful navvy' from whom he politely asks the way: 'Can you kindly direct me to Slagley?' Powerfully navvy: 'Ah can poonch the head of thee.' The tourist, we are told, retired hastily.[9]

Though less categorical in their classification, modern historians have confirmed to their own satisfaction the dualist character of working-class culture. The roughs have had no difficulty in registering their presence, appearing in various guises from the simply pathetic to the alarmingly violent,[10] but it is the respectables who have received more precise attention. The line of economic differentiation between the aristocracy of labour and the rest have been represented as more or less coterminous with the social divide between respectables and non-respectables, and historians have achieved a sharper focus on the former where they have reconstructed something of the experience of distinct communities or sub-cultures of working-class respectability.[11] We can also know the more specific human face of respectability through modern biographical studies and the rescue from obscurity of personal working-class testimonies.[12] Here, where conduct and belief cohere in the continuum of an individual life-history, is convincing evidence of respectability as a monolinear and perennial commitment of a broadly ideological or ethical nature. Yet the evidence now taken to support the idea of stable and exclusive constituency of working-class respectables is often little different in kind from that which confirmed the formulations of Victorian observers, for it is still for the most part anonymous and disembodied, episodic and elliptical. The reconstructed world of working-class respectability, though now more sophisticatedly assembled and interpreted, is still an artificial composite, put together from limited instances of respectable behaviour and its rhetoric, rather than from a sustained collective biography of its constituents. In the present state of knowledge this is a necessary and legitimate technique for the historian, but what is inferred from such a construct is more dubious; for it suggests a continuity in casting where there may only have been a continuity in performance. This inference echoes that of contemporary commentators, and we may more readily appreciate the probability of a present day misreading of the evidence if we examine the presuppositions that governed the Victorians' conception of social reality and their ordering of experience in everyday life. A simple ecological model of the urban process, derived from the writings of the Chicago School, defines the context.

II

In the nineteenth century, the expansion of the urban population and the development of a society ordered by the priorities of industrial growth fragmented social interaction, and the coherent and readily comprehensible pattern of social life shared within the small-scale traditional community was increasingly exchanged for a pattern of life notable for its discontinuities of experience in terms of time, space, and personnel. In the city, segregation and the introduction of new work routine compartmentalised social classes and the basic activities of work, leisure, and home life to such a degree that man the social actor was obliged to play out his encounters in an ever greater number of discrete situational settings.[13] According to Gerth and Mills, in the more intimate social milieu of the pre-industrial village or small town, 'the various situations in which men play roles are not so widely different from one another and are transparent to all . . .The variety of roles which any given person plays is not very wide, and each is translatable into the others.'[14] In such a world, men's conduct and intentions answer to an homogeneous 'vocabulary of motives'. In an industrial city, however, conduct is segmentalised and justified according to various and more private vocabularies of motive; the diversification of social context allows for a greater variability in personal behaviour as role activities become insulated from the continuous observation of actual and potential role others.[15]

Insulation was most pronounced in inter-class relationships: here physical discontinuities were compounded by the bourgeois concern to maintain social distance. But although there was frequent acknowledgment among middle-class commentators of how little they were acquainted with working men and their world – it was, in a much used phrase, 'terra incognita' – they had a rudimentary interpretative scheme of the territory, peopled with stereotypes that represented imaginary projections of the role-specific behaviour met with in the intermittent social exchanges of real life. Only rarely were they confronted with evidence which revealed their mistake in presuming upon a consistency in role progression that followed from the expectations of conventional behaviour in their own lives. The Birmingham manufacturer, William Sargant, realised as much when he discovered, by accident, that one of his steadiest and, as he had thought, most temperate workmen was a heavy drinker.

Most of us [recorded Sargant] know very little about what goes on among workmen in the evening. We see them in their places during the day, we find them always ready to labour when they are called upon, and we set them down as men of temperate habits; inferring from their regularity that they are not guilty of excesses in their leisure hours. It is sometimes startling to find that we are entirely mistaken.[16]

Sargant's surprise suggests how little cognisant of role discontinuities his contemporaries could be.

That the co-existence of seemingly contradictory modes of behaviour within a single life-style was not an aberration can be evidenced from other sources, particularly those relating to leisure-time activities, which provided a striking new area of free choice for all classes by the mid-Victorian period – 'a sort of neutral ground which we may fairly call our own', as one observer noted.[17] The leisure choice of one contemporary working man is recorded in 'Bill Banks' Day Out', a suggestive piece of documentary fiction by Thomas Wright, the 'Journeyman Engineer', published in 1868.[18] Bill is a London railwayman who goes 'St. Mondaying' with his wife and friends in Hampton Court. They meet outside a local pub, admire each other in their best dress, and start the excursion with a morning pint. They travel out to Hampton Court by hired van, complete with cornet player to enliven the journey. On arrival they tuck into a dinner provided by the van-owner at 2s 6d a head – 'a first-rater; beef and mutton and ham, and any quantity of rolls, and lots of fruit-tarts, in the way of eating, and bottled ale and small cask of porter to wash 'em down'. The harmony of the occasion is disturbed when Bill, somewhat flushed with drink, takes exception to the superior airs of a young shopman in the company; after a scuffle, peace is restored and the party continues, finishing up in late evening back in town, at the Alhambra, the famous Leicester Square music hall. Bill and his wife together with two friends share the cost of a cab home, enjoying the prospect of scandalising the neighbours by arriving in such style.

Retailed in the first person, the piece has an internal consistency which suggests how a working man at play could move through several different roles, all cohering into a single life-world, but each in turn likely to be interpreted by an outsider as the behaviour peculiar to a distinct, separate, and exclusive type within the working classes. On the evidence of his home life Banks would pass as the self-improving artisan: he is a considerable and intelligent reader who borrows books from the local Institute to supplement his own small library. In taking an excursion Bill appears at first to be a further credit to his class. His expenditure can be reckoned at between ten and fifteen shillings for him and his wife, yet the day out is not the reflex action of a poor family gobbling up a sudden windfall, but the happy product of careful budgeting which, so we gather, owes something to Mrs. Banks' good management. Hampton Court, an historic house on which Bill is well read, represents a 'rational' choice for a visit, and in their concern with their appearance the party displays that 'pardonable vanity' that reformers recommended as a tonic both for trade and self-respect.[19] Thereafter, however, Bill Banks' respectable image disintegrates, as he regresses into the time-honoured role of the English workman on a spree. To a middle-class observer he then would appear drunk, gluttonous, and unruly. Detected among the music hall crowd he would serve as an example of the feckless new breed of workingman who surrendered himself to the temptations of the 'fast' life. Thus might random snapshots of working men at play confirm the bourgeois categorisation of working-class life, whereas the synoptic documentary of Wright's account suggests a congruency that questions its reliability.

The easy association of rationality and traditional play patterns – respectability and non-respectability – represented above appears in institutional form in the case of the friendly societies, which retained much of the older style of conviviality while mostly commending themselves to middle-class observers as improving agencies in working-class life. At the national meeting of the Friendly Society of Ironfounders held in Bolton in 1866, the chairman opened proceedings by declaring that they were met for two principal objects: 'enjoyment and pleasure, and to show the country that the ironfounders were not behind other bodies of workpeople in this age of improvement'. Improvement here was measured on a different scale from that used by politicians and reformers – it came by the bellyful. Accordingly, the ironfounders demolished a mountain of food and indulged an impressive thirst. To cater to the delegates 'the whole length of the west side of the pavilion had been appropriated to a refreshment department, in which were to be seen a multitudinous array of glasses, jugs and beer barrels'. Afterwards the ironfounders and members of local allied trades disported themselves till daybreak. The local press made but few disapproving noises on reporting such occasions: 'After all their drawbacks,' concluded the *Bolton Chronicle* in a review of the Lancashire societies in the late seventies, 'they ... provide an education in the duties of citizenship through the practice of self-government.'[20] The consolidation of friendly societies into regional or national organisations of increasing financial probity encouraged observers in the belief that orthodox values of improvement were well on their way to superseding the obsolescent survivals of an older and intemperate way of life, the hangovers from a semi-barbarous folk culture which would soon be extinguished.

Yet working-class culture in its adaptation to an urban industrial setting was more additive than substitutive. What outsiders chose to see as anomalies were its normalities: to members of the friendly societies and other major institutions in common life, the concurrent pursuit of 'thinking and drinking', 'virtue and vice' represented not so much a conflict of value systems as a reconciliation. Thus did the working men's clubs of the eighties combine sociability with instruction, though their unabashed informality (the constant traffic, the cries of the pie-boy and the pot-boy, the smoking and bantering) – produced a bad press among visiting middle-class lecturers. For Frederick Rogers, an unbendingly respectable working-class autodidact, disenchantment came in the middle of his Sunday morning talk on Shakespeare, when the club chairman called a break to let the man come round with the beer.[21] The trappings of respectability were on occasions readily assumed in working-class life, but they did not mean the displacement of older conformities. Climbing into the sober garb of the Sunday suit, for example, was no prophylactic against the customary resort to the pub, and best clothes could be openly surrendered to the pawnbroker on Monday morning without loss of face.[22]

Where the working-class neighbourhoods of big cities later took on the closed and parochial character of 'urban villages', the possession of Sunday best clearly became an important ongoing test of status and identity,[23] but respectability could also function in a more limited and situational sense as a tactic for dealing with the external world beyond one's most immediate class and community reference group. It could, for example, be assumed as a defensive device. Mouthing a few passwords about respectability might secure immunity from the 'badgering' of middle-class charity workers or district visitors.[24] In the sensitive matter of dress, the accessories of respectability might offer some protection against arbitrary arrest or conviction for implication in one of the 'nuisances' which provoked recurrent purges of street life by the police – in cases of prosecution of the players and spectators of the street games in Bolton, police witnesses thought it material to inform the courts whether or not the defendants were apprehended with or without a jacket or collar on.[25]

Acknowledging respectability as a choice of role rather than a universal normative mode can make us more alert to its instrumental or calculative deployment in working-class relationships with outsiders. Signing the pledge or otherwise subscribing to tests of membership for middle-class sponsored associations for improvement would have passed as professions of or aspirations to respectability, yet may well have only represented a limited attachment to its norms. Lay workers in Bolton noted that occasional booms in Sunday School attendance could be attributed to the announcement of some treat or excursion and were never sustained beyond that point, and there were other reports in the same vein.[26] Among the early football teams formed by working men in the seventies and eighties a good number were connected with religious bodies, yet the short-lived nature of these connections and the ease with which they were severed suggests that, in the practical and eclectic fashion of their culture, working men used such institutions as a convenient and socially neutral locus for realising their own initiatives, taking calculated advantage of the various amenities at their mentors' disposal.[27] Thus, by meeting the role demands of their class superiors, working people could extract practical benefits often unobtainable from the resources of their own culture.

In arguing for a calculative function in working-class respectability the assumption is that working people were capable of playing at roles as much as role playing.[28] The recovery of intention is a difficult exercise but the application of Goffman's concept of role distance gives us some leverage on the problem.[29] Goffman points out how, in the interests of social expediency, the social actor can perform a role with sufficient conviction to meet the expectations of the role-other, while injecting some expression into the performance which conveys his psychic resistance to any fundamental attachment to the obligations of that role. The signs of detachment are often minuscule, and displayed in any number of possible deviations from the conventional grammar of social encounter. Goffman finds considerable evidence of this in relationships between social actors in situations governed by a clearly ascribed authority structure:

> At such times, we often find that although the subordinate is careful not to threaten those who are, in a sense, in charge of the situation, he may be just as careful to inject some expression to show, for any who care to see, that he is not capitulating completely to the (work) arrangement in which he finds himself. Sullenness, muttering, irony, joking, and sarcasm may allow one to show that something of oneself lies outside the constraints of the moment and outside the role within whose jurisdiction the moment occurs.[30]

Can anything like these innuendos of disaffection be detected in the interplay of the classes in mid-Victorian England? Perhaps. G. M. Young offered sound advice to the apprentice historian by stressing the need to read, read, and read in the sources of the period until one could almost hear the characters talk. What we must be careful to do here is to adjust our hearing to catch the tone of speech as much as its content. One of Canon Barnett's eager young settlement workers recorded the welcome he received from East End working men: 'We are,' said one of the latter, 'always pleased to see a gentleman.'[31] How gratifying to be so readily awarded the title and status of gentleman! How likely that the term was delivered with the slightest inflection of mock respect? Expressions of disassociation are there, says Goffman, 'for any who care to see', to which we might add, for any who are *capable* of seeing, or otherwise comprehending. What was recorded as quaint or curious in working-class life may well have had more significant social undertones than middle-class observers could perceive. Workers in the Black Country, reported one witness in the 1860s, had so little social intercourse with their betters that they were almost totally ignorant of the correct forms of address; thus when confronted with a bishop or senior officer of the church they addressed him as 'Madam'.[32] An example of backward manners or a jest inwardly savoured by an outwardly respectful working-class audience? Certainly the middle-class reader of this extract was unlikely to know that the misidentification of a bishop as a lady in an advanced state of pregnancy was a staple of the comic routines on the music halls.

If, at this point, it be objected that the sources will not bear the strain of such a reading, it can at least be countered that certain forms of source material advanced as evidence of respectable or compliant behaviour among the working classes have been awarded too much significance and most likely have also been misinterpreted. We have

recently been warned in convincing manner how inadequate and mis-
leading was the representation of contemporary city life in Victorian
magazine illustration; a combination of artistic convention and technical constraints served to distance the polite reader from social reality
and protect him or her from exposure to anything startling or threatening.[33] Similar caveats ought to be attached to the general run of
magazine and newspaper reporting in the period. Reporters relied on
the stock phrases of a narrowly stylised vocabulary, pairing noun and
modifier in standard fashion, in the interests of balance rather than
accuracy. When local worthies or philanthropists addressed gatherings
of working men, the clichés of Victorian journalism assured them of
'hearty thanks' and 'vociferous applause' though the actual response
may have been a good deal less encouraging.[34] Social reformers who
promoted institutions or occasions for rational recreation several times
found working-class behaviour less than auspicious and the sanctions of
respectability imperilled. One reformer commented on the difficulty of
maintaining a happy medium between 'weak tea and a rollicking free
and easy' and the bourgeois promoter of the Manchester Lyceums,
Benjamin Heywood, wrote to his son bemoaning the collapse of propriety in these 'improving' institutions:

The character of the thing is changed. I am glad you were there, however, for
old time's sake, but it is somewhat humiliating that the sober speakers should be
the stopgaps between the acts.[35]

When Emma Cons opened an extension of Tom Hughes' Cat and
Comfort coffee house in Drury Lane for working girls, the latter
'marked their appreciation of efforts made for their comfort by smash-
ing the lights, breaking the windows, and tearing the inside out of the
piano'.[36] Incidents like the above may have been exceptional, but they
do suggest the persistence of a considerable social tension in reportedly
fraternal exercises in respectability. The official reports of the Working
Men's Club and Institute Union (initially officered by the middle-class)
repeatedly emphasised the well-mannered behaviour of club audiences
at lectures and the respect accorded visiting middle-class speakers,
which suggests a need for reassurance that all was truly what it seemed.[37]
The unease of a bourgeois patron in the presence of working men can be
attributed to several factors, but one of them may well have been
apprehension at the tenuous hold of the normative sanctions of respectability, particularly in the new open-ended social territory of modern
leisure. To reverse another cliché, a good time was not had by all.

Middle-class discomfiture on these occasions was compounded by a more general fear for the security of their status in an operationally protean social order. 'The social sorrow of our times,' observed the Rev. J. Baldwin Brown, in charting the 'social revolution' of the mid-century, is that men do not know their places,

> no man knows surely either his neighbour's, or his own. There is no sort of fixity in any of the institutions of society, no sort of continence in any of its orders. No order keeps to itself; they all interlock and interpenetrate. All things are in constant flux: and above all things the habits, pursuits, callings and social status of men. We do not know where to find men, and large classes do not know where to find themselves. There are no broad platforms on which men stand together with those of the same rank and calling ... Now every man, every class tries to make a law for itself. There is a complete break-up and mixture of social orders.[38]

On close investigation, mid-Victorian England appears remarkable not only for its volatile social order but for the plasticity of its human geography. Thus there were as yet no adequate physical *cordons sanitaires* to protect the assumptions and apparatus of class superiority. Residential segregation provided some protection for the middle-class, but the suburbs did not yet offer services and job opportunities sufficient to relieve the necessity of business and social commuting to the city, where social hauteurs could be badly bruised in the heavy human traffic of the streets (carriage trade alone excepted). Letters to the Bolton press frequently complained at the inadequate policing of the town's thoroughfares and the prevalence of 'nuisances' – bad language (as noted above), the road-running nuisance, the snowballing nuisance, etc. On vacation, as we have seen above, the middle-class family could not be certain of territorial security, for the excursion train made all classes mobile, and custom and price differentials had not yet confirmed the class rating of specific resorts.[39] Where strong economic sanctions obtained, as at work, in the market place or – more commonly significant for the conditioning of social responses – in relationships with domestic servants in the home, interclass contacts conformed more closely to class protocol (though even here the master class was apprehensive of the subversive alter ego that lay behind the face of conformity).[40] Elsewhere in the social landscape encounters were much less personal, formalised, or predictable, and took place along a shifting and discontinuous situational frontier peopled by anonymous strangers.

To be abroad in this territory was not often physically dangerous, but it constituted something of a normative void whose uncertainties threatened the fundamental structure of social control, and it was a signal virtue of the respectable/non-respectable formulation that it imposed some conceptual order and stability on the bewildering and elliptical experience of city life.[41] By its criteria a man could assess the likely extent to which other members of the volatile and congested public milieu shared common expectations in face to face encounters. A good deal of the business of an urban industrial society could no longer wait on any meticulous examination of individual credentials, and the pattern of social encounter had in any case changed to the extent where the empirical confirmation of another's character was mostly beyond the reach of personal witness, but the inventory of respectable behaviour and appearance provided a mental checklist by which to read both status and intention, thereby expediting social transaction and reducing vulnerability to rebuff, exploitation, or worse. Contemporaries were far from unaware that men might take advantage of the discontinuities of big city life to default upon their respectability. In the 1850s Ewing Ritchie inveighed against the suburban businessmen who drank heavily in Town but passed as models of virtue in their home neighbourhoods, and Samuel Smiles' commandment 'Be what you seem' was a warning against the inherent duplicities of modern living.[42] But despite such misgivings the middle classes proceeded on the conviction that respectability was a social imperative whose internalised values commanded the conformity of an individual's actions beyond the public knowledge of his reference group. Encouraged by this model, the middle class felt able to extrapolate from the various instances of respectable behaviour in working-class life and presume upon a constituency of working-class respectables whose putative presence substantially extended the safety zone of social contact in their cognitive map of the city.

III

The opacity of working-class life and the need to believe obscured the deficiencies of such a thesis. There were undoubtedly working men and their families for whom respectability was a stable and regular way of life, but in this period they were most likely rarer birds than contemporaries or today's historians have allowed. Many men registered as respectables in the mental dossiers of middle-class observers were known as such on the evidence of a single role-performance, a performance perhaps regularly repeated, but in many cases, isolated and anonymous or both. Much of this behaviour answered to the established constraints and expectations of inter-class encounter, but formed part of an independent working-class culture with its own patterns of behavioural consistency and homogeneity, a culture with a tangential rather than an emulative relationship to that of the middle class. To the middle-class mind, role enactments of respectability were like so many beads which they restrung along axes of their own wishful construction: that the beads led in other directions or conformed to different patterns was something that the middle-class outsider could not easily have known. Mostly, one suspects, he did not want to know, for the concept of a regiment of working-class respectables recruited from the unlikely denizens of the 'terra incognita' of Victorian England was a necessary prop to the self-esteem of his own class, proof of the middle-class capacity to remake society in their own image, and a preservative too of the flattering fiction of an open society in which working men could advance to 'ostensible equality' with their betters. The myth of substantial working-class respectability served, moreover, as a source of reassurance in a period whose conventional appellation as an age of equipoise obscures the extent to which the bourgeoisie were still mindful of the social and political combustibility of the urban masses.[43] Identifying the respectable working man was more of a prescriptive than a descriptive exercise.

This need to believe reduced bourgeois sensitivity to calculative or instrumental adoptions of respectability by working people. Given this predisposition on the part of the role-other and the episodic or otherwise limited nature of most class exchanges, respectability was an undemanding role to play for working men who possessed the basic equipment in dress, speech, and demeanour which conformed to its standardized public image. In his social classification of *The Nether World*, George Gissing offered that the broad distinction lay between two great sections of working men – 'those who do, and those who do not, wear collars'.[44] However circumstantial, there is evidence that respectability was assumed or discarded as easily as the collar that was its symbolic accessory.

Before concluding, I must revert briefly to the defensive. The case made here depends upon the interlocking and retrospective application of behavioural models generated by twentieth-century American society, a unique culture, it may be argued, whose more loosely-textured social structure and higher rate and range of social and geographical mobility has produced more abrupt discontinuities and normative confusion than can wisely be allowed for mid-Victorian England. Perhaps then my argument only makes sense as a personal attempt to resolve the cultural schizophrenia that afflicts an expatriate Britisher teaching Victorian Studies in Canada. Yet the transposition is admissible on more than *ad hominem* grounds. Clearly the work of the Chicago School of the 1920s and 1930s is of that city and that era,[45] but the ideal type that it presented was influenced by the evidence of late nineteenth-century London – the *locus classicus* of Victorian behaviour – and its scheme of distinct patterns of urban segregation has recently been revalidated, not only for late- but for mid-Victorian England.[46] No Victorian formulated a role theory of behaviour, but the characteristic anxieties of contemporary literary consciousness do reveal an increasing sensitivity to the opacity of modern city life. By the eighties, novelists like Gissing plainly recognised that they could no longer assume the continuity between private consciousness and public reality that had typified an earlier society, and Stevenson's Jekyll and Hyde can be seen as a striking metaphor for the divided self in a new urban world, a moral fable that was quoted from a thousand pulpits.[47] Recently disclosed case histories of double lives are also significant, for their revelations provide more than a simple addition to our gallery of Other Victorians; they are the rattle of skeletons in a closet that may yet be found to contain innumerable other examples from an extensive seam of more or less 'moral' deviancy (Robert Park's coinage) that stretched through the life of the period, and was practised by all sorts and conditions of men and women. After all, Arthur Munby's inamorata, the maid of all work, Hannah Cullwick, proved just as capable of a double consciousness as her bohemian and eccentric master.[48]

But the test of this hypothesis on working-class respectability, particularly where it is represented as a manipulative mode, must depend upon its correlation with a broader range of concrete historical evidence. Given the nature of the case made here this will be no easy matter, but I hope enough has been said to encourage a greater sensitivity to the situational contexts of behaviour, particularly in inter-class relationships. What exactly were the short-run social and geographical mobilities of city living and how did they determine role progression? What were the sites and occasions of class encounter, whether by design or accident, in the individual trajectories of daily life? What was the vocabulary of class encounter, and when and how did it chime with the semi-official rhetoric or respectability? What were the cues in its non-verbal exchanges in the paralanguage of tone, and the silent language of gesture and appearance? We may find clues in music hall parody, in the graphic satire of popular periodicals, or in the behaviour of the marginal or economically unincorporated worker, the 'sort of working-class Bohemian' who Raphael Samuel discovered among the free spirits of Headington Quarry.[49] Certainly for the later period new questions could be asked in oral history interviews, for it is from studies of the individual that we may best discern the pattern of movement in and out of respectability and thus illuminate the broad territory that lies between its two idealised poles.

It can be admitted that however disjunctive or calculative the practice of respectability among the working class, taken *in toto* it denotes a measure of compliance with bourgeois norms that largely justifies its interpretation as a 'socially-soothing tendency'. But the recent analyses of respectability still underestimate the ambiguity of its operation in working-class life, and the extent to which it cloaked a form of deviancy or new style of counter-theatre.[50] Where its practice served to extract material and social benefits from class superiors it functioned as a kind of exploitation in reverse; where its returns offered more psychic satisfactions, it served as a kind of private saturnalia in a society that had all but extinguished carnival. Despite the tightening constraints of social organisation that mark the development of modern industrial society, its expansion provides a diversity of situational contexts whose lack of correspondence enables the individual to manipulate the social order in such a way as to preserve what Burns identifies as 'a kind of second-order self-realisation and autonomy'.[51] The preservation of a satisfying inner life in a self-contained working-class culture may have had more to do with the maintenance of social stability in mid-Victorian England than the blandishments of embourgeoisement or a collective modification of its norms. In the manner of their resistance to middle-class tutelage, working-class males may appear to be both less than doggedly heroic and more than boorishly bloody-minded – in truth, perhaps rather a shifty lot – but this interpretation may be more consistent with the changing patterns of consciousness and behaviour in a modern society than those we have yet been offered.

CHAPTER 3

Ally Sloper's Half-Holiday:
Comic art in the 1880s

Ally Sloper's Half-Holiday was a penny weekly comic paper published without a break from 1884 until 1916.[1] Among the most successful and long-lived of its kind in a very competitive sector of the new popular press, the paper's strength derived mainly from its eponymous hero whose agreeably outrageous picaresque adventures were celebrated weekly in its large front page cartoon. Together with a wide range of promotional schemes, these cartoon adventures made him one of the best known fictional personalities of the period, with a visual currency comparable to that of the Disney figures of a half-century later. To H. G. Wells, Sloper was the new urban John Bull, a secular saint whose feast fell on August Bank Holiday. To the American critic, Elizabeth Pennell, he was 'an original creation in this age of imitation . . . the great modern jester or popular type of England', and the cartoonist H. M. Bateman recalled: 'The big one was *Ally Sloper's Half-Holiday*, everyone grew up with that'. Indeed, Sloper achieved the apotheosis of the fictional character in that, no less than Pickwick or Sherlock Holmes, people believed he actually lived.[2] Yet despite his inescapable presence for contemporaries, Ally Sloper has gone unremarked by social historians. This is no reproach, for it is all too easy to disregard some of the most salient texts in a culture as too self-evidently typical to require further comment. Only after several years of unsought acquaintance has this still potent old rascal with the fairground face and antic figure finally elbowed his way into the direct focus of my own critical attentions, and challenged me to make a deeper sense of his popularity. This essay is based on a fairly close reading of the first ten years' run of the paper – the written as well as visual copy – though the illustrations reproduced here are drawn mostly from the years 1884–8.[3] The main aim has been to explain *Ally Sloper's Half-Holiday* in terms of its historically specific ideologies and codes and to suggest its importance as a prototype of a new commercial popular culture at a crucial point in the latter's growth and transformation. It is a historian's exercise in deconstructing the popular.

I

Plainly, by its very title, *ASHH* was a celebration of the new world of popular leisure whose modern shape and content were distinctly visible by the eighties.[4] The Saturday half-holiday together with Saturday night were displacing Sunday as the prime focus of social and recreational energies and marked the climax of the newly-defined 'weekend'. Capitalism now assured its workers more frequent and regular breathing space, with standardised instalments at the end of the day, the end of the week and, ideally, the end of the year, when an annual summer holiday clinched the new trade-off between work and leisure. By the 1880s too, there was more spare money to spend on the new spare time, due to increasing real wages and a fall in the price of basic commodities. The increased opportunities and resources for leisure taking were met by the provision of an extensive new range of consumer goods, services and institutions, the manufacture and marketing of which displayed a thorough-going commercialism and a considerable increase in the scale and specialisation of operations. By modern standards there were simply more things to do and enjoy in leisure time by the eighties than had been the case a generation or so previously.

Arguably too, the processes of capitalist growth and social differentiation that gave leisure and its institutions a distinct and separate place in modern life also gave it a new psychological or emotional saliency. An increase in mechanisation and the subdivision of labour, together with the impress of scientific management reduced the satisfactions of the work-place and concentrated social expectations onto 'life off the job'. Changes in the emotional content and associations of leisure can be further understood as the expression of class-specific modes of behaviour in the making and remaking of the major social formations of the period, yet it is at this point too that the collectively-prescribed leisure forms of an older way of life were yielding to a more generalised and indefinite condition of freedom, increasingly given over to the more or less conscious construction of an individual or family-based life style. If class yet remained a powerful determinant in shaping leisure choice, the search for an appropriate style was also perceived in other terms, as the oppositions and ambiguities of class stratification gave way to finer definitions of individual status within and against the more amorphous mass groupings of the modern world.[5]

If the experience of leisure was becoming more atomised, it was also – by a complementary process – becoming increasingly homogenised. Indeed by the 1890s we had moved into a new era of a mass or common culture whose artefacts were designed by a new breed of entrepreneurs to appeal to the widest possible audience irrespective of class or other divisive market variables. By this account, culture was now the product of an industry rather than the product of experience and its content was defined by the lowest common denominators of popular taste rather than the particularised expressive needs of a diversity of cultures. Mass culture is the ultimate of those omnibus categories that too often collapse necessary considerations of continuity and differentiation, but it is useful in describing one of the major forces engaged in the profound social transformations that took place from the 1880s, in which working-class culture and much else was remade.[6]

Yet if we may agree on this major shift in the development of popular culture, we still know very little about its precise dynamics. How exactly did the artefacts of this new age capture not only the mass, but the individual within the mass, for this was the difficult double mechanism necessary for success. What too was the nature of the popular mentality with which the artefact engaged? In studying leisure as a prime focus for this transformation of culture it is necessary not only to inventorise the changes in its forms, organisation, economics and technology but the changes in the consciousness of its participants. What particular models of identity or behaviour were most compelling among those purveyed? What social roles and rituals were most frequently reproduced in leisure, and what resources and expectations were brought to bear in their performance? How did people impart significance and meaning to such experience? How did older cultural forms colour the new and what were the more particular configurations within the broad outlines of this mass culture?[7]

ASHH may provide a valuable entrée to the field. It offers a running commentary on the general expansion of leisure and popular culture while providing a specific case history in the development of the popular press, a central indicator and agent of change in the period. It also provides a mirror to the world of the new entertainment industry of the music hall and popular theatre in which it was engrossed. By its personalised focus upon a principal character and his companions, one is given some sense of continuity and direction in a field whose materials are massive and infinitely miscellaneous. Above all, the visual form dramatises experience in a compact and immediate fashion that gives the historian some sense of a particular way of life in action, however conventionalised.

Historians generally have been slow to exploit graphic evidence and where it is provided it most often serves as illustration for points adduced from other materials rather than as substantive evidence in its own right with a considerable interpretative potential. If this is true of the use of formal art, it is even more true of the historian's use of the vernacular arts of the pictorial and cartoon press, which in this period – with a few recent and honourable exceptions – seem reduced to the merely supplementary parade of cuts from the *Illustrated London News* and *Punch*, or self-contained selections from these journals that glorify them as unique and comprehensive mirrors of their age.[8] To extend the range of enquiry involves considerable problems of sources, methodology and interpretation; but the popular ideography of the later nineteenth century should not be neglected, for images no less than print proliferated in the period and clearly shaped as well as reflected the mores and behaviour of the crowd. Georg Simmel remarked of the new anonymous promiscuity of railway compartments and omnibuses that life in the great cities showed a greater preponderance of occasions to *see* rather than *hear* people, to look at each other without talking. Modern social life, he maintained, increased in ever growing degree the role of mere visual impressions in reading others. This suggests the importance of recognising specific socio-visual sensibilities in history, and suggests further the necessary appreciation of graphic models and stereotypes as powerful reference points in the social evaluations and transactions of popular life.[9]

II

ASHH first appeared in May 1884 as an illustrated comic weekly selling for a penny. One of several similarly styled contemporaries selling at that price, it stood in clear line of inspirational descent from *Punch*, though with fewer and larger pages, cheapened in the quality of its production and content, and clearly aimed at a more numerous lower class readership.[10] It was, according to the legend under the paper's masthead, 'founded and conducted by Gilbert Dalziel', who remained the proprietor until 1903, but the *Half-Holiday* owed a good deal of its unique identity and success to two others: Charles Ross who probably did most of the writing and editing, and was the inventor of the original Ally Sloper; and W. G. Baxter, the principal illustrator, who gave the latter his definitive style and persona as the most popular cartoon character of the period.

Of the three men, Baxter is the least known, though the surviving details of his life put him in the romantic-pathetic tradition of the rootless young artist-illustrator drawn to London from the provinces, and killed off early by a mixture of consumption, drink, and overwork. Born in Ireland of English parents he spent a brief period in America as a child but was brought up in Buxton, Derbyshire. As a young man he moved to Manchester to take his articles as an architect, and his early cartoons were published in a local comic journal there. When it failed he moved to London as an illustrator of greeting cards, but was soon under the employ of Charles Ross, then editor of the magazine *Judy*. In turn Ross hired him for the *Half-Holiday* to which he made such a signal contribution until his death at 32 in 1888, four years after the paper started. He was also, one obituary noted, an amateur actor of note; like Cruikshank he may have considered this an alternative career to that of graphic artist.[11]

Charles Ross was an older man than Baxter with an established if inadequately rewarded place among the minor litterateurs of the capital. Like several of his kind, when young, he had combined a writing career with the post of civil servant. His magazine, *Judy, the London Serio-Comic Journal*, founded in 1867, was one of the few cheaper rivals to *Punch* which enjoyed any lengthy success in these earlier years. In addition to his journalism and illustrations, Ross wrote satirical verse, novels and plays and was at one time part of the management of the Surrey Theatre. Ally Sloper was among the various creations that appeared in the first numbers of *Judy*. However, as David Kunzle has established, against the common report, the great majority of the Sloper cartoons that appeared in *Judy* and various spin-offs up to the late 1870s were drawn by Ross's wife, the actress Marie Duval, a singular achievement in a male dominated occupation.[12] Ross mostly provided the written copy. The publisher Tinsley recalled him as 'very clever, but very nervous' and despite his considerable talents and enterprise he appears to have been bested by Dalziel as an entrepreneur. Though Charles Ross was to make a good deal of money from the *Half-Holiday* he lost most of it in theatrical ventures.[13]

Gilbert Dalziel was the son of one of the brothers Dalziel, the distinguished firm of wood engravers who made their name in fine art illustration. Despite the recognition which their quality work received in the mid-Victorian art and literary world they were often disappointed by low sales and were seeking more remunerative work by the 1870s. In 1870, the brothers bought up *Fun* (paying £6,000 for the goodwill and copyright from the paper's founder, who went on to make his fortune selling Spratt's Dog Biscuits – an interesting glimpse into the business opportunities of the period). *Fun* was another illustrated comic weekly dating from 1865; more radical than *Punch*, it had its own style and audience and was clearly regarded as a valuable property, though still less successful than the older, more established paper. The Dalziel family groomed young Gilbert to take eventual control of the new venture. Thus after formal schooling including a spell at the Slade, Gilbert worked first in the family studios but was soon serving as apprentice editor in *Fun*. In 1872 the Dalziels bought up Charles Ross's *Judy*, and Gilbert was then sent to serve under him. The *Half-Holiday* seems to have been the young Dalziel's first independent undertaking, and probably his most successful. Among other later ventures, he succeeded to the control of *Judy* which he revivified with a new more refined image, while launching at least two other comic papers at the end of the market where the 'penny dreadful' was succeeded by the 'half penny dreadfuller' following Harmsworth's introduction of *Comic Cuts* in 1890. Both bold and shrewd, he was said to have made £30,000 out of the *Half-Holiday* alone, but his methods brought him into dispute with Ross who in 1888 set up his own magazine in direct rivalry to *Half-Holiday* in price and format. Ross was later moved to sue his former associate.[14]

It was then Dalziel who conceived and modelled the new paper and set out to test and exploit new market formulae, but it seems plain enough that the social tone of the paper was more obviously a reflection of the experience and style of the other two men than of the successful businessman who employed them. Ross and Baxter, though of different generations, belonged to the sub-culture of Bohemian London with its clannish network of favoured clubs, taverns and theatres, and its finely cultivated sense of its own individual and collective identity vis à vis the conventions of respectable bourgeois society and its penumbra of petty imitators. Comic papers had long been a typical product of this world where, as the modern historian of *Punch* puts it, 'merry fellows met other merry fellows in taverns and talked plans', but the frequent failure of such ventures reinforced the insecurities of its members with their uncertain social and professional status.[15] The odds against Bohemian entrepreneurship became longer as the century progressed and the capitalisation of such projects became more daunting. The patent success of *Punch* (and its more dignified pictorial contemporary, the *Illustrated London News*) had conferred a new and glamorous social promi- nence on its leading contributors by the seventies that made it an even more seductive model of journalistic and social achievement, at a time when the chances of duplicating its success grew more remote. Ross probably, and Baxter certainly never enjoyed the relative prosperity and éclat that came with membership of the elect of their profession, and neither rose above the middle reaches of Bohemia. In such a situation merry fellows could soon become bitter fellows, and though neither Ross nor Baxter evinced the splenetic social hostilities of a *libelliste*, there are signs of their resentment and frustration, not least in Ross's dealings with Dalziel. The ambiguities and tensions in the social content of *Ally Sloper's Half-Holiday* reflect something of this compound of aspiration and insecurity that marks the careers of the paper's progenitors.

We are talking here also of characteristics that most clearly identify the social mentality of the lower middle class, the group that formed the paper's main readership and more generally seem to have functioned as the pilot group in the creation of a mass market.[16] Evidence for the social composition of the readership is mostly circumstantial, though convincing enough, but there is more specific evidence in the printed list of winners of the twenty watches given away each week by the paper over the four year period from 1886–1890. Applicants completed a form requiring name, address, age, occupation (if any) and the length of time they had subscribed to the paper. There are obvious problems in assessing this sample for there is no clue as to the principles (if any) of selection, though readers' complaints about the results of other competi- tions may have led the editor to make the list here as wide ranging and inclusive as possible. Thus the geographical pattern tended to remain fixed in the proportion of metropolitan to provincial winners (15/85%). Distribution by age and sex was similarly stable: rarely more than 20% of the winners were younger than 16 or older than 30, while women comprised some 15–20% of the names. In both these categories however the proportions probably conformed more exactly to the actual reader- ship profile than did those for geographical distribution. Composition by occupation is much harder to determine. Self-labelling no doubt allowed for a good deal of status inflation, ambiguity and facetiousness and the very wide range of occupations represented here may again have been due to editorial design. But we do learn that the readership of the *Half-Holiday* included such diverse callings as surgical instrument maker and billiard table repairer, brewer and lace manufacturer, solicitor and railway signalman, officers' mess waiter and dealer in horse flesh, french polisher and ploughman, governess and mill girl. The biggest general group comprised clerks, tradesmen and shopworkers, but a considerable number of working-class trades also appeared in the lists, and the paper was obviously very popular with working people. It was reported as commonly available in barber shops, then social centres of some importance in working-class districts. Working men's clubs invited Sloper to address their members, and trades and friendly societies solicited his attendance at their demonstrations.[17]

At this point, it is important to note too that the *Half-Holiday* was read among the middle classes. Sloper was a cult figure in 'upper Bohemia'; William Morris and Burne-Jones, among others, were fans. Recalling his youth in the haute bourgeoisie of Clifton, Bristol, Montagu Summers emphasised that of all the papers, daily and weekly, 'our favorite was *Ally Sloper*', commending its 'wisdom mingled with merriment'. The sense of cultural overlap becomes stronger when we learn that society artists regularly set aside time to draw cartoons for the *Half-Holiday* and other popular papers, welcoming the cash, but protecting their reputations by leaving their work unsigned.[18] Sloper's appeal worked simultaneously on a variety of social constituencies.

The giving away of watches (engraved, of course, with a true likeness of that Friend of Man, Ally Sloper) was only one example of an extensive offering of competitions, bonuses, prizes and stunts with which the paper sought to engage the loyalties and participation of its readership, gain publicity and boost its circulation. Other give-aways, usually bearing the Sloper motif, included pipes, cigarettes, sheet music, pairs of trousers, oil paintings and, on one occasion, a nanny goat. Readers were provided with a graphology service, a matrimonial agency and free insurance premiums – the paper itself doubled as a railway accident policy for £150 payable in the event of death, should the paper be found on the corpse at the time. Competitions with often handsome cash prizes invited submissions of readers' verse, essays, stories, love letters, drawings and photographs. Full length portraits of Ally and other members of his family were available for the price of postage, and the paper published various supplements and almanacks. Sloper also awarded his own weekly Order of Merit to deserving public figures. The Friend of Man himself delivered the certificate with its huge wax seal; played by an actor impersonator he drove up by coach to a fanfare on the post horn played by his son.[19] Such devices were not unknown at an earlier date and were used by other papers of the time, but their extent, insistency and relentless novelty mark *ASHH* as one of the aggressive pioneers of mass sales techniques.

Ally Sloper's image quickly entered the public domain. His likeness appeared on a great range of commodities – buttons, pipes, umbrellas, jars of pickles, boxes of matches, snuff boxes, doorstops. He was impersonated on the music hall, in pantomime and circus, and was displayed in fireworks at the Crystal Palace and seaside resorts. He replaced Guy Fawkes on bonfire night and he and his wife were substituted for Punch and Judy in street puppet shows. Dalziel apparently could not or did not effect any control over commercial exploitation of his hero's likeness and Ally Sloper never seems to have achieved apotheosis as a registered trade mark, though the paper proved quick enough to jump on its own bandwagon in holding an International Exhibition at the Royal Aquarium in 1888, displaying the already vast range of commercial articles bearing his image. Such schemes and the gratuitous momentum of popular taste and its small time hucksters gave Ally Sloper his high visibility in late Victorian and Edwardian popular culture. Within five years of its launching, the *Half-Holiday* boasted a circulation in excess of 340,000, and in the ten years under review here it continued to claim the largest circulation of any illustrated paper in Great Britain, with extensive sales abroad. Though we may question the claims of Ross's son that Sloper publications of all kinds reached annual sales of over 52 million by the nineties, *ASHH* was plainly a best-seller. Harmsworth tried to buy it out before producing his own comic papers.[20]

Though he enjoyed a new prominence and persona in the *Half-Holiday*, Ally Sloper did not burst unknown or unannounced on the late-Victorian public, for he had an earlier history, both as an individual cartoon character and as a social type descended from an earlier popular culture. Marie Duval's cartoons in *Judy* from the late 1860s quickly secured Sloper's popular celebrity and he was featured in several supplements, summer numbers, almanacks and the like under his own name. Duval's style was primitive but resourceful and effective, and it was she who established the distinctive visual signature of the new anti-hero, his bulbous nose, decrepit umbrella and grotesquely ballooned top hat. Lower class in background, Ally Sloper made his living as a small time confidence trickster – to slope, according to Partridge, meant in the 1850s to loiter, and by the seventies it meant also to decamp from lodgings without payment. He was depicted operating various dubious businesses – loan services, betting offices, cheap theatres – in company with a Jewish confederate Ikey Mo. Often drawn in a family portrait, he was nonetheless quite prepared to see his wife and children consigned to the workhouse, and regularly collected on her burial expenses from unwary benefit societies. There was some doubt as to whether Sloper was legally married; certainly he never allowed his family obligations to interfere with his interest in the ladies. He operated his nefarious schemes in the City but retired after work (and between his periodic arrests) to his home in suburban Battersea. Here then, in his first incarnation, Sloper is a minor deviant challenging Victorian pretensions of respectability, operating on the fringes of legality in the familiar topography of the capital. Though we are clearly meant to laugh at him there are features of his behaviour which may have given the still predominantly middle-class readers of *Judy* some disquiet (as well as confirmed their prejudices), for his petty roguery is at times overlain by the indiscriminate loutishness of a working man on the spree, as he clings drunkenly to a lamppost or falls backwards through a milliner's window.

But through whatever range of associations Sloper's image communicated to his public, in his days in *Judy* his character seems most strongly grounded in conventions of the 'low-life' school of enquiry reinvigorated by Egan and Cruikshank's Tom and Jerry series in the 1820s, and carried through in the work of many other writers and artists, including Dickens.[21] Ally and Ikey are colourful curiosities from the deeps; their exploits are a warning against the traps and deceits of big city life yet they are less threatening or sinister than Sykes and Fagan whose characterisations they may have echoed.

The rebirth of Ally Sloper in his own paper in 1884 maintained some continuity with his previous characterisation, but the considerable changes in his image bespeak significant shifts in popular taste. If not entirely a reformed character, he is the most inoffensive of recidivists, whose depredations are incidental rather than systematic. There is some suggestion that his reluctance to surrender his voluminous umbrella to servants or cloakroom attendants belies its utility as a cache for loot. In the early years of the *Half-Holiday* Ally frequently advised readers to help themselves to the paper while the newsagent's back was turned, and there were tips on how to engineer free cab trips and other rip-offs around town. There were acknowledgments of previous delinquencies: Sloper had once been a waiter at the Vauxhall pleasure gardens, so we are told, but he left 'because of a misunderstanding over a ham'. But the role of unreformed felon mostly falls to Ikey Mo. There is also some displacement of Sloper's proletarian antecedents. Though he occasionally appears in coster's dress and his home life and address remain relatively humble, he is rarely in any unequivocal sense represented as working class – he had become a man of the people, which is something different. His wife, forever wedded to her talismanic bottle of Bass Ale, seems resolutely plebeian but the role of working man now falls exclusively upon William McGoosely, an addition to the cast, and a genial but irredeemable derelict – probably Irish – who haunts the Moocher's Arms.[22]

More significant, however, than the dilution of his low-life persona, is Sloper's assumption of the manners and style of the fast life. Overnight he becomes something of the man about town with an appropriately expanded wardrobe and a more fashionable range of haunts. Thus Sloper becomes less of a sloven and more of a Gent. Such a role answers to a complex heredity. The Gent as a social type had first been noticed on London streets in the 1830s and 1840s. 'A second hand, shopworn imitation of the dandy', according to Ellen Moers, he was drawn 'from the very bottom of the respectable class, the scrubby clerks, apprentices and medical students.' Here was a butt for the comic journalism of the day. Thus Albert Smith, a member of the *Punch* coterie, in his *History of the Gent* of 1847, pilloried the 'rude untutored man' who 'by combinations of chance and cultivation' achieves a spurious gentility advertised by his pursuit of what he takes to be modish pleasure in what he thinks to be modish dress. Thackeray's *Book of Snobs* was a similar exercise. The pretensions of the upstart clerk remained an obvious target for popular satire, yet at the same time, behaviour that at first seemed aberrant and absurd became increasingly institutionalised as a self-sufficient and indigenously authentic style among the expanding lower middle class and more self-regarding members of the working class. The popularity of the heavy swell or lion comique who dominated the music hall stage in the sixties provides some confirmation of this, though his message was ambiguous. The immaculately dressed and champagne befuelled Swell displayed an aristocratic savoir faire and an effortless and unlimited command of the resources of the good life that mocked the aspirations of the upstart clerk who essayed the same style, yet the Swell seems also to have validated what he mocked.[23] Charles Ross ran a series in *Judy* in the seventies on the Rorty (fast) Life among the 'latchkey class' in a tone at once deprecating and indulgent. A further popular variant appeared in the same decade in A. J. Milliken's *Punch* stories of 'Arry, the Cockney

Cad, a lower class rake of ebullient vulgarity.[24] The gent, the swell, the toff, the masher, the rorty plunger and the cad were all variations of a type that together represented a sizeable constituency by the eighties, and not just in London, for by then jolly dogs were parading down provincial promenades as well as the Strand. Easily parodied though he was, the gent had become sui generis, and Ally Sloper was his fitting and timely embodiment. In his new image Sloper also represented a significant conflation of low and high life conventions within a single figure, where previously they had served to distinguish separate and contrasting characters.

Given the literary and theatrical interests of his progenitors, the refurbishment of Ally Sloper may have involved the assimilation of other and more recherché models. It is possible to see in him elements of the traditional or court fool, of Pantalone and, of course, Punchinella of the Commedia dell'Arte. The theme of interaction between high and low life invites comparison with Daumier's Robert Macaire. Suggested home grown models include another mid-Victorian comic figure cum con-man, Billy Barlow and, less plausibly, *Punch's* early strip character, Dumb Crambo. Some commentators detect a plain line of descent from either Pickwick – who had also become a mania with endless commodities carrying his name or likeness – or Micawber.[25] Whatever his cultural or stylistic lineage, Ally Sloper was yet more than the sum of his tributary parts, for he had his own unique and particular genius.

III

In the new paper, Sloper assumed a more substantial and confident form – 'a pygmy become giant'.[26] He appeared weekly in the 'big cut' on the front page, in action with an expanded cast of supporting characters in a much greater variety of settings. The cartoons often resemble the genre paintings of formal art in their compressed narrative qualities that invite the reader's own elaboration of a story line, and there is a good deal of sharply observed detail. The artwork was more sophisticated and the layout of the eight page paper was much cleaner than that of many of its rivals at the same price. Inside, Ally's doings were further recorded in print, and his daughter, Tootsie, an actress on the halls, provided a diary which also featured family affairs, news of the theatre and life about town. For the rest, the paper offered the usual miscellany of bizarre news items, short stories, jokes and riddles, light verse and correspondence, with a further leavening of smaller cartoons

MARGATE, AHOY!

"*Steamers leave London for Margate and Ramsgate every Tuesday, Thursday, and Saturday at 11 a.m., calling at Blackwall Pier, and returning from Ramsgate at 11 a.m., and Margate about noon every Monday, Wednesday, and Friday.*"—Advt., Daily Paper.

The Fam'ly, airy, light, and gay, The Old 'Un, Tootsie, Snook, Bob, Bill,	McGoose' and Boy set sail one day— The Old 'Un near the Nore was ill!

Figure 1   'Margate Ahoy', from W. G. Baxter, *Fifty Sloper Cartoons*, London, 1888.

and illustrations. Popular magazines were frequently short of copy and plagiarism was common. The *Half-Holiday* solved this problem by re-cycling material from *Judy*, a practice which makes assessment of changing emphases in tone and style more uncertain, though much of the paper's content seems fresh and topical.

In company with different combinations of his family and associates, Sloper spends his year in progress through the calendar of London social events with seasonal excursions to provincial resorts. Ally regularly takes in the new season at the Royal Academy, the Lord Mayor's Show, the various exhibitions that proliferated in this period, the Boat Race, Henley, the Derby, Ascot and the Eton and Harrow match. On occasions, in mock heroic manner, he himself takes to the field, and appears playing football or running in some pedestrian enclosure. In the summer he makes his progress around the resorts in remarkably comprehensive fashion, from Scarborough to Ilfracombe (figure 1, 'Margate Ahoy!'). The predetermined round is punctuated by time out to exploit topical issues, as Ally assembles his own relief expedition for the Nile, takes his place as judge for a society breach of promise case, or runs for Parliament. The year ends with the famous Christmas party back at Battersea and a visit to the pantomime.

Clearly, *ASHH* followed established practice in capitalising upon the mystique and glamour of the metropolis, but here was a London minus the slums and rookeries, and minus the East End. The contrast of extremes in London life that had featured so prominently in the previous popular literary tradition, and which so powerfully exercised the consciences of social reformers and the middle-class public of the eighties, has no place in the social topography of the *Half-Holiday*. The contrast to the opulence and glitter of the West End is now Battersea, a gateway to south London suburbia rather than the resort of the dangerous classes. The London we get is in fact very much the tourist's or day-tripper's London of the major landmarks up West, though in the specious way of the modern guide book it also purports to offer an insider's view of the city – 'the London the tourist never sees': all of this without the frisson of risk for the unwary that coloured older guides to life in Town.[27] But while paying considerable attention to the capital, Ally's interest in life out of Town and his annual progress around the resorts show a keen concern to reach a national audience, and by the nineties the itinerary included visits to major provincial centres and chummy encounters with the local worthies of Birmingham and Manchester.

In this and other ways the world of Sloper and his cartoons is inclusive rather than exclusive. Thus McGoosely, though a derelict, is always included in the family's Christmas celebrations, sitting down together with the aristocratic trio of Lord Bob, Dook Snook and Honourable Billy. These three have been drawn to Sloper by the charms of his daughter and her ready supply of actress friends, but Ally is totally unawed by their presence and their common role is that of supernumerary. In the text, Tootsie, who is engaged to Lord Bob, frequently mocks them for their shabby behaviour. The Dook is said to have let his town house to a co-op grocer and is reduced to sponging off Sloper's daughter. The effect is to collapse social distinctions at the top end of the scale,

MASHING 'EM AT MARGATE.

" *The goings on at Margate this week, my dear, have been simply disgraceful. It appears that Poor Papa was mashing them on the jetty, and while twirling his umbrella round in a light and careless manner, accidentally hit a Peer of the Realm, who is staying at Margate with his aunt, on the head. Mamma, who was lunching at the time, was very nearly killed.*"

—ANOTHER ONE OF TOOTSIE'S.

Figure 2 'Mashing 'em at Margate', from W. G. Baxter, *Fifty Sloper Cartoons*, London, 1888.

an effect demonstrated more forcibly when Sloper accidentally fells a peer of the realm with his umbrella on Margate pier (figure 2, 'Mashing 'em at Margate'). There are other episodes of accidental violence at the expense of the privileged, but in general any such hostilities are repressed, and where Sloper is depicted in the company of actual members of the upper class and high society (in one cartoon he takes tea with the Queen and he is depicted several times on nodding acquaintance with the Prince of Wales) the effect again is primarily that of reducing social distance. The great, including such unlikely candidates as Gladstone, shown guffawing over the first edition of the paper, are represented as chums who are happily co-opted into his populist world. In this case too, politics as well as rank is demystified.[28] (Figure 3, 'Back again

BACK AGAIN AT SCHOOL.

PROFESSOR SLOPER:—*In addition to the other important Studies which will be proceeded with, the position of affairs in Egypt, and the course of policy adopted, will demand immediate attention. So hurry up, boys, please!"*

Figure 3   'Back Again at School', from W. G. Baxter, *Fifty Sloper Cartoons*, London, 1888.

School' – Bright, Childers, Chamberlain and Harcourt follow Gladstone.) The interviews that Ally conducts with the recipients of his Order of Merit (embracing a wide range of prominent public figures; political, legal, theatrical and literary including – I pick at random under the latter head – Zola and Ruskin) were reported in a tone that suggests a meeting of back-slapping equals. Not that *ASHH* was free from discrimination, for there were frequent dismissive references in the text to various minorities beneath the salt: foreigners, the Salvation Army, socialists, servants, and strikers generally. However, such examples probably reinforce rather than invalidate the model of petty bourgeois populism, and the main cartoon set the paper's general tone of affable inclusivism.

Sloper's annual round includes a mix of fashionable and homely pleasures, but here again, just as his style in mixing with his social superiors essentially domesticates them and brings them within reach, so too his easy access to the physical territory of the rich suggests that the enclosure at Ascot, or the pavilion at Lord's, or a seat at a Mansion House banquet is within the range of common experience. (It was the traditional privilege of the jester to move with all sorts and conditions of men, but the scope of Sloper's venues and visitations is far more comprehensive.) True, the text often suggests minor tactical difficulties, and one of Sloper's many titles was Most Frequently Kicked Out Man in Europe, but it is significant that he invariably gets in in the first place, and struts his stuff through the precincts of privilege mostly unhindered. Such episodes may also have operated on a different level for they provide a vicarious form of conspicuous consumption, rehearsing the names and scenes of the haute monde for the vulgar, at one remove from actuality, but this still constitutes in some measure a democratisation of experience. Tootsie is a crucial mediator here. She, too, has her own social circuit – lunch at Romanos, dinner at the Cri(terion) – but her diary gives the inside story of all occasions in detail, in a manner both awed and matter of fact. Thus she contrives to be both mystifying and mundane, and this capacity to at once impress and yet reassure her readers may be a key property of much of the popular culture of an emerging mass society.

Thus an initial review of Ally Sloper's picaresque adventures can suggest that the world of fashionable pleasure is accessible and amenable. Indeed, some episodes further suggest that such a world can be possessed and dominated. Consider our hero and the world of things. In J. A. Banks' memorable phrase, the social aspirations of a newly prosperous mid-Victorian bourgeoisie generated a new range of material accessories with which to reinforce their status claims, what he called 'the paraphernalia of gentility'. Much of this was deployed and managed by servants but it also presumably demanded new social skills among its owners. What Ally frequently displays, despite occasional embarrassments or 'fixes', is a superb aplomb in mastering various items of this paraphernalia. Take for example the cartoon 'All There at Brighton' (figure 4) where he tools his hired brougham along the King's Road. It may be ramshackle and unpaid for, and drawn by a drayhorse, but Sloper is far from non-plussed. The matter of the hire charge is disregarded with an aristocratic disdain for the vulgar details of com-

ALL THERE AT BRIGHTON.

" *Yes, dear, Poor Pa is down at Brighton, and has been recommended to drive as much as possible.   Until the Livery Stable person wants his bill settled, Poor Pa says he will.   Tottie Goodenough met Poor Pa by accident, and went for a drive along the King's Road.   She says that " Snatcher," with spots painted on him, looks just like a real carriage dog, or better even, and that everyone at Brighton appears to know Poor Pa.*"
—EXTRACT FROM TOOTSIE'S CORRESPONDENCE.

Figure 4   'All There at Brighton', from W. G. Baxter, *Fifty Sloper Cartoons*, London, 1888.

merce, the family has (with some ingenuity) been pressed into service to provide a groom and carriage dog, and Ally is accompanied on his excursion by a pretty woman (thus duplicating a condition that Dr. Johnson considered the closest thing to heaven on earth). The whole exercise is accomplished with spirit and command and though the caption suggests Tootsie's mortifications and the street urchins regard the spectacle as uproarious, the two most prominent (and distinguished looking) spectators register respect. Ally is that remarkable phenomenon, the welcome arriviste, and again we are shown how an outwardly daunting world can be co-opted or indeed conquered.

It may well be that the principal appeal of Sloper's adventures lay in such representations of the common man in excelsis, yet to leave it at that would be to miss the complexity of an artefact that spoke to a mixed class readership, beaming a complex of meanings, at once ambiguous and complementary. Thus while the same cartoon might flatter and encourage the lowly aspirant to the good life, it could also work to amuse and comfort his social superior. To Gordon Roe, whose middle-class artist father drew for *ASHH* in the nineties, Sloper impressed only by his failures: 'he ever tried to carry off life in style, only to be thwarted, exposed, tripped up and generally plunged in the liquid'.[29] This is a reminder that misadventure often alternated with triumph in the comic cycle of Sloper's festive kingdom. From this position, and mindful of the genre's invitation to narrative projection, we can look again at 'All There at Brighton'. Sloper is all there, but only just: the old joker is barely in control, and will surely self-destruct in the next frame! The genteel spectators are bemused by the happily inevitable. The threat posed to middle-class status and exclusivity by the expansion of popular leisure since the mid-century had often been symbolically represented in the figure of the boorish working-class excursionist, and bourgeois repugnance at the invasion of the leisure space was part of their greater unease at the political and economic advance of the masses. There are still some disturbing features in the cartoon – the hint of violence in the savage device of the fishhooks on the whip's end, and the rogue erectile tissue of the horse's tail, a visual pun that amplifies the phallic symbolism of Sloper's nose. But the comic effect reduces the sense of threat, alleviating anxiety at any real penetration from below, and suggesting how unlikely it is that the lumpen leisure class can ever master the social skills of their betters.

Another and more significant element in the paraphernalia of gentility (or sub-gentility) with which Sloper is constantly engaged is dress. Again the central message would seem to be one of reassurance, but a reassurance that works in different ways at different levels. In the matter of dress, as in so much of the material history of popular culture, we are as yet poorly served and probably misled. While it may be broadly true that in this era it was becoming difficult to tell a man's class by his dress, this emphasis on democratisation disregards the infinitude of fine gradations of style and status that obtained beneath a superficial uniformity. This was certainly true, as we know, for the young shopmen in *Kipps* whose conversation was dominated by the minutiae of fashion. Such minutiae could, to the initiated, have a quite disproportionate social resonance, for in considering dress in this period we are dealing with a material culture of almost uniquely acute and extensive social specificity. To catch something of the precisely differentiated social colour and function of a gentleman's wardrobe, turn to Tom Stoppard's *Travesties* and listen to Henry Carr's almost rhapsodic inventory of his various pairs of trousers; then read the stories in the *Half-Holiday* and ponder the particular signals flashed by a two guinea Lincoln and Bennett (hat), a new tourist suit at £1 19s 9d, or a pair of Denkins' nine and eleven penny 'flannel bags'. Consumption in today's capitalist society, so we are told, confers a state of grace, but the sentiment was well understood in the early 1880s, if we are to judge from the well-dressed lady on holiday who speaks to us from a cartoon in *Judy* (6 August 1884). 'The consciousness of being well dressed', she offers, 'causes an inward peace of mind which religion is powerless to bestow.' 'Just so' murmurs an editorial voice. The problem for the young swell was not only to be well dressed in the sense of meeting the proprieties (particularly in the matter of formal dress), but that he needed to display something unconventional (properly unconventional one is tempted to say) by which to advertise his individuality and bohemian disregard for the orthodox. Plainly too, from the itemising of prices evidenced above, this had to be accomplished within a very modest budget. In addition, dress had to be complemented with an appropriate manner or bearing – at best, it demanded 'dash', than which, as Denry Machin mused, few things were more mysterious.[30]

At first glance Sloper's diverse and garish wardrobe would seem to lie outside any finely shaded social classification, being rather the theatrical properties of the clown. Plainly the reader was meant to laugh at some aspects of Sloper's appearance, as we can still do where it is bizarre or incongruous – such as the watchchain that could moor a barge. With a little knowledge of the history of dress we can also spot the persistent anachronisms of the frock coat and the neck stock. Given the detailed treatment of costume in the cartoons and the sensibilities of the time, it would not be surprising to learn that Sloper's dress was studded with various other less obvious solecisms for contemporaries to spot as proof of his misdirected attempts at gentility, in the way that a butler's tie and trousers distinguished him from his gentleman employer. For middle-class readers, Ally Sloper was probably more than simply funny looking; he was a graceless catalogue of errors in taste that marked the common man as incorrigibly common and made the cultural lines of class exclusivity seem still secure against democracy.

But again, we should allow for different readings of the same image. Sloper's dress may have been intended and read by some as a parody of the ineffable bad taste of the bookmaker, the publican and the stage army of vulgar swells, but there is nothing in his demeanour that suggests the conscious copyist or slave of fashion. What impresses is Sloper's unabashed sartorial confidence. His splendidly eclectic wardrobe serves him admirably in whatever role he plays and he proves himself a master of the accessories – monocle, watchchain, hat and gloves, cigar and, most notably, the umbrella. For Sloper it is the umbrella, the symbolic insignia of the city clerk, that gives him additional powers, serving variously as a truncheon, cane, slap-stick, wand, hold-all and auxiliary phallus. In the manner of modern sub-cultures that make their own selection and combination from the dominant culture, Sloper creates his own style and conventions, and encourages others to do likewise. The characteristic insouciance of the Friend of Man may well have relieved some of the discomfitures associated with correctness of dress.

For all his pursuit of *la vie élégante* and its fashionable round, Sloper is unashamedly given to more fundamental pleasures. He has a great love of the bottle. His regular tipple is unsweetened gin, though he drinks whatever is going: champagne of course at the races, Bovril and sherry at the Gaiety, iced chablis on the river.[31] He suffers from a more or less permanent hangover. Proposals to tax drink move him to one of his infrequent political protests. On one occasion he is arrested for being drunk and disorderly, though later acquitted. In 'Turning Over a New Leaf' (figure 5) a repentant Sloper sets off for church – with Lord Bob and Tootsie in the rear – but is somewhat delayed by McGoosely and the counter attractions of the Moochers Arms. His drinking is half celebrated and half connived at – it is an understandable weakness. Sloper's own unabashed enthusiasm for strong drink may represent one of the irreducibly plebeian features of his behaviour and a corrective to undue delusions of refinement, but it may also reflect the persistent drinking that took place in the commercial world, particularly in the City.

The other pleasure which openly conflicts with the tests of respectability is Sloper's philandering. Immune to his wife's scolding, Ally flirts outrageously with the ladies and is the frequent consort of Tootsie's actress friends, the Girls from the Friv(olity Theatre). On occasions this remarkable man is invested with a magnetic and indeed omnipotent appeal for adoring groups of young women – witness his visit to the Health Exhibition, where Sloper is the cynosure and the other males

TURNING OVER A NEW LEAF.

" *My dear, you would never believe it, Poor Pa is no longer the man he was. We attribute it to a new hat; but all feel sincerely glad. As Ma says, there is a time for all things. We were accidentally three-quarters of an hour late last Sunday, and caused some attention to be directed towards us. But that need not occur again.*"

—EXTRACT FROM TOOTSIE'S CORRESPONDENCE.

Figure 5   'Turning Over a New Leaf', from W. G. Baxter, *Fifty Sloper Cartoons*,
London, 1888.

are faceless and emasculated (figure 6, 'Ally at the Healtheries'). Neither his grotesque appearance nor his age are allowed to blind us to his sexual appetite – the spats he sometimes wears enhance his goatish image, and though old he is clearly not spent, for he fathered twins in the early years of the paper. At times the cartoons suggest a good deal more than flirtation or 'spooning'. Thus the prominent and much ravaged nose that otherwise advertised his taste for drink could be quite plainly and alarmingly phallic. It is most appropriately tumescent on Derby Day as Sloper brandishes his ejaculatory bottle of champagne (figure 7, 'The First Favorite Everywhere'). As represented in *ASHH* this was not the sanitised and sentimentalised festival of Frith's painting,

ALLY AT THE HEALTHERIES.

The success of the " Half-Holiday" enables dear old SLOPER *to attend the Wednesday Evening Fêtes.   It will be observed that he has not lost sight of the fact that* DRESS *is one of the Features of the Exhibition.*

Figure 6   'Ally at the Healtheries', from W. G. Baxter, *Fifty Sloper Cartoons*, London, 1888.

THE FIRST FAVOURITE EVERYWHERE.

I. Moses, Esq.—*Now, then, my Sportive Noblemen and Festive Dames! Plank down the plebeian penny! Beg, borrow, or steal, or even work for it—but get it, anyway, and plank it down.   A moral certainty:—*

SLOPER **1**

THE REST NOWHERE.

Figure 7   'The First Favourite Everywhere', from W. G. Baxter, *Fifty Sloper Cartoons*, London, 1888.

but a traditional celebration of licence when, as Taine remarked, we may see in every Englishman 'the beast that explodes'.[32]

For all Ally's engaging satyriasis, the paper commonly traded in a more cosmetic form of sexuality: it dealt in glamour, that particular product of modernity. It was an early pin-up magazine, and in its first year received letters from tradesmen who protested at its pictures of young women for distracting their apprentices. The girls who appear in the main cartoon and in such series as 'Fashion Fancies', 'Girls Sloper Has Kissed', 'Girls from the Friv' etc. were all of a type – enchanting yet remote, alluring yet daunting in the perfection and indeed purity of their stylised voluptuousness. They belong to a fantasy world, idealised and distant. Yet here again the paper works to collapse distance, and Tootsie is the mediator. In her diary she takes the reader 'Behind the Scenes' at the Friv and elsewhere. Here is a world of many meaningful glances (or 'eyework' as she puts it, in happy anticipation of Goffman's term), a world of considerable sexual promise. She herself writes under the byline of The Well Regulated Girl, suggesting a calculated permissiveness that gets no one into trouble.[33] She is portrayed visually in the same style as her peers, yet for all her glamour and worldliness Tootsie in her diary often evinces a masculine matiness which suggests a ready understanding of men on their own terms. Tootsie is both a sex symbol and yet really one of the chaps, thus encouraging a belief in the reduction of sexual as well as social distance in a society characterised by a high degree of tension and formality in its sexual relationships.

We are back again to what seems to be the *Half-Holiday*'s major function, that of encouraging its readers to make light of the various problems of negotiating the more sophisticated world of social encounter that constituted modern leisure. It should be noted too how little the pleasures of Sloper's personal world were inhibited by the intrusion of work, of which little of any kind was seen to be done, though his leisure was so strenuous that it could be interpreted as a substitute (Pennell was struck by the seriousness with which he pursued his amusements). His income, so we gather, was derived from his editorial duties, but they were rarely made explicit. When temporarily short of funds, he resorts to freeloading, pawning, cadging and a simple Micawberish faith in providence – at no time does he appear seriously embarrassed or discommoded by the problem or its remedies. But if the good life generally proceeds triumphantly for Sloper and his family, the anxieties that he set out to allay continued to surface in other departments of the paper.

The stories and smaller cartoons that, together with the commentaries and correspondence, made up the rest of the paper, are also instructive, for all their miscellaneity. Time and again they demonstrate the considerable social energies invested in leisure. Young men and women are momentarily transformed as they pass from the routine and subordination of their working lives to the freedom and opportunity of this ephemeral but enchanting new social world. Tibbins the humble City clerk blooms into Captain Tickleby, habitué of Pall Mall and Monte Carlo, as he steps off the train for his week in Folkestone. Miss Becky Solomons from the fried fish shop becomes the beautiful Re-

becca on the promenade at Margate, and servant girls on their day off
disport themselves grandly in their mistresses' clothes. Men and women
not only put their working lives behind them but often too are shown
shrugging off what are represented as the equally burdensome demands
of marriage and family while they snatch briefly at pleasure and adventure. The seaside is the commonest site for such escapes. Here plainly
was a new popular school of manners where life became theatre and
new roles and identities were experimented with.

There are tensions here as well. Pleasures are all too episodic – and
all too dear. 'Love is exceedingly nice', wrote the winner of an essay
contest on How I Spent Whit Monday, 'but awfully expensive', a
reminder of Fred Willis' emphasis that in those days the Boy Always
Paid.[34] There is an element of risk in many of the adventures: the
contriving of an illicit holiday is discovered by an employer; an assumed
identity is collapsed in dramatic fashion; a husband's holiday liaison
with a servant girl is similarly disclosed. Thus the discontinuities and
anonymity of modern life that facilitate these adventures are at times no
security against fate and coincidence. But retribution here is more of a
dramatic convention than a moral judgment, for in general deception
and dissimulation are connived at, almost as necessary social skills –
indeed, virtue is sometimes more despised than rewarded. This is part
of the considerable ambiguities of tone that infect the stories. While the
characters are mostly treated with indulgence, there is frequent scorn
and contempt for those whose performance cannot match their presumptions. Thus of one would-be swell, we are told, 'He has the
manners of a vet and the look of an ostler, with the high bred tone of a
solicitor's clerk.' There are also many contemptuous reminders of the
gaffes of the uninitiated, like buying the 'gooseberry champagne'
specially manufactured for the credulous on Boat Race Day.

The social world represented here is enormously enticing, but often
expensive, anomic and ruled by chance; the pitfalls for the unworldly
are many. But again readers could take comfort and assurance from
Tootsie, whose weekly confection may well have had as much to do
with the paper's success as the tableaux vivants of her more notorious
father. Though not without pretensions herself, Tootsie makes us privy
to her own thoughts and intentions (and those of her father) while she
moves about in the fashionable world. Plainly, the diary form is a key
device in sustaining this effect. Through this the reader can negotiate
the sophisticated and uncertain world of social encounter at second
hand, enjoying the benefit and security of her intimacy amidst the

falsities and pretensions of others. You are in the privileged position of her confidante, enfolded together in an exquisite complicity. Another powerful source of comfort here must be that, for all her showbiz exoticism, Tootsie is one of a family, and the sense of membership of the family that comes with the weekly insights of the diary strengthens the reader's sense of identification and special status. The symbolic and dramatic formula of the family as the knowable unit in the crowd was to become a commonplace in later popular culture. Though not unexplored before, it receives a new emphasis from the chronicles of the Sloper ménage and the graphic snapshots from their family album.

IV

Ally Sloper's Half-Holiday creates its own symbolic and ideological world. It celebrates leisure as a new area for adventure and fulfilment, a self-contained world of experience in which the individual can fashion a way of life of his or her own choosing; leisure here is a laboratory of social styles. There are strong elements of fantasy and wish-fulfilment, but it is a manageable fantasy, grounded in the concrete particulars of the real world. *ASHH* is the vade-mecum to the pleasures of this new freedom, giving a ritualised agenda of its principal sites and occasions, its appropriate activities and accessories, and its particular aesthetic of display and consumption. Almost literally the paper makes the individual reader feel at home in this heady new domain. Yet its freedoms are far from open-ended, for though the world of Ally Sloper is energised by his spirit of play and exuberance, it is also one of considerable constraints, not least that of an implicit psychic economy that programs and contains its joys and expectations. It is an almost manically optimistic world which has repressed its conflicts but cannot escape its contradictions.

Just as Sloper's image represents a conflation of high and low life, so too the new leisure world he inhabits is a compound of their cultural milieux. Though answering crudely to the antique stereotypes of patrician/plebeian and aristocratic/folk, they are here reworked and reflect a new social reality. High life in *ASHH* is a bourgeois appropriation and modification of older aristocratic forms. It is the world of the London season with particular emphasis on the newly-fashionable sporting calendar and its tributes to the contests of the reformed and embourgeoised universities and public schools. The various grand exhibitions celebrate enterprise and progress in tandem with their entertainments. There is a nod to art and culture (as fashionable commodities) at the Royal Academy, and some suggestion of ideals of service in the attention to the rituals of Parliament and the flummery of the Lord Mayor's show. Life at a less eventful level is spent in the round of fashionable restaurants and theatres. There is a certain risqué tone to the reporting, but there is no recklessness or abandon, no real licence or excess. It is a bourgeois version of the classical Good Life – self-consciously genteel and indulgently materialist. (Though new, like the remade working-class culture of the period, it is a way of life that has become sanctified as 'traditional' and needs serious historical study.) As both contrast and complement to this reworked vision of life at the top, *ASHH* offers a chronicle and gazetteer of a reworked low-life. This, as we have seen, is no longer sited principally in the rookeries of central or east end London, but in the 'transpontine' suburb of Battersea. Its round of pleasures take in the pub and various low dives but the new playground of the seaside is a more frequent and significant setting. There is an overt delight in boozing, wenching and gambling, but this revised formulation of low life has largely shed its associations of deviancy and violence. Above all, it is a life now anchored in domesticity and the family, however uneasily, for its pleasures are often snatched at in defiance of domestic constraints. Pleasure here does answer the promptings of basic human appetites more than in high life, but it is also more closely defined in terms of its constraints – of family obligations, of money, work, manners, and time. Leisure is more abruptly episodic in this world, qualifying less for the label of the Good Life with its sustained trajectory of pleasure and comfort, than that of the Good Time with its compulsive intervals of whoopee.

The ubiquitous Ally Sloper straddles and reconciles the two worlds, collapsing distinctions of class and caste, age and grace, in a new fraternity of the playful. Sloper himself owns to no single class identity. He is plebeian without being classbound, perhaps the first demotic hero of the period who is neither criminal nor faithful servant, though he bears the marks of both. His adventures denote a new pattern in the otherwise traditional mode of the urban picaresque: whereas previously the reader had been taken on a tour of low life by an escort from the high born, he was now treated to a guided tour of high life by one of the underlings. Moreover, this new guide is totally uninhibited by any sense of deference or undue liberty, and it brings three witless and redundant aristos in tow. In his compulsive quest for pleasure, Sloper assumes another novel heroic role, reconciling the myth of the romantic individual and his life-search with the unromantic routines of suburban domesticity. Sloper's adventures fuse the epic and the diurnal, the odyssey with the day excursion to Brighton. In this further attempt to both collapse and elasticate the range of experience we have perhaps the Friend of Man's ultimate conceit, a theme at once poetic and absurd that seems to prefigure new genres in modern literature, and a rich field for comic expression in modern popular culture – what James Joyce noted as 'the ennoblement of the mock-heroic'.[35]

Thus Sloper's career sublimates the popular appetite for pleasure, suggesting how the common man can engross this new world of democratised leisure and live the Good Life for himself. There is in the Sloper cartoons something of a visual rhetoric of progress and democracy, to be realised in play, in a society which is one big and mostly – warts and all – happy family. Leisure is the new utopia and other sites are ceded or evacuated; work is the unspoken but tolerable incubus, politics are simply redundant. 'We all try to be clever in our prophecies,' ran a caption in the election year of 1886, 'but the fact is, honestly speaking, we none of us know anything about it . . . what on earth does it matter as long as *Ally Sloper's Half-Holiday* comes out every Saturday, and bangs all feeble and flabby imitations into a cocked hat.' Ally Sloper is dauntlessly egalitarian, but since he eschews any explicit political or class consciousness, the effect is not that of the World Turned Upside Down, but rather of the world transformed into everyone's front parlour. The *Half-Holiday*'s populism is inclusive but innocuous.

While less obviously disabling, there are also ways in which the particular commodity and cultural forms of *ASHH* interact with and help construct an ideology that carefully regulates the expectations encouraged by the confident irruptions of the Friend of Man. Leisure is the great bonanza, but its prizes are doled out in penny packets through the commodity form of the periodical, whose very periodicity is a secondary determinant of considerable significance, at once obvious and unnoticed. The *Half-Holiday*, as we have seen, has its own rhythms and climaxes but its episodes are nonetheless extruded at a regular weekly pace within the confines of a uniform format – a kind of portion control of pleasure in which appetites are stimulated and yet flattened out and contained in a half-way house between instant and deferred gratification. Regularity here generates an assurance of opportunity if not of fulfilment; under this regimen, there is always a next time, always another bite at the cherry, always another half-holiday. Indeed, Sloper's mix of coups and calamities may have induced a kind of benign fatalism

– 'you win some, you lose some' – in which any larger vision or confidence is curtailed. This is the mentality of the punter, not the man who would conquer the world. Ultimately too Sloper is the prisoner of his own cultural form; he is a comic hero whose assertive, at times almost anarchic, role can never escape self-parody. Thus the comic lens always leaves the reader with an alibi: the text can be taken as some kind of model for action that is otherwise inconceivable, or it can be enjoyed and set aside as merely comic and eccentric and beyond the bounds of realisation.

Overall the paper's appeal was clearly widespread and spoke to several social positions. More particularly we can speculate on its appeal to the young. Recalling his own youth in the early years of this century, Richard Church observed: 'The day-school-boy, and especially the board school boy in a close, petty family circle of little or no culture and social contacts, is doomed to late development as an adult with worldly confidence or authority.'[36] The newly extended years of dependence in schools mostly staffed by women and homes largely run by mothers made the transition to a man's world of work and play and the fashioning of an appropriate masculine identity a particularly critical transition for the late Victorian youth. What Sloper may have offered is less the missing father-figure than the raffish old uncle who could offer a relationship akin to that between father and son and without the inhibitions; Sloper is the greenhorn's guide to life on the town.[37] In another guise *ASHH* appealed to the outwardly secure middle class. Sloper could be *their* clown, bringing an acceptable whiff of saturnalia to a glamorised picture of their new leisure world, dispelling the spectre of the hooligan or communard, and assuaging the acute political and social anxieties of the 1880s by representing popular aspirations in comic form. It is surely no mere coincidence that the original conception and subsequent refurbishment of Ally Sloper came in 1867 and 1884 respectively, the years of the second and third reform bills with their mass extension of the franchise.

By its general accessibility of style and content, the *Half-Holiday* reached for and captured a broadly based popular market, yet paradoxically its success may well have lain in its ability to suggest a certain exclusivity for its proto-mass audience. There was a decided complicity of tone, a sense that its news and gossip were dispensed strictly entre nous. The paper's column of answers to correspondents suggests a high degree of reader participation and considerable identification with the Sloper ménage. Thus *ASHH* generated a particular community of interest that fulfilled something of the surrogate social functions of the family, the private club, and the voluntary association. The paper's operators, by coincidence or design, had learned the trick of selling identity and membership via a mass medium, of preserving gemein-schaft in gesellschaft.

Plainly, *ASHH* fulfils the commonest function of modern popular culture by its insistent message of flattery and reassurance. Even so, it did not exorcise all the anxieties it sought to allay, and may have served to aggravate them. The paper's content showed that those who might wish to be free faced daunting material and social constraints in a world of leisure that was already extensively commoditised and commercial-ised, and the cultural convergence that it championed was opposed by the reinforcement of class distinctions in culture that came in the 1880s, no doubt in defence against the pretensions it represented. In its parody of the ideals of competitive gentility it seemed often to reinforce what it mocked, and as a conduct manual it could only have frustrated the novitiate, for it spoke with a knowingness that disallowed precise in-struction – knowingness, that persistent tone in much of nineteenth-century popular culture, would seem to be the petty élitism of the populist. Moreover, while Sloper's self-confidence encouraged readers to believe in themselves, the rest of the paper warned them against believing in others. In modern marketing strategy, those who trade in reassurance also take care to perpetuate the anxieties that demand it. In the history of the *Half-Holiday* in those years, there is more than a suggestion of such manipulation, and in this as in several other features of its operation it does seem to qualify as a prototype for much of the cultural product of modern consumer capitalism.

This may be a more than sufficient account of Sloper's place in the popular culture of the period, but there are a number of avenues left unexplored. It would be interesting to learn the connections and opposi-tions through which the *Half-Holiday* interacted with other texts and practices – those of the music hall, theatre, the more fashionable illustrated press, high art and photography and advertising, and beyond that with political and social forms and their ideologies. What too, are the shifts in Sloper's relationship with his audience and social context in the nineties and beyond; when does he become obsolete, why does he die? What are the later manifestations of the type, fictional or otherwise (figure 8)?[38]

'Master of his fate, Captain of his soul', Ally Sloper is a complex and tightly wound metaphor for the vulgarised liberal ideology of mass

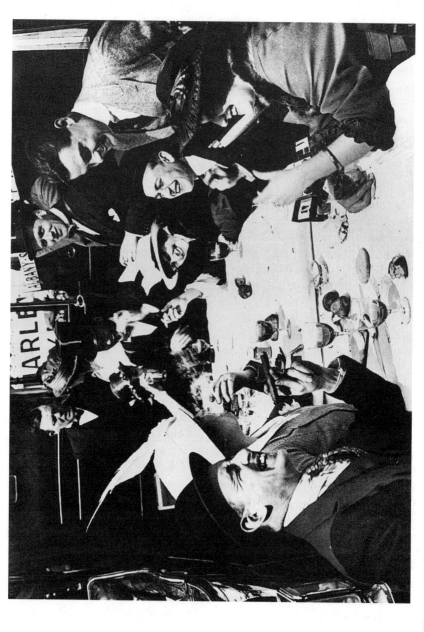

Figure 8   Performing the Good Time for the last time? Doing a Sloper at the Derby, 1914. 'A scene from the course', Horace Nicholls.

individualism with all its hopes and contradictions. An exuberant marauder in the extended margins of a social order that was learning to accommodate and exploit play as it had controlled and exploited work, Sloper gives graphic realisation to what Wells described as Mr. Polly's 'restless craving for joy and leisure', while creating a potent identity that is more vigorously drawn than most such characterisations of an essentially petit-bourgeois sensibility. The Friend of Man is a powerful antidote to priggishness, respectability, and suburban torpor, yet he is reactionary as well as liberating and the *Half-Holiday* may well be read as a hegemonic text. But it is also a fluid text which keeps its questions open even when they may be closed; certainly it is more than flatly formulaic or merely opportunist. We are frequently told that the best of popular culture evinces a distinctive vitality, a judgment that until recently and still too often is a substitute for any further critical conclusions. But, yes, the abiding impression left by Ally Sloper is one of vitality, of enormous social and physical energy. Each week Sloper fairly leaps off the page, a dynamic contrast to those other contemporaries that have been offered as paradigms of the Common Man – Leno and Chaplin, the little men that life kicks around and consoles with small pleasures.[39] Though superficially tamed, Homo Slopens is a creature of instinct, appetite and spontaneity; in a world of rationalised and routinised leisure he preserves the spirit of licence and the carnivalesque, and suggests something of the latent social force of the lower classes in late Victorian society. Maybe that is why William Morris enjoyed him.[40]

CHAPTER 4

Business and good fellowship in the London music hall

In his address to the audience at his grand benefit night in 1869, William 'Billy' Holland, the proprietor of the Canterbury music hall in London, 'first begged permission to substitute the word "Friends" for Ladies and Gentlemen, and then very properly remarked that when prices are raised on benefit night, a man finds out who are really his friends'.[1] In this artful reconciliation of the ingratiating and the obligating, the affective and the instrumental, Holland animated an ideological motif central to the culture and operation of early music hall, for in this world the language of friendship was the language of business.

Though music hall is much celebrated for its legendary *bonhomie*, there has been little analysis of the specific dynamics of its sociability – how it worked and what it meant. This essay attempts to understand friendship in the music hall as a distinctive stylistic and operational code in what is characterised as a socially intensive industry. It concentrates on the role of the London proprietors in an era of sucess *c.* 1860–85, their conduct of business and their relationships with the performers, other music hall workers, the audience and the community. Particular attention is paid to the ritual occasion of the benefit night, which disclosed the contradictions of business and good fellowship while celebrating their mutuality, and the essay concludes with some general observations on the significance of friendship to the culture of the period.

Though still something of a novelty, music hall was a well established institution by the 1860s.[2] Garnering its miscellaneous fare from a range of other entertainments, it had begun to take shape as a separate business in the concert rooms and singing saloons of public houses in the 1830s and '40s in response to a surge in popular demand from a rapidly expanding urban population. By the 1850s the more enterprising publicans were providing larger and more elaborate premises and charging directly for entertainment that was increasingly performed by specialised professionals. Older histories give pride of place to Charles Morton as founding father of the newly styled 'music hall', nominating his Canterbury Hall, opened in south London in 1852, as the first of its kind. Though indeed a prominent figure, Morton's enterprise was matched and in part anticipated by other publican-entrepreneurs, not only in London but in the industrial north and midlands where growth was similarly rapid, extensive and dramatic. Within little more than a decade or so, music hall had entered its first major boom, displaying all the elements of a prototype modern entertainment industry in terms of scale, investment and ethos. Profit minded proprietors did sensational deals with high-profile star performers who played to adoring mass audiences in large handsomely appointed halls; their appearances were booked country-wide by their agents and were publicised in a trade press defending this improved modern recreation against charges of corrupting public morals and civilised taste.

For all the vigour of provincial music hall, these developments were most conspicuous in London. Morton continues to claim attention with his move to the West End, where he opened the Oxford in 1861 as the first purpose built music hall. But again, there were many others on the move and on the make, exploiting the capital's greatly expanded leisure market and its unequalled concentration of numbers and resources. More heavily populated (and extensively reported) than elsewhere, London's music-hall community constituted a recognisable sub-culture, providing us with a case study of the negotiations between the often traditional set of practices and the imperatives of liberal capitalism.

I

Although neither they nor the record were reticent on their behalf, the proprietors have received little attention in music hall history compared with that lavished on performers and the sacred sites of the halls themselves.[3] There is unfortunately no space here for an adequate group biography; what is offered is a brief sketch of the London proprietor or 'caterer', as he was called, as an occupational and social type.

The majority of metropolitan proprietors from this period were drawn from the swarming world of small to medium-sized independent businesses in the service and retail trades. A number of them entered music-hall management through the theatre or showmanship, but among some very mixed and mobile careers the commonest way-station en route to full-blown proprietorship was that of publican, and the identification with the licensed trade remained strong. Most of the halls were run conjointly with the taverns with which they shared their sites, and the new caterers gave freely of their halls and services to the extensive social and charitable functions of the trade.

In social terms, the bigger proprietors had made it from the classic petty bourgeoisie to the more substantial commercial middle class. Capital-investing, property-controlling, servant-owning, the successful caterer celebrated the myth of the self-made man in a career open to talent; 'I, gentlemen,' declared Frederick Strange – who had started as a waiter, then made a fortune as a refreshment contractor at the Crystal Palace before running the monster Alhambra – 'have been . . . the architect of my own position'.[4] Yet though the rise of the music hall entrepreneur took him to the comforts and conceits of the 'paraphernalia of gentility' and commissions in the Volunteers, this self-aggrandisement was balanced with a continuing dedication to the small businessman's traditions of public service and mutuality in the intimate networks of the pub, the friendly society, the masonic lodge and the local vestry. Here service was a gregarious and social act undertaken with one's fellows in the ritual conviviality of dinners, toasts and testimonials.

The self-made man who retains the common touch is no very exceptional phenomenon, but in the music hall proprietor the mix was translated into a distinctive style in which personality was less the mark of the colourful individual than a common element in the modus operandi of a type. Central to this style was an effulgent social presence. Personal attention to the service of food and drink seems to have diminished to a token echo of the publican's traditional role as host, but the proprietor was habitually on the premises, his presence sometimes amplified in the appointments of the hall – Morton's monogram was reproduced in relief around the walls of the Oxford, and Morris Syers was represented in a life-size oil portrait. Proprietors took the chair on benefit night and readily allowed themselves to be called on stage. On their own territory they were formidable figures, as was noted of the boss of the Foresters in the East End: 'When I go I like to see Mr. Fort on the premises . . . his authoritative strut and the air of deliberate confidence in which he floats is very refreshing'.[5]

Presence and self-advertisement were further amplified by conspicuous consumption, not only in the accessories that took the proprietor away from the halls and his public – the broughams, the estate and the yacht – but in the manner of his dress, his eating and his drinking which was open to intimate public witness. Walter Besant's fictional caterer, Emmanuel Leweson, was discovered 'gorgeously attired in a brown velvet coat and white waistcoat with a great profusion of gold chain and studs . . . in his hand was a tumbler of iced soda and brandy'.[6] This is hardly a caricature, for many proprietors were known for their grand style: Holland and Crowder of the Paragon modelled themselves explicitly on Napoleon III in dress, manner and moustache. Fulsome eating and drinking were further emblems of success, and the symbolic role of gorging, guzzling and smoking was celebrated in the items habitually chosen for presentation at proprietorial dinners: engraved goblets, decanters, canteens of cutlery, cigar cutters and silver snuff boxes. Drink, of course, was the essential fuel of good fellowship. The chairman was the arch imbiber whose direct function it was to generate profit by the glassful, and it was said that proprietors kept their business head by taking their drinks from the 'sober' rather than the 'drunken' tap. But the signs of indulgence were plain enough in what one trade paper described as 'their grog-blossomed faces'.[7]

Yet what we now register as consumption, the proprietor would have represented as provision. One of the most frequent terms of congratulation in the sub-culture was liberality. Thus Holland and Sweasey were extolled on one of their dinner nights as proprietors of 'great judgement and liberality'. Judgment in music hall language could mean the ability to read the public taste, to know when to drop ballet and promote gymnasts, to know how to compile a programme of the widest appeal. In part, then, it meant intuition, but in a more basic sense it stood for rationality and calculation, values that were meant to complement or temper those of liberality with its sense of lavish and spontaneous expenditure. But in music hall it was the latter, the values of social rather than economic man, that were most applauded. After extricating himself from the Canterbury at a loss, Holland was reproached for his 'lack of judgment . . . his terrible mistake in giving 2/-worth of entertainment for a 1/-', and was urged to 'study a little economy'. Since this verdict was delivered amid the agreeable debris of yet another proprietorial blow-out, it was clearly more commendation than reproof.[8] If the proprietor indulged and regaled himself, it was partly as a symbolic exemplification of the good life in which *all* were invited to share. Fulsome public provision – monster programmes, the best in food and drink, luxurious amenities and, as we shall see, generous dispensations as friend and benefactor – these were the marks of the proprietor as public caterer. Ballooning liberality might at times float dangerously free from the restraints of conventional business sense or 'judgement', yet in the political and emotional economy of the music hall, liberality *was* good business. Through style as much as practice the proprietor contrived to represent himself as host of a great feast whilst simultaneously charging for it.

Liberality of provision was an important part of playing the big man who lived life beyond the scale of ordinary men. Music hall, declared the agent Didcott, could never be a success if run like a tallow chandlery; it had to be run 'on the heroic method'.[9] Caterers were as often cautious as reckless, but they did court risk in a more cavalier style than other entrepreneurs, and in true heroic tradition were called upon to confront the defeats as well as triumphs of the venturer. Holland lost £7,000 in three days when his bullfights at the Agricultural Hall flopped, a singular improvidence on the part of a man who was president of the Music Hall Provident Fund.[10] But this was not a matter of lamentation in Holland's account; it was part of the ups and downs of the showman's life, a matter of luck good or bad. This is the philosophy of the gambler, and the close relationship between the halls and gambling is well established. Here was a carry-over from the publican's membership of the sporting fraternity and, it may be argued, no index to his values in his metamorphosis as caterer; or gambling might be taken to evince a rational as much as a providential view of the world, a miniature reproduction of the mysteries of the market situation which might explain its appeal for the proprietor as a transference skill for the modern entrepreneur, rather than identify such enthusiasm as evidence of an important variation on the type. But the gambler in the music hall proprietor does suggest strongly a view of life as successive turns of the wheel of fortune rather than a condition that yields to long-term rational strategy. Such a perspective may well induce fatalism, but for these men it seems invariably to have generated confidence and resilience, for if they believed in luck they also believed in their abilities to seize the main chance and turn their luck to good account.[11]

As a self-invented élite, the proprietors were a yeasty, swanky lot, who in the face of a good deal of hostility in the larger world manufactured much of their own status. Though parvenu in fortune and manner, their roots in the ancient and (by its own lights) respectable trade of the publican gave them security of identity and the social skills to sustain their economic opportunism. Their image was that of the big man with the big heart doing things in a big way, representing himself as both larger than life and humanity itself. It is not Charles Morton, the over-celebrated and, by one account, 'severe and dogmatic' father of the halls who is the typical figure here, but the extravagant Billy Holland, the 'Emperor of Lambeth', who appropriated the mantle of Gladstone as well as Napoleon by styling himself the 'People's William' and claiming a mission to improve the condition of the working classes. The independent music hall proprietor of the period was a liberal populist, believing in the natural merits of the open market and competitive self-advancement, whilst claiming an unselfish dedication to his public through lavish personal service. It was an effective role, not only as a source of esteem, but as a means of control.

II

We turn now to examine the business in which the proprietors operated. Data for this period is scattered, inadequate and unreliable, but some general features seem plain.[12] Overall the history of London's halls in these years, though not without its alarms and casualties, seems to offer an almost perennial success story amid the mixed fortunes of the national economy. In the 1860s, their number increased more than three-fold to more than forty, and, as the mid-Victorian boom gave way to the Great Depression after 1873, the metropolitan halls retained their buoyancy, holding steady or declining only slightly in number, while audience capacity and the value and profitability of their property continued to rise. Amid reports of a further general down-swing in trade at the end of the 1870s, the music hall press found the halls, east and west, in flourishing condition. 'Everyone is talking about the profits made by music hall proprietors', noted the *Entr'acte*, amazed at 'where it all comes from in hard times like these', adding that Graydon of the recently enlarged Middlesex was negotiating for a small truck to deliver his takings to the bank.[13] In 1885, as the depression in London deepened, Edwin Villiers opened the luxurious new London Pavilion, and saw his confidence amply rewarded. Yet the trade press was forever warning that music hall was 'a perilous business', and the jeremiads deserve attention. As the capital's indigenous and tourist population grew in number, purchasing power and expectations in these years, the market for entertainment of all kinds not only provided greater entrepreneurial opportunity but grew more volatile and competitive. Moreover, the fact that fluctuations in the music hall industry tended to be personal, localised or seasonal rather than industry-wide and dependent on the general economy, may have contributed to the conviction that, whatever its great prizes, this was a particularly capricious and idiosyncratic business.

Certainly the costs of entry were considerable and rising, whether by building or buying in. Extensions and refurbishment were increasingly expensive, the general rise in London property prices after 1870 drove up overheads, and rates rose sharply with the revaluation of 1870. The average capitalisation of halls listed in evidence to the Select Committee of 1866 was close to £10,000, but leading halls required much greater outlays. An aspirant proprietor might take a smaller or declining property for a few thousand, but the general escalation of costs was signalled dramatically in 1878 when the Board of Works paid £109,347 for the site of the London Pavilion.[14]

Significantly, despite the rising costs, there was little recourse to the formal capital market and the new device of limited liability; raising finance for the halls in this period was a mostly private, informal (and thus unfortunately obscure) business. Though there were several proposals for company formation in the 1860s and 1870s, only three reached incorporation, two of which soon failed. More generally, capital was raised by the individual owner himself or in partnership, with what was called 'the usual leg-up given by brewers and distillers', a suggestion that the latter subventions were necessary but not sufficient.[15] Family money was a customary way of expanding personal capital, and beyond kin the caterer may have looked for funds from the professional men about town who figure among the notables in prospectuses and at table.[16] Another source may have been the more numerous component in the guest lists, the provisioning trades – grocers, biscuit and soft drink manufacturers, proprietors of cigar divans, wine and spirit merchants. Profits from the latter trade had been boosted by Gladstone's deregulation measures in 1860, and a number of merchants were parties in music hall promotion, including perhaps the last of London's old-style grandees, George Adney Payne.[17] The role of the other trades seems to have been as necessary auxiliaries, part of the closely interested local business community that sustained the halls in other ways, by its custom, confidence and credit.

Whatever the costs, proprietors seemed to tap a ready supply of venture capital, without extensive resort to institutional funds or incorporation. In such a personalised and capricious business, direction seemed no doubt best committed to the capable hands of the big man, unencumbered by the counterweight (and expenses) of company management. And after all, this was show business, where the potential investor was himself probably an *habitué* and rational calculations might be secondary to the thrills of linking destinies with the charismatic figure of the caterer. There is a telling recollection of Holland riding the wheel of fortune in the 1860s and 1870s; after many financial failures, we are told, 'he invariably reappeared, sphinx-like, irreproachably groomed and waxed, with some confiding creature ready to finance him'.[18]

After the costs of setting up in a hall came the costs of keeping up the hall. The demands on circulating rather than fixed capital were also considerable. 'Whoever takes a hall', advised the *Entr'acte*, 'will need to be furnished with plenty of the ready.' Certainly, the big salaries of the stars, the doubling of the number of acts on the programme, and the increasing sophistication and scale of the staging drove production costs higher. In 1885 one estimate put the salary bill for artistes at a West-End hall at from £150 to £250 per week. To this would be added the bill for musicians and numerous other staff, backstage and front of house. There were also bills for gas, advertising and printing. The proprietor was said to cover these costs with takings at the door, and to look for his profit in the 'wet' money spent on drinks and refreshments.[19] Though there are some estimates of expenditure on these items there are no figures for the cost of their provision; given the range of drinks, tobacco, confectionery and 'other substantials', this would have been considerable. It is most likely that it was in this department that proprietors elasticated their assets by relying a good deal on credit and goodwill.

The important functions of credit, cash flow and business confidence come to light in an action in 1869 for slander and consequent commercial injury brought by Charles Sinclair, proprietor of Sinclair's Music Hall, off Edgware Road, against Bennett, pork butcher in the neighbourhood:

The slander complained of was that the defendant said that the plaintiff has been arrested for debt and carried in a cab to Whitecross Street prison, whereby the plaintiff was injured in his credit. He could show that in consequence of the report getting into circulation, Mr. Stack, a tradesman in the neighbourhood, who used to cash the plaintiff's cheques, refused to do so. Mr. Rawlings, who supplied the plaintiff with cider and perry, to be consumed in the Music Hall; Mr. Harris, who supplied him with cigars; and other tradesmen withdrew from supplying him with goods.

Unable to cash his cheque, Sinclair 'was put to great inconvenience for money with which to pay his performers, and two of the band actually left him on account of the report'. Bennett the butcher, who was alleged to have an interest in a rival theatre close by, rang the death knell on his neighbour by announcing his tale to a crowded bar in the local pub, where Sinclair had previously been negotiating with a solicitor representing another artist and small-time impresario who owed him money. 'Professor' Sinclair won the case but received only a farthing damages, and did his best to repair his damaged reputation by holding 'A Proprietor's Tradesman's Bespeak' or benefit at which 'there were many friends and guest artists, all of whom made some allusion to the proprietor's goodness of heart, upright dealing in business matters and honourable conduct'. Sinclair went bankrupt the following year when it was reported that most of his debts were for money lent.[20] Sinclair's hall was small and obviously something of a hand-to-mouth operation, yet bigger men were as anxious to protect their credit and the reputation on which it rested. Syers wrote to the *Era* to correct their underestimate of his profits, for 'your former report might shake my credit if left unchanged', and Villiers clearly moved heaven and earth to secure the attendance of Stanley Vickers as chair at the dinner celebrating the rebuilding of the South London in 1869. Vickers was not only an MP – genuflection – but Villiers's principal supplier of 'gallons of wine and gin', and his fulsome testimony to the proprietor's 'honour and probity' was urgently adduced to counter those who were trying to 'talk him out of business'.[21]

The business relationship between proprietor and performer was both critical and complex. In theory the performer was dependent but not subordinate, but the proprietor's tightening control of market access made the fiction of an equitable relationship hard to sustain, and the conventions of good fellowship had to be worked more feverishly to obscure incipient conflict and exploitation. The rise of the agent meant greater formalisation of business and contract, but many hiring agreements were still no more than a verbal exchange made face to face over a drink. In Didcott's telling description, proprietors and artists of this era transacted their business 'like farmers at a fair'.[22] The rapid and competitive growth of the halls in London may have given performers some leverage on the market in the 1860s, an advantage certainly enjoyed by the new stars. The turns system discouraged the establishment of permanent or seasonal companies, and the necessarily piecemeal assembly of programmes might make the proprietor more dependent upon the co-operation of key artists. Holland publicly acknowledged the magnanimity of the star Nellie Power who made him a gift of her services for a week over and above the terms of her engagement, and there were other signs of the exchange of favours and an amiable mutuality of interest.[23]

More often, however, the proprietor held the upper hand and the artist was the supplicant. 'Moans of a Manager', a piece in the trade press from 1870 derides the importunate pro soliciting for a job or 'shop' at a time when a bulge in supply coincident with a levelling off in the number of halls may well have compounded the insecurities of a generally overstocked profession. The piece goes on to tell how, after he has been hired, the pro turns from ingratiation to calumny and accuses the manager of 'taking half his "screw" '.[24] Summary depredations were indeed common as proprietors squeezed labour costs when business was thin: fines were imposed, unexpected commissions were levied, performers were kept waiting late for 'treasury' on Saturday night to keep up the drinking that could be discounted from their pay, and refreshment tickets or free passes might be substituted for cash.[25] Amid the clichés of companionable equality one voice spoke forthrightly and illuminatingly about where real authority lay. Fort of the Foresters Hall (he of the authoritative strut) brought a number of actions in the mid-1870s to vindicate the rights of proprietors over performers. In one case he complained that he had been misreported in saying a certain artist was his tool, offering in correction that 'Miss Thorne does as I tell her . . . she is my servant'.[26]

Music hall was increasingly labour-intensive and the proprietor had charge of numerous staff. In 1862 one of the largest halls was said to employ eighty staff, the majority of which would have been in service rather than production roles.[27] Here organisation was overtly hierarchical – 'Caste is everywhere, even in the music halls' – with authority passing down through a general manager or chairman to individual subcontractors. The status of staff was more obviously that of servant than was that of the performers, though musicians as artistic labour occupied a more ambiguous position. With low or no money wages, staff were often dependent on perquisites and tips from customers and performers, or on pilfering and embezzlement.[28] Proprietors sought to win honesty and loyalty by their paternal largess – fêtes and outings for employees became regular features in the music hall calendar, and in the 1860s proprietors began to extend the privileges of the benefit performance to individuals and groups among their support staff.

The final important relationship considered here was that of the proprietor and the neighbourhood community. Here, as already suggested, status, credit and custom were sensitively connected. A hall's function as ready source of entertainment – permanent, casual or bye –

enhanced the proprietor's local status, as did his seat on the vestry or the board of guardians. Certainly the neighbourhood connection was crucial in maintaining a core of regular custom. It is plain that as in Morton's campaign to lure the fashionable supper-room set across the water to the Canterbury, proprietors set out to extend the constituency of their audience upwards and outwards, offering superior and separate amenities for a putative middle-class clientele and special deals for the new leisure traffic on the underground and suburban railways. But the courting of local custom was still essential even for the big halls. The *Entr'acte* scorned grandiose schemes for attracting 'society', maintaining that those who had succeeded in London music hall made local business their priority.[29]

The most obvious favour and symbol in the cultivation of local identification was the free list, the issue of complimentary passes or 'orders'. Already in disrepute in the theatre where it had originated, the practice flourished in the halls where it was claimed that those on the list were more profitable customers than those who paid at the door. Membership of the free list – and even better, the recognition that brought with it a 'face pass', or the practice of 'going in on the nod' – meant almost certain election to the élite of local *habitués*. The group comprised mainly tradesmen and their sons, plus clerks and shop-boys, the young men presumably entering initially on passes given to their fathers and employers in return for exhibiting bills for the hall. Dressed in flamboyant gentish style, the in-crowd eschewed the common folk at their tables and clustered at the side bars exchanging knowing nods with the chairman, shaking hands with the guv'nor himself, and enjoying the privilege of buying them drinks.[30] Standing treats in such company conferred manhood, established status, and filled the music hall tills. In this and other ways the generosity of the proprietor to his friends redounded to his considerable advantage.

Music hall may be usefully termed a socially intensive industry; whatever the degree of its needs for capital or labour, an exceptionally and continuously high input of social energy and skill in the direct mediation of its personal and structural relationships was a necessary condition of its establishment and effective conduct. Carrying out business on the halls was a complex and demanding social exercise, a matter of self-advertisement and personal contact, the exchange of favours and gestures of good feeling, the nursing of networks and the wooing of public confidence. In this milieu, drink and kind words were as potent a currency as cash and contract. Life in this often bogus yet compelling social world was, more so than in the routine metaphor, a dramatic performance, whose roles were rehearsed daily in the bars, the street and the press as much as on the stage, but they found concentrated and ritual expression in the institution of the benefit night.

III

The benefit night was a traditional practice inherited from the theatre at which the proceeds would be given to a particular member, associate or servant of the company. The amenities of the theatre and the services of the others – lessee, players and staff – were in theory provided free, while prices were raised. The benefit or bespeak functioned variously as a speculative device, a reward for distinction, a supplement or substitute for salary, or aid in relief of distress when it was frequently extended to those outside the profession. Whether a star or one of 'the small people', the beneficiary was given the run of the stage. But while by the mid-century the benefit was falling into disfavour in the theatre for allegedly alienating the public and depressing salaries, it flourished mightily in the London music halls.[31]

Though the benefit system on the halls duplicated many of its features in the theatre, it was here more obviously the instrument of the proprietor. Proprietorial benefits were the great events in the calendar, held annually as a matter of course and on other notable occasions – farewells, inaugurations, seasonal re-openings. The free list was suspended and prices were raised, frequently threefold and sometimes more; boxes and best seats might be put up for auction. Most of these 'bens' were sell-outs and some were extended to two nights to accommodate the crowds. Halls were specially decorated and bills greatly extended. At the Middlesex, in October 1883, Graydon presented fifty-six artists in thirty-six turns over five-and-a-half hours.[32] The programme was supervised by a fellow proprietor or one of the big agents, and other visiting managers – the *Era* counted sixteen in attendance for another of Graydon's benefits – would in turn preside as chairman, leaving the beneficiary free to receive various gifts and testimonials, to make his address and generally to disport himself among his public. At the conclusion of the entertainment (which might run till 3 AM by special licence), the artists and special guests would be given supper and more toasts and speeches.

The functions and significance of the proprietorial benefit were various. The most obvious economic function was to raise extra money and this was clearly acknowledged where benefits were held to give direct relief to proprietors in need, as in consequence of some particular calamity or a more general reversal of fortune. Thus Villiers took a benefit after a fire at the South London; Weston and Holland announced benefits to remedy their heroic indebtedness. More covertly, the benefit could be used to rescue the marginal operation. Creditors might be prevailed upon to take the high-priced tickets in part-payment, and the prices of liquor and refreshments could be raised, though there was less precedent for this and more popular resistance. More generally, the benefit was regarded as necessary and justified to make good the season's out-of-pocket expenditures. 'Benefits here, benefits there, benefits everywhere', declared the *Entr'acte*, 'and of great benefit they are to those hard drinking managers and artists who rely upon expenses attending the proper following of their employment.'[33] Whether for charitable need, overhead expenses or simple profit, the occasional report of the 'take' at proprietorial benefits suggests that London's caterers did well: Fort cleared £400 over two nights in 1874 (at a previous benefit he also received a diamond ring and breastpin worth 175 guineas); Mrs. Poole at the South London took £561 12s 9d. in 1887.[34]

Yet benefits were not represented as simply money-making. Any gain was implicitly justified as a proper return on previous favours and good service. This function as an annual night of reckoning was made plain by John Wilton of Wilton's in 1862, when he explained: 'There are a great number of tradesmen and others who derive great benefit from my establishment, and others upon whom I confer favours. It is to enable these persons to acknowledge those favours that I take a Benefit.'[35] There are suggestions that this return of favours might be pursued somewhat aggressively, but though patrons were no doubt variously obliged and solicited to take tickets, the protocols of friendship put some limit on the proprietor's presumption. Tribute volunteered clearly signified more than tribute exacted, and the response from artists as well as customers was a public test of popular favour, as Holland recognised in his pride at the turn-out for a benefit of his in 1872 at the North Woolwich:

He had not issued a single ticket but depended entirely on the public; he had not asked a single artiste to come and assist him, but many had volunteered their services, and it was a pleasure to know he was as well thought of by the profession as by the public . . . he had tested the esteem with which they regarded him and the value they placed on his services as their caterer.[36]

Though its production might involve much haggling, importuning and moral blackmail, the benefit night was a great celebration of fraternal good feeling at which all were enfolded in the language and sentiments of friendship. Charles Merion, manager at the Met, said on his benefit: 'It seemed like a great meeting of friends, for wherever he turned he saw faces that he knew and people with whom he would like to shake hands.' It was also typical of such occasions that managers spoke not only of renewing friendships but of reconciling differences among their kind. Frederick Strange, for example, as a guest of Holland and Sweazey at the Royal in 1866, declared himself delighted 'to preside over so many friends ... and to have the opportunity of setting an example to others of doing away with some of the great many jealousies that exist among our music hall proprietors.' 'Although', continued Strange, 'every man of business does the best he can for himself, it always can be done without undermining his neighbours.' Sanders at the opening of the Islington Philharmonic in 1860 professed himself 'glad to see his friend Weston and other friends who had come to give support; and if they were rivals, he knew they all felt they were rivals in a good cause (Cheers).'[37]

There was none the less a continuing note of competition at proprietorial benefits, though far from confounding the good intentions we may allow that it added to the piquancy of such encounters. Proprietors would rehearse their common interests at such occasions and declare the liberal and progressive ideals of their calling; the host and beneficiary would be lauded as an exemplar of such values, and in turn would compliment his peers for their generosity in releasing their artists to appear on his bill. But within the *bonhomie* the host strove nonetheless to outfeast the others and score heavily in the relentless trade war between establishments. Thus the length and quality of the programme, the number and names of those in attendance and the level of prices all reflected upon the reputation of the proprietor and his effective command of the services and respect of others. As in the exchange systems observed in traditional societies, the proprietorial benefit registered the separateness, even the hostility of its chief participants even as it served to integrate them. It was like an inverted potlatch or kula, a competitive as well as fraternal display, but overall it served to renew and reinforce power at the top.[38]

Next in line as frequent beneficiaries were the performers. For them, too, the benefit was an occasion for raising extra money, the friendly exploitation of mutuality, and recognition and advancement of standing in the profession and at large. Perhaps most of all an artist's benefit night was a prime vehicle for self-advertisement. Bills and posters proclaimed the name of the favoured one. Beneficiaries met their public at the door, arrayed in their best finery, 'giving away smiles and portraits'. Here was a showcase for their talent in front of an unusual concentration of their peers (who also took turns in the presidential chair), proprietors and agents. After successful bens the pros would be seen in handsome new togs, treating themselves and others to 'big feeds' and drinks at the Oxford matinee or betting heavily at the Victoria Club. For the stars, who regularly held benefits at the end of an engagement or before provincial tours, financial returns were often handsome. At the Cambridge one night, Walter Laburnum was said to have taken £70 at the door, 'while the private sale of tickets was something fabulous'. At a sell-out at another East End hall, Jenny Hill was reported 'like the king of the nursery story, counting out her money'.39 But in return the system made heavy demands on performers of any prominence. Writing to the *Entr'acte*, a successful pro declared the 'bespeak' system a nuisance, for he claimed to be pestered to contribute his services on average twice a week.40 Mutuality had its price, most obviously for the performers, whose services were of course central to the operation.

The anxieties and abuses of the benefit system were more problematical for the lesser performer. A financial profit was far from assured. The stars could command a 'full clear' or genuinely 'complimentary' benefit with the proprietor waiving all house costs (such gestures were compensated by his monopoly on drink profits) but the minor artist was lucky to secure the remission of even a fraction of these, and might have to foot all running expenses. Some managers demanded their pre-payment, and there were in any case the additional costs of advertising. The first call on friends therefore might be for cash to float the benefit 'granted' by the proprietor, after which they would, if performers, be solicited for their services on the programme. The appearance of a big name was crucial for success, but attracting the services of artists outside the circle of one's intimates was tricky. It was customary to approach an artist and ask his or her terms for an appearance, hoping that any fee would be waived. Paying for services, however big the name, might wreck the budget; but with no fees involved, the guest might not turn up, to the great embarrassment of the beneficiary who would have given the star top billing and ran the risk of charges of misrepresentation. And in the final accounting, the beneficiary had to beware of the unscrupulous proprietor who would falsify the figures or pad the costs. For the small fry then, the benefit might 'increase their vanity, without assisting their pocket'.⁴¹ Overall, too, it was the rank and file who could least afford to forgo a night's salary in what were becoming in many cases involuntary levies rather than a mutual exchange of services.

Although criticisms of the music hall benefit system grew among artists, they continued to give it their support. *In extremis*, the benefit was still the most reliable source of relief and one which avoided the stigma of direct charity. For the greenhorn, the benefit afforded a chance of exposure to the big time as a fill-in during the 'waits' (the turns system complicated the scheduling, and benefit programmes often defied efficient stage management). But, as one pro remonstrated with his fellows, such eagerness was soon converted into toadyism and ignobility:

> You would like to be associated, even in ever so small a way, with influential people, and will nearly cringe to them to be allowed to take an unpaid part in a performance under good patronage, though you would shrink from allowing your name to be used on behalf of a distressed brother to whom you might be of real service.

According to another critic, even 'the Great Guns' solicited for appearance would rather be out of pocket than absent from the benefit programmes of the 'men of power'.⁴²

If the real benefits of this exercise in collective self-help seemed to be made to flow more readily upwards, the system did have some redistributive effect, not only across but downwards to the 'small people' of the halls. Not-so-small people such as the chairman might have an annual benefit in their terms of engagement, but the privilege was rapidly extended in the 1860s to cover a wide range of minor functionaries and service staff – under-managers, cashiers, money- and check-takers, carpenters, machinists and waiters. In a marginal business such benefits may have been important in meeting running costs; easing the problem of cash flow in a money-poor operation by functioning as a supplement to or in lieu of wages. But the more likely function was that of building the proprietor's local reputation through his benevolent manipulation of the gift relationship. Again benevolences had to be paid for, and staff might find their annual bonanza and the brief glory of a summons on stage small compensation for their involuntary 'assistance' at other bens throughout the year. Musicians seem to have suffered most (which may have accounted for their reputation as particularly importunate demanders of tips or 'prossers') for their only return seems to have been a putative share in the conductor's benefit.

Music halls were also common venues for benefits held by or in aid of local societies. We get a glimpse of this under-recorded function from John Wilton, who was proud 'that during the last twelve months no less than eighty nights have been set apart for some philanthropic purpose or another – either for benefitting the funds of a friendly society or improving the conditions of some distressed private individual'.[43] Wilton meant this as a tribute to his working-class clientele, but proprietors also derived credit for throwing their halls open to such use, as well as from other forms of relief. Holland, who brewed up soup for the unemployed in 1886, was applauded for holding a benefit for the Newcastle workers who struck for the nine-hour day in 1871, and Crowder was commended by the unions for 'allowing the workingmen free use of his hall for the ventilation of their trade and labour grievances'.[44] The profession as a whole, together with its public, were everready with benefits and subscriptions for the victims of local and national calamities – the painter who broke his leg, the victims of colliery disasters and shipwrecks, the unemployed Lancashire workers in the cotton famine.

In all of these variations on the benefit, the proprietor played his part, made his contribution, and took his credit. To a degree he was servant as well as master of the system, and it may be argued that the nexus of custom and mutuality exemplified in the good fellowship of the benefit night was part of a traditional ideology and practice on the halls that muted and diffused the rationalising thrust of modern capitalism. (It is significant that Morton, with his austere personal style and early use of written contracts, rarely held a personal bespeak and thus would seem to have avoided its clinging mesh of obligations.) But in the overall arithmetic of its reciprocities we may rightly suspect that, by fair means or foul, it was the big man who derived the greatest returns from the benefit.

By the 1880s the benefit system was badly overloaded and more actively resisted. Its occasions became fewer, and its forms changed. It was less the conflict of interests that brought about its decline than the increasing scale and bureaucratisation of music hall that made the rituals of friendship and mutuality a cosmetic rather than an essential way of doing business.

The top men of the new syndicated halls were directors rather than proprietors, and more often accountants than publicans. They raised capital on the stock market, not from their cronies, and were more concerned to advertise their probity to a board and shareholders than to impress their good fellowship on the local butcher in the stalls bar. They had less direct contact with artists, who were hired by agents and booking managers, and who were now more concerned to formalise contracts and business dealings. The profession also increasingly withheld its services from the benefit, setting up its own autonomous welfare institutions which relieved some of its dependence both on management and public.[45]

The surviving forms of the benefit bore the mark of this more rational and distanced mode of business. Personal benefits were mostly restricted to long-serving unit managers in the combines whose local standing reproduced something of the substance of the early owner-proprietors.[46] Benefit performances for other staff were long gone, and though the annual paternalist beanfeast remained, the new big men were rarely there to play their role. At a staff outing from the South London in 1902, an official apologised for the directors' absence: 'Mr. Payne is on holiday, Mr. Tozer has gout, Mr. Newson-Smith has a very arkward day . . .'.[47] Charitable benefits found a new form in the special matinée. Held more for national than local causes, they attracted more distinguished patronage, which flattered the industry's leaders into attendance (though it renewed performers' accusations of exploitation).[48] The combines reduced their favours to the local community in other ways. After Crowder's Paragon incorporated with the Canterbury, working-class societies reported that charges for holding their annual benefit had doubled, a percentage was charged on the take, and various restrictions were now imposed by 'the none too courteous management'.[49] By this time, in the mid-1890s, free orders had also been cut back in most London halls – though one of the dispossessed pulled a revolver to protest at the affront!

From the turn of the century, the industry looked back indulgently on the old style personal proprietor. The syndicate director Henry Tozer recalled: 'They all in their youth loved and admired him, his glossy hat, his substantial jewellery, his glowing affability, and his habitual spoof.' But now, in the words of another of the new men, 'the old blatant music hall manager . . . has given place to the sharp but courteous business man'. Even so, the type they romanticised with his affability and spoof, had been no less of a businessman.[50]

IV

Friendship – 'a voluntary, close and enduring relationship' – is a ubiquitous and self-evident phenomenon, yet its history and sociology are still waiting to be written.[51] In terms of its own particular history, music-hall friendship would seem to be a descendant of two observable eighteenth-century forms. The first is that institutionalised in the popular and numerous Friendly Societies.[52] Friendship here was collective in sentiment and purpose. Within a rule-bound body, members (mostly artisanal and petty bourgeois) gathered to promote conviviality (ritualised and ceremonial), while pooling their resources to protect the welfare and security of the individuals within the group. The second form was more middle- or upper-class.[53] Similar in its combination of the affective and instrumental, it was less institutionalised, sociable in a different style, and based on personal contact within looser and more extensive networks of family, kin and other dependants and associates. 'Friend' meant specifically one with whom to exchange favours, in the form of goods, services and, in an age of patronage, place. The use of the word in this context is particularly interesting, for its implicit equality elides the social discriminations of rank through which patronage was mediated.

Music hall friendship was both a derivation and a reworking of the two strands with their complementary yet also divergent ideologies. Music hall's direct descent from the pub as provident club and the popular theatre as 'republic of players' made for a tighter, less differentiated sense of mutuality in the tradition of the friendly societies. But at the same time, the rivalrous vanities of the performers and the palpable ambition of the caterers in a singularly competitive and insecure business made for a more self-conscious individualism within the common nexus of regard that seems to derive from the other, more bourgeois strand. Thus part separated, part integrated, a process of as it were individual mutuality was always in negotiation amid the larger collective mutuality that constituted music-hall friendship.

Characteristically fulsome in sentiment, music-hall friendship was nonetheless explicit in its demands, as the transactions of the benefit night make plain. Then, as Holland declared, you found out who your friends really were; then you called them to account for the debts and credits in the ledger – the metaphor came to life in the name of one East End pub music hall, The Bank of Friendship. The system, though less rule-bound than a Friendly Society, was still highly normative. For all its candour on some occasions, the language of friendship was often more slippery; as in the exchanges of patronage in a previous era, it was a useful fiction in the exercise of discriminatory power for its sentiments flattered inferiors, and appeased or bemused the exploited. Thus its equalising rhetoric obscured the asymmetrical distribution of advantage in the gift relationship of the benefit system. Moreover, in a time of transition between relationships of place and service on the one hand, and contract and employment on the other, 'friend' was likely to be an even more useful term to cover confusion and ignorance, or simply to evade.

The rhetoric of music-hall friendship was all-inclusive, promising universal membership. In this we can recognise a genial cognate of other omnibus and ideal categories of Victorian Britain as a liberal democracy – associationism, social citizenship, respectability – combining the properties of voluntarism, equality, dignity and earned inclusion. Of particular importance to the halls in this respect was that friendship included women. Again the usage may well have been hegemonic and a cloak or lever in economic and emotional exploitation, but it may also have served to defuse or elide tensions of gender and sexuality. Though there are notable ambiguities in this context, early nineteenth-century literature suggests that friendship could denote a sexually disinterested protective function.[54]

But there can be no inclusion without exclusion, no friends without enemies, or at least non-friends – the 'chums and rotters' of one account – and music-hall friendship was both all-embracing and select. One appropriate analogy here might be freemasonry (much practised in the profession) with its ideals of universal brotherhood and its practice of exclusion. The halls, however, were not a closed institution on this model but a more fluid, sub-cultural world which for all the density of its local ties was also, particularly in London, a mobile and ever-recomposing community. Music hall was both parochial and cosmopolitan in a way which generated chronic tensions in relationships. The tightness of the neighbourhood connection intensified rather than ventilated differences of interest, while the growth of industry, the ready flow of recruits, entrepreneurial and artistic, and the particular pattern of production in the turns system brought constant shifts and intensification in rivalry and competition. The device and rhetoric of friendship were thus probably more extensively invoked in direct proportion to the growth in the dynamic and fissionable properties of the music-hall world. Colin MacInnes, in his study of the songs of the halls, noted that 'there are more invocations of friendship after a row has happened, than among friends who've never much quarrelled at all'.[55]

Again in the wider context of a modern urbanising and arguably more impersonal society, friendship was a complex metaphor of recognition and identity, a free order or 'face pass' to membership of a community, or in Victor Turner's less structured sense, *'communitas'*.[56] Sociological definitions leave out the property of trust which is part of the ideal of friendship, and which promised stability and certitude in music hall's slippery and capricious microcosm of a larger world. The deceits and emptiness of many relationships in contrast to the ideal could be desolating. 'Friends, what friends? I have none', was the despairing cry of the great star George Leybourne, and the authentic voice of alienation in a business that was as abrasive as it was emollient.[57] That friendship was often an illusion, a fragile membrane of good intentions, made its desirability all the more intense.

Friendship in the halls was in any case being redefined in this period as the industry was rationalised and the extension of the sub-culture diluted intimacy. It became more a private than a public interchange, a matter of withdrawal rather than display. Indeed, a distinction not only of degree but of kind creeps into music hall discourse from the 1870s. The *Era* saw the audience at one of Syer's benefits as comprising the 'general public and particular friends' and the sense of a divergent if complementary set of categories became more common.[58] At a benefit for Villiers, the paper distinguished between 'an inner circle and the public in general'. 'Privately his social qualifications may render him an object deserving homage from his friends; publicly his management may have been conducted with energy, with talent and with success; and the two sections of the public actuated by different desires, unite to do honour to the occasion'.[59] This is more than a differentiation between a proprietor's cronies and the rest; it represents the lapsing of friendship as an instrument of everyday business and music hall community. Friendship was replaced by civility.

Yet it would be too simplistic to see in this line of development the almost inevitable triumph of the rational and contractual in social relationships, the victory of *gesellschaft* over *gemeinschaft*. Friendship remained a common theme in the music hall canon and popular literature, and the language of pals and chums ('Thank God, for a trusty one', wrote Kipling), was translated from sentiment into action in the pals' battalions of 1914. *Gemeinschaft* and *gesellschaft* are in any case not necessarily specific historical and mutually exclusive conditions, but co-existing states of experience.[60] People fashion affective relationships within the most depersonalised social systems; conversely, the appeal of amiable inclusion is likely to be a necessary interpellation or hook in any scheme that seeks to make a business out of pleasure. This was certainly true for Billy Holland and the other big men of London music hall who made friendship a powerful engine of a new form of capitalism – capitalism with a beaming human face.

CHAPTER 5

Champagne Charlie and the music-hall swell song

In his commentary on Gustave Doré's famous pictures of life in London in 1872, Blanchard Jerrold reports with distaste his sightings of 'grotesque imitations of that general enemy known as "swell"'. Some twenty years later, the performers who had become the first big music-hall stars by celebrating this social type in song were looked back on with revulsion. These *'lions comiques'*, in one recollection, 'were the most vulgar and objectionable creatures that ever faced the public . . . Champagne Charlie and the rest of them became the rage and turned the music halls into veritable sinks.'[1] Some modern writers have not liked the swell songs and their performers any better, seeing them as a reactionary diversion from the development of an authentic and combative working-class culture.[2] Clearly here is a phenomenon which made a powerful impact upon polite and popular consciousness. This essay tries to understand why this was so. It concentrates on the making of the swell song as a performance type that constituted its own ideology in the sense of a shifting yet coherent cluster of meanings, constructed and contested in action, both within the music hall and the larger social and cultural world of which it was part. As previously, we are addressing music hall in an era of vigorous growth when it already manifested many of the features of a modern entertainment industry, including the manufacture of hit songs and their singers.[3]

I

The swell song remained in the repertoire in several variants throughout the history of the halls, but it was at its most vigorous and eruptive in the 1860s and 1870s. Typically, the swell was a lordly figure of resplendent dress and confident air, whose exploits centred on drink and women; time, work and money scarcely intrude as the swell struts his way across town in the company of other 'jolly dogs'. The swell song was a major feature in the repertoire of a new generation of comic singers who rose to fame in the mid 1860s. Young men in their early twenties, they were the darlings of the first music-hall boom, while the professional finish of their performances provided a new standard of comic realism. The two most notable in the contest for popular favour were George Leybourne and Alfred Vance, who made their metropolitan debuts within a few months of each other in 1864–5.

Of the two, Leybourne has left the more vivid impression.[4] He dominated the music-hall stage for most of his lifetime, and his classic hit *Champagne Charlie* both defined his own life and provided one of the more durable images of the era. Often said to hail from Wolverhampton, Leybourne was in fact born in Gateshead in the North-east in 1842, the son of a currier and part-time theatre musician. His early life remains obscure, but he worked first as an engine-fitter, then as an entertainer in the North and Midlands under the stage name of Joe Saunders. There are differing accounts of what or who first brought him to London, but he seems initially to have carried on his trade as an engineer while playing the smaller halls and penny gaffs of the East End.[5] His debut in the big halls came in early 1865, when he was noticed at the Metropolitan, Edgeware Road, doing a mechanical donkey act, an obvious transplant of his craft training; the following year he appeared dancing on stilts as Chang, the Chinese Giant. Though a Geordie and devotee of Ned Corvan, Leybourne never seems to have drawn on his home culture for his act – several commentators thought him a cockney – yet it is plain that throughout his career he was a performer of considerable versatility. Among other talents he was a fine ballad singer, but his comic singing brought him his greatest success and it was *Champagne Charlie* in 1866 that first made him a star and won the 'volcanic appreciation' of music-hall audiences (figure 9).[6]

In 1868, in one of the legendary moments of music-hall history, George Leybourne, 'The Original Champagne Charlie', was signed to an exclusive twelve-month engagement at the Canterbury by William 'Billy' Holland, the flamboyant 'People's Caterer', who placarded London with details of the terms. Among the duties that were to earn him £1,000 for the year, the contract stated that 'George Leybourne shall every day, and at all reasonable times and places when required so to do, appear in a carriage, drawn by four horses, driven by two postillions, and attended by his grooms'. Thus every evening Leybourne left his home in Islington to be driven down to Lambeth by barouche. He was to be the swell off as well as on stage, bedecked in fur-collared coat and

THE ORIGINAL "CHAMPAGNE CHARLIE."

Figure 9   'The Original Champagne Charlie', from *Entr'acte*, 24 August 1872.

diamond solitaire, and plying his public with champagne provided by
wine shippers eager for publicity. Leybourne was 'bound in heavy pains
and penalties not to appear at any other Music Hall or place of
amusement without the express permission of Wm. Holland'.[7] He did,
however, play several other London halls concurrently, no doubt under
a farming agreement between Holland and Charles Roberts, his agent,
who also promoted him in concerts at the more respectable venue of St.
James's Hall and despatched him on a tour of provincial music halls in
1869. Heavily booked for as many as six London halls in a night,
'Leybourne the pluralist' had to plead with enthusiastic audiences to
release him so that he could meet his schedules across town. He
repeated his success in the North and the Midlands, similarly parading
himself in carriage and four, and commanding big salaries. Combined
nightly appearances at Leeds and Bradford were said to have made him
a weekly salary of £100 upwards. Provincial proprietors exulted at his
popularity: 'Simply announce Leybourne, and in spite of the weather,
the doors are besieged; open them and in half an hour's time, the hall is
packed and money refused.'[8]

Tall and handsome, genial and unaffected in manner, and with what
Jenny Hill recalled as 'a curious faculty of filling a stage',[9] Leybourne
sustained his star status into the next decade, though he paid dearly for
his success. He was acclaimed in Paris, appeared before the Prince of
Wales, and acquired a country estate. The trade press censured him for
his vulgarity, some of his fellow artists thought him guilty of sharp
practice, and proprietors became uneasy about his unpunctuality, but
his public loved him. According to an oft-repeated story, Leybourne in
private despaired of the emptiness of his success and the absence of
true friendship amid the milling crowds. Yet he remained the good
fellow of his most successful stage role. Notably generous with hand-
outs as well as the drink, he was dubbed 'honorary high almoner to the
profession'. Eager to enlarge on any irony that confers a tidy pathos on
the life of a star, some have seen a metaphor for the decline of
Leybourne's career in the setting of one of his later songs, where the
erstwhile swell sang the praises of life in a teashop – 'Ting a ling' rather
than 'Slap Bang'.[10] Quite apart from the likelihood that the song was
more an effective parody than a dying fall, the evidence is that despite
collapses in health and some decline in favour Leybourne sustained the
vigour of his stage characterisations to the end. The true pathos of his
career needs no invention. Reports of his several indispositions attributed them to consumption, but his death certificate records exhaus-

tion and abscess (cirrhosis?) of the liver. He died penniless, at the age of forty-two.

A less engaging character than Leybourne, Alfred Peck Stevens, the Great Vance, was his biggest rival.[11] Born in London in 1839, he started work as a solicitor's clerk, then played a variety of roles in the theatre before transferring to music hall in a blackfaced double act with his brother. By 1864 he was drawing big crowds as a solo comedian, notably at the Metropolitan. Like Leybourne, Vance was a versatile performer; he enjoyed much success as a stage cockney and was a master of the vernacular 'cellar flap' dance, but he won most acclaim with his swell songs.

Hired by Charles Morton for the Oxford in 1866 as a counter-attraction to Leybourne, Vance challenged his rival with his own hymn to champagne, *Clicquot, Clicquot! That's The Wine For Me*. The two then worked their way in competitive antiphony down the wine list. A less aggressive and more mannered performer than the other lions comiques, Vance also established a considerable reputation as a popular concert artist, appearing before more select audiences in London and conducting annual tours of the provinces with his own concert party.[12] He hardly seems to have modified his repertoire for his respectable clientele and still played his swell and his cockney – 'the dainty exquisite and the rugged vulgarian' – back to back, though the reviews applauded him more as an actor than a vocalist.

Like his rival, Vance was an accomplished showman with a talent for self-advertisement – he drove to his engagements behind a pair of cream-coloured ponies with smartly liveried boy grooms.[13] Unlike Leybourne, Vance managed his own career and seems to have taken himself more seriously. Although he also was indicted for vulgarity, his general persona was less roguish than Leybourne's. The minister at his funeral revealed how as an aspirant performer himself he had been deterred from seeking a professional career after a lecture by Vance on its moral hazards, suggesting the latter's caution in negotiating his own path to success. In the 1870s his absences from the halls grew longer; on his more frequent returns in the 1880s the reviews were still complimentary, and his latter-day success seems to have been more durable than Leybourne's. He died from a heart attack in the wings of the Sun music hall in Knightsbridge in 1888. Though still said to command a high salary, he left a total estate of £39 7s 5d.

A number of other performers were billed as lions comiques and included swell songs in their repertoire. Of these G. H. MacDermott enjoyed comparable notoriety, though his greater speciality was the topical song. Arthur Lloyd was noted for the accuracy of his impressions based on exhaustive scrutiny of everyday life, and was an early success with his hit about the cockney swell *Immensikoff, the Shoreditch Toff.* Harry Rickards made his name in the late 1860s as a parodist of Champagne Charlie, and pioneered a notable variation on the type in his portrayal of the military toff, *Captain Jinks of the Horse Marines.* Other contemporary comic stars were Jolly John Nash, Tom Maclagen, Harry Liston and Ned Hammond. Also important were a number of women performers who specialised in male impersonations and are discussed below.[14]

II

This brief review of the emergence of the lions comiques accords at several points with a conventionalised picture of modern showbusiness as a voraciously commercialised institution. We see leading entrepreneurs competing for novel attractions as they slug it out in a trade war for control of the big London houses. The comic singer is slicked up, hit songs are delivered by professional writers, and the new package is advertised in sensational fashion. Agents exploit their charges, and sponsors promote their product by identification with the star and new images of conspicuous consumption. And yes, amid the money and the success and the hype, the star is confronted with the emptiness of it all, knows alienation, and dies an exhausted commodity, himself no better that a spent champagne bottle. However crude and one-sided the picture is, we need to acknowledge the powerful role of the forces of production in the making of the swell songs and their singers.

Music-hall promotion in London in the boom years of the 1860s was a highly personalised and competitive business dominated by a feisty cadre of proprietorial grandees.[15] When Weston of Weston's Music Hall in Holborn contested Morton's opening of the Oxford in Oxford Street in 1861, the clash was represented in the prints as a prize fight for the West Central Stakes. There was talk that Weston and other managers had tried to suborn the magistracy in order to deny Morton a licence.[16] Undoubtedly there was a seamy side to the trade war but the bid to capture and hold audiences relied on the more public tactics of out-shining and out-shouting your rivals. Here the proprietor traded upon his own expansive presence, playing host and servant to the crowd, publicising himself, his amenities and his entertainments at lavish dinners and benefits where he himself was the star.

Morton essayed a more temperate personal style, but his contemporaries had little regard for restraint. Ned Weston, who was seen by some as the more dominant figure of the early 1860s, provided champagne on the house and invited the public to his suburban estate in Kentish Town. Extravagance and over-speculation contributed to his decline, and he was forced to sell his Holborn hall to William Holland in 1866. The most flamboyant of all the London caterers, Billy Holland specialised in taking on fading establishments, undertaking expensive renovations and mounting bold new programmes; in his time, he sought to galvanise the London public with Blondin, bull-fighting and barmaid competitions. Arguably, in buying up the 'exclusive' services of George Leybourne in 1868 to revive the depressed fortunes of the Canterbury, Holland was doing more than seeking just another publicity coup; he was promoting a style and image that pointed up the grand manner of the caterer, flattering the big man and his public alike, suggesting a community of bluff and carefree revellers. In promoting Champagne Charlie, Holland was promoting himself and the general business of pleasure.

Though far from being puppets, it seems obvious enough that the performers were ready accomplices in the manufacture and marketing of the swell. The swell, as already noted, was not the only role in their repertoire, but it was the one which gave them their sharpest identity with their public and, crucially, within their own profession. The more successful performers were sharing, often in quite spectacular fashion, in the music-hall boom, but it was still a fiercely competitive and insecure way to make a living. With the proliferation of halls in London and the provinces, the profession increased in number and mobility, and in this ever-widening and over-populated world, the artist too had to shout louder to be heard.[17] It became essential to advertise, to be known to be in circulation. Not to advertise could 'kill' an artist, generating rumours of sickness, retirement or death; Leybourne more than once returned from the dead to read his obituaries with relish. Advertising was a matter of posters and placards, of column inches in the trade press, coloured portraits on sheet music, and the distribution of cartes de visite (introduced in 1859) bearing the artist's photograph. Even so, the star of the 1860s was far from relying on the mere reproduction of himself, because much of the necessary advertisement had to be done by personal presence.

If earnings and opportunities at the top grew in pace with the expansion of the industry, the monitoring and construction of professional success lay with a relatively small and still physically knowable nexus of interests in London, an inner world of top proprietors, agents, pressmen and fellow and sister artists.

Two mutually reinforcing innovations of the period did much to institutionalise this world. In 1870 the Oxford under Morris Syer began its regular Saturday matinees for professionals. It was an occasion for the audition of new talent, and 'reunion' among established members of the profession; all those in the business were admitted free. The year before had seen the publication of a new trade paper, the *London Entr'acte*, unique among a cluster of similar productions in the 1860s for its durability. It did not displace the *Era* but its reporting concerned itself much more with personalities and gossip than its staider contemporary. Much of the *Entr'acte*'s colourful copy came from the Oxford matinees.[18] For those in the know its allusions and innuendoes recorded the making, bending and breaking of innumerable deals and reputations. The atmosphere at the Oxford was one of feverish glamour and display as the performers, proprietors, chairmen and agents disported themselves in their best finery and put away much food and drink. The mix of big names, supplicant new talent and an admiring public also provided an ideal setting for conspicuous treating and other generosities. Here the grand style of the swell was the definitive style. Thus to master it on stage as well as with the company at the Oxford bars gave the performer as it were a double presence in his professional community.

But the swell was not just a vehicle devised to gratify the self-images of the music-hall world – he was derived from life, and already had a long history. Partridge dates the term from the early years of the century when it denoted a fashionably dressed man or woman of the upper classes, and though subsequent usage broadened its meaning considerably it always retained some sense of derivation from a genteel or aristocratic archetype. Beyond that it is possible to give the type some further specificity under three counts. The swell was defined in terms of dress, and where this was a meticulous and obsessive preoccupation which marked him off from the common herd we may talk of the swell firstly as dandy (or 'dandizette', though the term was increasingly reserved for men). The languid upper-class swell of this type had long been played as the effete fop of English stage comedy, and was a frequent comic target in pantomime in the early century,[19] but he achieved apotheosis in 1861 with E. A. Sothern's great popular success as Lord Dundreary in Taylor's *Our American Cousin*. His make-up and wardrobe were widely imitated, and Dundreary's centre parting and side whiskers were adopted by the lions comiques.[20]

In a second variant, as rake or man about town, the swell was considerably more boisterous and obtrusive. Here he stands in line with the drinking songs of the eighteenth century and the exploits of Corinthian Tom in Pierce Egan's tales of the 1820s as the lordling hell-bent on the good time.[21] There is much horse-play, drinking and laughing and a good deal of noise in general. An actual site for these forays into low life in the 1830s and 1840s were the song-and-supper rooms around the Strand, important if minor antecedents of the music hall and all-male Bohemia for those who wished to escape convention. The collection of bawdy songs that made up the programme for one of these notorious establishments, the Coal Hole, was subtitled *The Swell's Album*. Another leading room, Evans's, later became a principal rendezvous for upper-class hooligans in the ritual excesses of boat-race night. This type was met with early in the music hall; when Morton opened the Oxford he was confronted by the swell who would sweep the board of crockery and glasses that he might pay for the damage and exclaim 'Damn the expense!'[22]

Lastly we come to the swell as counterfeit. Though located originally among the *ton*, the term swell carried an early suggestion of the bogus, particularly in the appellation 'swell mob', denoting a class of pickpockets who dressed in style to escape detection as they mingled with their fashionable victims.[23] But the sham swell was more commonly registered as a social rather than a criminal menace. He appeared in great numbers on London streets in the 1830s and 1840s as the much despised 'gent'. As Ellen Moers puts it, 'this was a label pasted on young men on the bottom of the respectable class, the scrubby clerks, apprentices and medical students who scraped along on less than £50 a year, calling themselves (hopefully) gents, and their betters (admiringly) swells.' Albert Smith in his *History of the Gent* of 1847 pilloried the type for a spurious gentility of dress and manner, and a *Punch* cartoon registered the phenomenon as 'A Most Alarming Swelling'.[24] But the upstart clerk and his kind would not go away, for they already constituted a sizeable, self-conscious consumer group with its own emergent sub-culture.[25] Certainly these gents and would-be swells found a haven in the early music halls and singing saloons. *The Town* in 1838 noted the proliferation of 'Cockney swells' – mostly linen-drapers' assistants and shop men – at the Castle in Regent Street. J. Ewing Ritchie, an early music-hall hater, recorded 'juvenile swells' at the Eagle Tavern in 1857 and again at a hall in Hungerford Market where he noted 'one or two awful young swells with excruciating all-rounders' (a type of collar).[26] A programme from the Victoria Saloon in Old Street in 1843 announces the appearance of a comic singer as 'The Modern Slap Up Swell', and several titles show that the swell was the subject of popular song before the arrival of the lions comiques.[27]

In his several guises the swell was well known in life and literature by the 1860s, suggesting in a single word both an ideal and its debasement. Inside and outside the halls the lion comique and the swell song had some interesting cultural stock to exploit.[28]

An obvious entrée to the songs themselves is *Champagne Charlie*, written by Leybourne with music by Alfred Lee, published in late 1866, and remaining a popular item in Leybourne's repertoire till his death.[29]

> I've seen a deal of gaiety
> Throughout my noisy life,
> With all my grand accomplishments
> I never could get a wife.
> The thing I most excell in is
> The PRFG game,
> A noise all night, in bed all day,
> And swimming in Champagne.
>
> CHORUS:
> For Champagne Charlie is my name,
> Champagne Charlie is my game,
> Good for any game at night, my boys,
> Good for any game at night, my boys,
> For Champagne Charlie is my name,
> Champagne Charlie is my game,
> Good for any game at night, my boys,
> Who'll come and join me in a spree?
>
> The way I gained my title's
> By a hobby which I've got
> Of never letting others pay
> However long the shot;
> Whoever drinks at my expense
> Are treated all the same,
> From Dukes and lords, to cabmen down,
> I make them drink Champagne.
>
> From Coffee and from Supper Rooms,
> From Poplar to Pall Mall,
> The girls, on seeing me, exclaim
> 'Oh, what a Champagne Swell!'
> The notion 'tis of everyone
> If 'twere not for my name,
> And causing so much to be drunk,
> They'd never make Champagne.

> Some epicures like Burgundy,
> Hock, Claret, and Mosell,
> But Moet's vintage only
> Satisfies this Champagne swell.
> What matters if to bed I go
> Dull head and muddled thick,
> A bottle in the morning
> Sets me right then very quick.
>
> Perhaps you fancy what I say
> Is nothing else but chaff,
> And only done, like other songs
> To merely raise a laugh.
> To prove that I am not in jest,
> Each man a bottle of Cham.
> I'll stand fizz round, yes that I will,
> And stand it like a lamb.

It seems a simple enough text, with the exception of the obscure cabalistic reference to the 'PRFG game' (a good bottle for the reader with the most convincing gloss!).[30] It is a tale of heroic consumption in which our champion keeps the champagne industry afloat virtually singlethroatedly – by his own prowess (he swims in it), and by his generosity in treating others. As the new and unrivalled elixir of the drinking man, champagne despatches hangovers and brings instant renewal. Appropriately befuelled, men may conquer the night and obliterate the day. Under Charlie's leadership (note the chummy and disarming diminutive) the invitation is open to all, though the nature of nocturnal exploit is vague: it is certainly noisy, may well be daring and will generally put the 'boys' on their mettle. It will impress the girls. There is no great literary artifice here – no 'beaded bubbles winking at the brim' – no narrative development, and the music is a simple and repetitive march tune. Its popularity was nonetheless, in the puffery of the day, 'immense', and it received its ultimate accolade from the Salvation Army who appropriated it for a hymn tune.

How are we to explain the remarkable success of this unremarkable song? My method here has been to relate it to others of its type, to understand their range of connotation or web of associated meanings within a particular social and historical context, to reconstruct the dynamics of their performance, reception and use, and to extend this exercise to define the swell song as a genre, as well as register the specifics of its most notable hit.[31]

Like many others of its type, *Champagne Charlie* was most obviously a song of release and action. The release is from the almost literally unspeakable purgatory of the daytime; for Charlie it is merely a recuperative interlude, though for most it must have implied work. The action is that of the boys on the spree, 'good for any game at night'. In Vance's *Slap Bang, Here We Are Again*, which celebrated 'our British Gentlemen', the action was more specific, for 'They play cricket, box and torture cocks' before repairing to the Opera, then Evans's. Together with the zest for traditional manly sports goes the role of the swell as man about town combining the fashionable with the fashionably disreputable. The ritual delinquencies that went with the latter role are suggested in the song sheet cover of another Vance hit, *Jolly Dogs Galop*, where the jolly dogs are shown in retreat from the police; *The Swell*, published in Birmingham in 1867, also recounts a brush with the law after the boys refuse to pay a cabman.[32] The action (over a wide if predictable territory) also involves a great deal of noise. Champagne Charlie makes a noise all night, Vance's *Howling Swell* announces himself with 'Crash, smash!' (no doubt as a follow up to 'Slap bang!') and J. H. Milburn sang *Come Along Boys, Let's Make a Noise.*

But above all else in these songs of licence, action meant drinking. Here champagne was king. Other drinks were celebrated, but it was champagne that was installed as the sovereign cordial of the good time and the only tipple for the real swell. Leybourne, whose repertoire included anti-temperance as well as drinking songs, drank the stuff by the pint tankard, and we may recall Ned Weston the proprietor treating his customers to champagne on the house. Waiters placed bottles on all the tables in every part of the house, reported the *Era* under the title 'Champagne for the Million', adding that it was a gesture 'which seemed utterly incomprehensible to the visitors'.[33] Within a few years there could have been few music-hall goers who were not familiar with the idea and image of champagne – if not with its consumption.

Champagne had a long-established reputation as a fashionable drink. Charles Townsend, the eighteenth-century wit and politico, had previously enjoyed the title of 'Champagne Charley'. It had been a favourite of the marcaronis and dandies (Beau Brummell had reputedly cleaned his boots with it); it was sold at Vauxhall, prescribed at the spas, and later celebrated by Byron. Only the best people could afford it. A drop in prices in the 1840s and 1850s doubled its consumption, but the great breakthrough came after 1861 when Gladstone reduced the tariff, bringing champagne within reach of the middle classes (Gladstone himself took a quart with his dinner).[34] Sales grew dramatically and were duly recorded in the *Era* together with warnings of cheap imitations made from gooseberries or rhubarb. Whatever its provenance, champagne was on regular sale at music halls by the mid 1860s from 6 to 10 shillings a bottle. In 1864, for example, it was to be had not only in the famous Canterbury music hall in Lambeth, but also in the Canterbury music hall in Sheffield, where a certain W. Revill was advertised singing *The Glorious Vintage of Champagne* to the cutlers and grinders who comprised the 300 capacity crowd of this modest establishment.[35]

The consumption of champagne among working people either inside or outside the music halls cannot have been extensive, whatever the promotion stunts of the wine shippers and the endorsements by music-hall celebrities, but its myth was democratised. Some working men lived the myth briefly during the wages boom of the early 1870s when there were indignant reports of miners indulging in 'sealskin jackets and bottles of champagne', and champagne did appear on the shelves of some co-operative stores by the 1880s.[36]

The majority no doubt took their ease with less exalted drinks, yet even here significant changes in taste complemented the language of the champagne shippers who stressed its properties of lightness and purity – the *Era* extolled champagne as 'a great restorative' whose 'intoxicating effects were rapid but transient'. Changes in brewing and the cheaper production of glass were already producing a new emphasis on 'drinking by the eye' and a growing preference for sparkling, lighter-bodied beers over traditional heavy-bodied brews. The champagne of the new beers was Bass Pale Ale introduced nationally in the late 1860s and commended in glowing terms by that otherwise sober journal of improvement and reform, the *Beehive*. The 'light, sparkling exhilarating beer', proclaimed an editorial in the working-class paper, 'satisfied thirst, refreshes the spirits and suits the stomach', suggesting further that 'it induces habits of temperance and moderation.' Champagne and beer alike were thus represented in the rhetoric of an emergent mass consumerism with the emphasis placed on lightness and brightness and the benign and easeful experience of consumption.[37] Champagne, of course, was made to promise this and more. In the years of the first great music-hall boom, 'fizz' symbolised glamour and high success – 'Will it fizz?' meaning, will it go, was the expression music-hall people used of any new venture throughout the rest of the century.

The reactions of one working-class audience to a comic singer's invitation to drink champagne was noted by Walter Tomlinson in a Manchester hall in the 1880s:

The exquisite fitness of this query to such an audience seems to tickle the fancy of the ladies, and one near us observes to her companion with good-humoured sarcasm, 'Oh yes! of course we has champagne for supper every night reglar!'[38]

It is the good humour that counts. If they could not share directly in its bounties, songs about champagne flattered them by its invocation of high life, and its invitation to vicarious participation.

Being a swell or lion comique required more than making appropriate noises and drinking appropriate drinks – as Charles Norman sang in 1868 (in the Star at Bermondsey), *So Much Depends Upon The Style In Which Its Done*. Dress and bearing were of central importance. The stage swell paraded all the apparatus of genteel apparel, though variation and distortion were common where the object was parody. Thus Arthur Lloyd often performed in bizarre dress and make-up, sporting a coat with exaggerated lapels, an outlandish silk choker and 'a forty Cardigan power moustache'. In his song *The Dancing Swell*, Harry Liston was reported as wearing 'a pair of unmentionables (trousers) which no one outside of Hanwell (a lunatic asylum) would think of putting on'.[39] Clothes were of course among the fundamental properties of stage comedy and trousers were inherently comic, particularly where their incumbent suffered for fashion's sake. 'How did you get those trousers on and did it hurt you much?' sang George Leybourne in his *Comet of the West* (End), and the same question might have been asked of the gaudy striped pants he wears in the song cover to *Champagne Charlie*. Presumably a direct rendering of his stage costume for the song, it depicts Leybourne in collar and tie, waistcoat and cutaway jacket, sporting a set of Dundreary whiskers, a cigar, a cane, and the cut-down top hat with the curly brim that became known popularly as a champagne charlie hat.

Here it seems that Leybourne was to some extent sending up the swell style, but in other similar roles he could be irreproachably genteel, and was most frequently recollected for his studied portrayal of the society gentleman. 'George', recalled Percy Fitzgerald in the 1890s, 'was never seen out of a dress suit', adding that there was a common belief that he took part in the brilliant scene enacted on stage. This enduring image derives no doubt from Holland's successful promotion of Leybourne off as well as on stage, but the dress suit and the appropriate manner of its wearing was as much a necessary accomplishment for the lions comiques as for the parodies they wrought upon it. Vance wore formal evening dress for several of his songs and was recalled as 'the best groomed comic singer ever to grace the halls' (though his feet were said to be distinctly bigger than the fashionably Lilliputian size of his song-cover portraits). Jolly John Nash later claimed to have been one of the first vocal comedians to adopt society's evening dress, so we may accept that it was something of an innovation in music-hall stage costume.[40]

The appropriation of gentility could be suggested by association as well as emulation. Several of the most popular swell songs were set in the specific territory of fashionable society. Vance had a great hit in *Walking in the Zoo*, at a time when London's zoological gardens were the preserve of an exclusive private society – 'zoo' was the lyricist's vulgar contraction, said to be a term offensive to the ears of its select membership. Vance also went *Lounging in the Aq*(uarium), a favourite haunt of fashionable men about town, and Rickards sang of *Doing the Academy* and *Strolling in the Burlington* (Arcade).

Just as this transcription of fashionable life could in part be actualised with a glass of cheap champagne, so too was its approximation democratised through the new availability of cheap tailoring. The market leaders were Elias Moses and Son. Since the 1840s they had been servicing the 'gent' from their several emporia in central London, offering ready-made menswear which aped the fashionable line and drew the fire of the satirists for its ill-bred affectations.[41] By the 1860s there were several large firms in the market and their advertisements appeared regularly in the *Era*, the *Entr'acte* and the working-class *Beehive*. The theatres and music halls provided them with a prime showcase for their products and the stars were eagerly wooed for their endorsements. Sothern's dressing room was crowded with salesmen as tailors and haberdashers sought to create a fashion through some new addition to Dundreary's wardrobe.[42] Moses' ads claimed the patronage of a number of stars, and Vance got free suits in return for plugs for his tailor, Edward Groves, who had shops next door to the Canterbury and Metropolitan halls. Arthur Lloyd hymned two other firms in *Immensikoff*, his hit about the Shoreditch toff, and Jenny Hill's similar hit, *'Arry*, spelt out costs: 2 guineas for a suit, 13s for 'bags'. The halls were particularly sensible to the claims of fashion, its provisioners and prices.

The range and exuberance of the popular wardrobe grew in other ways. The introduction of aniline dyes in the 1860s affected the dress of all classes, but it contributed mightily to the profusion of boldly coloured cravats, waistcoats and trousers so beloved of the swell on and off stage (and now vividly reproduced on the song covers through the parallel innovation of colour lithography). The new technology of electroplating brought cheap 'Birmingham' jewellery to the masses, providing a new element of display in popular dress. Another vital accessory came within easier reach in the 1860s, when Gladstone took two-thirds off the duty of manufactured tobacco and gave the nation a cheap cigar.

We may note also a new attention to self-presentation. The spread of photography no doubt encouraged this – photographers were already reaching downmarket in the 1850s and 1860s through fairground booths – but the music hall in particular intensified the interest, for it was in one respect quite literally the mirror of fashion. From its early days the music hall had made extensive use of mirror glass, a feature inherited from the gin palace. As well as providing a greater illusion of space and comfort, the mirrors made for an increased self-consciousness of bearing and appearance. 'All round the hall', remarked a review of the refurbished Middlesex in 1872, 'handsome mirrors reflect the glittering lights, and offer abundant opportunities for self-admiration.'[43] As the lion comique paraded his fashionable self on stage, members of his audience could with a sidelong glance decide how their own image matched up to that of their hero.

For the performer, boldness and singularity of dress were useful in making immediate impact upon an audience subject to a range of distractions within the hall, while it also gave opportunity for several forms of stage business. Vance made great play with large handkerchiefs which he pulled from his waistcoat. Hats, canes and monocles could be variously adjusted, twirled or manipulated, and gloves (lavender) – their putting on and taking off – were frequently noted as part of the stage business of the swell. Leybourne was complimented for 'the majestic sweep of his handplay'.[44] The significance of all this is elusive. Mastery of the genteel wardrobe and its accessories was an accomplishment that would add to the authenticity of the stage portrayal of the swell; it would also be prime territory of comic parody. But dress and its manipulation had its own code on the halls, though clues for its deciphering are few. One critic reprimanded Vance for the vulgarity of his handkerchief play – littering the stage with them, he said, 'suggested a state of undress'. Was this the intended message, commonly understood, or the reaction of a singular, over-heated imagination? There was also suggestive business with the cane; the performer might extend the knob of his cane across the footlights as a surrogate handshake to members of the audience. Such sartorial-cum-gestural innuendoes were likely important features in the performance of swell as well as other comic songs.[45]

The full manner of performance is of course difficult if not impossible to reconstruct. We have the text and the music and some indicators of vocal style in the surviving conventions of music-hall type performances. But we have no record of what Barthes calls the particular 'grain' or materiality of the voice, and only occasional printed and presumably bowdlerised snatches of the 'spoken' or patter which the comique would have slipped in between verses (Leybourne was particularly notorious for his interpolations and spontaneous exchanges with the audience). Yet it seems plain enough that swell songs were delivered robustly, even aggressively. The previously noted emphasis on noise-making in the songs certainly suggests this, though this may have been a functional as well as stylistic device, as performers strove to cut through the din of a self-absorbed audience and noisy environment. Certain lyrics and song covers suggest a languid style of delivery as in Leybourne's *Cool Burgundy Ben* and Vance's *Lord Swoon*, but the more obviously bacchanalian songs were vocally and physically more assertive, sometimes with direct audience encouragement – thus it became common for the crowd to interject a shouted 'Yes!' at the end of each line in the chorus to *Champagne Charlie*.

Swell songs came with a distinctive body language. An interesting guide to comic singing from 1869, for those who wished to reproduce the music-hall style in the drawing-room, considered Vance the prime exemplar of 'Gentleman comedy' – significantly Leybourne is absent from the list of appropriate models – and noted 'a kind of pliability of body' in the former.[46] For most performers on the halls this would have been an understatement. Jerrold remarked of the swell in the penny gaff that the song came 'with a jerk at the beginning of each line, in true street style', a style readily reproduced on the halls to judge from the periodical *Fun* (7 October 1871) which noted 'The staring, flaring, glaring, swearing popular Lion Comique'. We may take it that the swell postured and strutted on stage, very much the male peacock.

Plainly the swell songs offered a particular construction of gender and sexuality. The novelist, William Pett Ridge, looking back on them, declared that they 'gloried in sex' as well as drink.[47] On the face of it, the swell is the rogue male, playing the field and resisting entrapment by marriage – 'With all my grand accomplishments,' sings Champagne Charlie in inverted parody of the spinster's lament, 'I never could get a wife.'[48] Undoubtedly the nature of the swell's sexual exploits were amplified by innuendo, patter and gesture, but the record here is sparse and elliptical with little more than the occasional report suggesting the miming of a conquest, as in the arm encircling the waist of some accommodating barmaid.

On the evidence of the text, however, partial though it may be, the swell's relations with women are far from predatory. 'The girls on seeing me, exclaim/"Oh, what a Champagne Swell"' – to be acclaimed or adored by women seems enough. The swell – and the built-in tumescence of the label can hardly have gone unexploited in the patter of the comique dealing with an audience well schooled in bawdy and scattered with prostitutes – was cocksure but unconsummating. His was the sexuality of display, perhaps of provocation, but not obviously of engagement. Is this sex for those who don't want it, or sex for those who can't get it, or sex for those who couldn't handle it if they did? There is some correspondence here with the predicament of the young clerk in the city as revealed in the letters to the *Daily Telegraph* in the late 1860s on the Young Man of the Day.[49] Often a newcomer to London, he found contact with females of his own station restricted by tight parental control, while marriage was being longer deferred by rising financial requirements. If it is likely that he was also deterred by the formalities of respectable dalliance, it may well be that he was too wary, too impecunious, or too inhibited to avail himself of a prostitute's services. In his involuntary abstinence he may have salvaged some masculine pride from identifying with the assertive but disengaged sexuality of the lion comique. The stage swell conducted a drama of masculine display, a form of collective narcissism – that of men showing off to other men.

Is there further meaning to be squeezed out of the swell song as songtext-cum-performance type? Current critical practice emphasises the polysemic properties of the most obvious of cultural forms, demonstrating how these can be made to reveal deeper structures of complementary and oppositional relationships within wider systems of signification and text/context interdependency. Such analysis demands attention not only to the author/performer, but to the reader/receiver as crucial agent in the construction of meaning. Before turning to consider the music-hall audience in this role, I should perhaps step outside the cautious practice of the historian with his nose pressed up close against the sources, and offer some bolder interpretive scheme in the spirit of the structuralist disciple who urges that such analysis should possess 'surprise value'.[50] What does strike me in larger symbolic terms about the swell song is the inherent tension between images of indulgence and constraint. On the one hand there is the licence of champagne-induced pleasure and the way in which it is literally bodied forth in performance, on the other is the constrictive nature of the dress in which the authentic good time is pursued – the formality and corset-like line of evening dress and the grip of the collar, the 'excruciating all-rounder' of Ritchie's report. This could be read as expressive of a deeper tension within capitalism itself on the admissibility of pleasure and consumption in a work-centred culture. No great surprise in this, perhaps, but I turn for that to gorgeous George himself, who concluded *Champagne Charlie* by brandishing a bottle fitted with a device that exploded the cork to order, a final ejaculatory flourish whose Barthian *signifiance* I leave to the critical imagination of the reader.[51]

IV

Thus the swell song engaged with its audience through a wealth of social, material and stylistic connotations, encapsulated within the part realistic, part idealised, part parodied, but instantly recognisable persona of the lion comique. Leybourne and company reflected and produced a particular definition of a contemporary social type, showing how it might be lived out through a specific repertoire of behaviour, appearance and manner, and exalting its particular masculinity to an admiring bachelor sub-culture within the halls. Yet the swell songs also engaged the attention of other constituencies in the audience, while within their more obvious target groups their meaning was often shifting and ambiguous.

To understand the further reach of the swell song and its ambiguities it is necessary to emphasise how endemic was the element of parody in music-hall song and performance. Any popular style or hit was immediately vulnerable – *Champagne Charlie* was instantly parodied on stage, and Leybourne's carriage and four was mocked by Walter Laburnum who drove a cart and a pair of donkeys in its wake. We have seen too, in passing, how the swell songs and their performance might carry an element of self-parody. In some of the songs, however, the thrust of parody was much more scathing and direct, while in performance a number of them allowed a mixed interpretation in which the role was offered for applause or derision simultaneously, according to the varying discriminations of a composite audience.

Like its more vengeful brother satire, parody operated in two basic directions, neatly rendered in our contemporary usage as to send up or to put down. Thus it might exaggerate pretension to the point of absurdity, or it might choose the alternative tactic of reducing what was represented as extraordinary to the commonplace (as with Laburnum's donkeys and trap). Songs like Vance's *Lord Swoon* operated through hyperbole to parody the swell at his most effete, but a commoner sub-type was the deflationary song which exploited what we may recall as one of the long-standing historical-cum-literary categories in which the swell was known – that of the counterfeit.

The swell as sham, the gent as fraud – as we have seen, these had been ready targets for attack from outside, but they drew a good deal of fire from inside the halls too. Swell songs, commented the *Era* (20 August 1865), 'frequently draw forth satirical remarks and odious comparisons between the real and the ideal'. The stratagems and sacrifices to which those of modest means were forced to resort in pursuit of the ideal provided obvious humorous capital. *How Does He Do It?*, sang G. H. Macdermott of a certain son and heir to two pie shops in Surrey who paraded as a toff in the West End: 'His name is Jones, but he asserts/'Tis Henri Montmorency.' Maintaining appearances on a slender or nonexistent budget was a common theme: as Walter Laburnum's *Fashionable Fred* proclaimed, 'I have a decent coat/Though I haven't got a groat.' But the note of indulgence, and even applause for these small-scale social heroics, was seldom more than a hairline away from a mockery that could be quite devastating. Parody became particularly explosive in the acts of the female swells, the male impersonators who aped the lions comique. Their acts were in themselves parodies, but their specific impact came in the way they pressed home their mockery of the swell as counterfeit, charging not only that he was less than the real thing in terms of dress and manner, but that crucially he was less than a man.

Male impersonation was an integral part of the English theatrical tradition, and its particular embodiment on the halls in the form of the fashionable young man was to become one of the major performance types in nineteenth- and twentieth-century variety.[52] In this and its variants it is a complex phenomenon that deserves much fuller treatment than can be accommodated here. But it does seem that the female as gent was a more disturbing characterisation in the 1860s and 1870s than in its later apotheosis in Vesta Tilley. On one level, of course, we may take in that the role flattered the men in the audience. What could be more admirable than that a woman should want to take on the attributes of the superior sex (with the saving clause that this was an episode at play rather than a real social challenge)? Casting a woman as 'one of the chaps' also served to reduce distance and the difficulties of formal address between the sexes, suggesting that she might be manageable on male terms rather than as an unpredictable female. But as might be expected in this role there were considerable ambiguities and, in the particular context we are dealing with, the honorary chap might turn round and savage those presumed to be 'his' pals.

This comes across strongly in the songs of Nellie Power, whose career as one of the earliest female stars on the halls derived largely from her swell impersonations. (Others noted in playing the role were Kate Harley, Jenny Stanley, Fanny Leslie, Louie Sherrington, Annie Hind, and Ellie Wesner.) Nellie Power made her name originally in the late 1860s doing imitations of George Leybourne, and in 1872 she had her first independent hit with *Tiddy fol Lol* which celebrated the doings of a real swell: 'He's got ten thousand a year, tiddy fol lol/Drinks champagne at the bars/Smokes Intimidad cigars'. The anonymous hero of the song was the son of a tailor called Brown, but in other matters his credentials were impeccable. He is also acquitted on the implicit charge of doubtful masculinity: 'Though he looks and dresses well/He's no lardy dardy swell.' It was to this latter theme that Power returned in her next and biggest hit, *The City Toff or The Crutch and Toothpick*. This pilloried the imitation swell both for his paltry style and his effeminacy:

> And he wears a penny flower in his coat, lah di dah!
> And a penny paper collar round his throat, lah di dah!
> In his hand a penny stick,
> In his mouth a penny pick,
> And a penny in his pocket, lah di dah!

The song remained a hit for two years, selling a thousand copies a day according to its author, E. V. Page, who pocketed £500 in royalties. The song certainly hit home with the subject of its caricature, for on one occasion a young man in the audience was so incensed that he hurled a soda water syphon at Nelly Power.[53]

Though this seems an exceptional incident, it is plain that the swell song exploited the tensions generated by the ambiguities and oppositions of class, status, gender and generation. Circumstantially at least, it seems that the oppositions lay not just between the performer and his or her target group but between sections of the audience. Most songs were less openly provocative than Nelly Power's, but in large mixed urban audiences they could be read in ways that excited a variety of cross-cutting responses. To working-class spectators, a man like Leybourne could demonstrate the triumph of the natural gentleman in his convincing portrayal of upper-class manners, while remaining one of them – according to Chance Newton he often reverted to his 'mechanic manner'. At the same time, as we have seen, Champagne Charlie was a compelling role-model for the young clerks in the audience. But if the swell song exemplified and validated a certain style, it also drew attention to those like the young clerks who might fall pathetically short of the ideal. If Leybourne might have appealed to workers as an example of what one working-class commentator, Thomas Wright, the Journeyman Engineer, called a 'genuine swell . . . a being to be admired', his performance might also have confirmed them in their distaste for what Wright called 'the cheap imitation swell (who was) fit only to be kicked'.[54] In this Wright was also attacking the youth of his own class for such affectations, adding a generational tension to the mix. One of the earliest notices of Nelly Power's success with *The Crutch and Toothpick* was from the Cambridge music hall in the East End, where Leybourne had been a great hit as Champagne Charlie. It was a hall with a strong working-class following, but with a good number of clerks in its audience too.[55] We can perhaps now understand why such halls gave the swell songs their popular momentum.

Perhaps too it was in such halls that clerks got their own back for any aspersions on their social skills, by enjoying themselves at the expense of another variant in the genre, the coster swell. Again, this is an important type in itself, and at this point was a more vigorous representation than the sentimentalised cockney of the late century. It was commonly played back to back with the society swell as in Vance's 'dainty exquisite and rugged vulgarian'. Another notable coster swell act of the period was Lloyd's *Immensikoff, the Shoreditch Toff* from 1873 (at the peak of the wages boom). Most of the song proclaims the superior style of his wardrobe, and was clearly the stuff of parody – thus the song cover shows him in all the conventional apparatus of the swell, but he carries a club in place of a cane. One writer, reviewing another song of the type, *Spicey Bill*, noted the singer's extensive patter which included much attention to his 'toggery . . . the while wiping his nose on his sleeve'.[56] One can almost hear the sniggers from the clerks.

But again, parody might march hand in hand with validation, further exploiting sectional antipathies within the audience. Jenny Hill enjoyed nationwide success with a coster song (also the result of meticulous observation) called *'Arry* (E. V. Page again), introduced in the early eighties but no doubt inspired by the series of comic stories written by A.

J. Milliken in *Punch* in the 1870s; their hero, also an 'Arry, became established in the language as a shorthand for the stereotype cockney swell, and indeed in general for the working man as lout on the spree.[57] One reviewer clearly read Hill's song on these terms: 'We should like all the 'Arrys in London to see her in character and to learn how ridiculous they are.'[58] However, though some might see the song as a put-down, it contained within it a jaunty defence of its hero:

> The Upper Ten may jeer and say
> What cads the 'Arries are,
> But the 'Arries *work* and *pay their way*
> While doing the lah-di-dah.

Did hearty proletarian cheers then drown the sniggers of the counter jumpers? Certainly the coster swell was not an automatic figure of fun among his cockney fellows. The costermonger was not in fact strictly a proletarian, but a penny capitalist with a necessary streak of competitive individualism. His trade demanded a certain style and self-advertisement of which the swell might be a natural projection, and the surge of casual migrants into London in this period may have added a further note of defensive pride. Thus what from outside might be seen as a caricature may well have appeared within its own culture as the celebration of an authentic indigenous type. From this angle, the cockney swell was neither a lout nor a buffoon, but the small man writ large.

V

In the swell song, music hall began to establish its own distinctive voice. Together with other modes within the broad field of comic song it marked a shift away from the leisurely narrative of the ballad tradition to a more episodic or situational representation.[59] The song was no longer that of a traditional air but one commercially produced by a professional song writer, the words by a professional performer or lyricist. The text was now less literary or poetic, and comes off the page poorly, relying as it did on performance *and* reception to detonate the charges that lie in the compressions and ellipses of its otherwise unremarkable language. (Singers were frequently taken by surprise at the way the audiences would 'manufacture' meanings unsuspected by the performer.) The swell songs exploited a range of cues that drew the audience into active recognition of its own various social selves, and directly exploited the sympathies and distances within and between them. As a genre, its form can only be satisfactorily defined in terms of performance and use.

In content, the swell song is one of male exploit and display; in both, its historic and contemporary models are aristocratic or upper class though the style is never merely imitative, but rather an appropriation. In its actions there is a sense of licence, particularly where they echo the traditional exploits of lordlings about town, thumbing their nose at authority and tasting the forbidden pleasures of low life. But the licence of the swell song seems less hell-bent and destructive (either of self or others), and more a matter of the indulgences of a self-regarding and mock-heroic male freemasonry, excused, if excuse were necessary, in the disarming and egalitarian language of the 'boys' on the spree. In display, the songs celebrate the new availability and consumption of the externals of fashionable life, demonstrating how they were to be mastered while wryly acknowledging the difficulties of this exercise. In the arch and knowing manner of the halls, the songs and their singers provided a style manual for those who sought status and identity in appearances.

In all, the genre projected a potent if slippery ideology of pleasure and social identity, which fused a traditional utopianism with the wakening yet uncertain expectations of a modern industrial society. The swell was a product of a larger system of liberal capitalism that was now affording its subordinates a greater share of its economic surplus, while offering a fuller sense of membership through the extension of the franchise (1867) and various middle-class schemes of cultural association or 'social citizenship'.[60] Although a rogue and arrivist branch of the system, the music-hall industry echoed the mainstream discourse of consensual liberalism, but in a language and symbolism shorn of the latter's moralising and conditional gradualism. Thus within the ancient conceit of the common man as king for the day – or lord for the night – the swell song transcended the short-run gratifications of the traditional good time and offered its own sensational vision of a more permanent world of progress and plenty. It is a measure of the plausibility of such a vision that the swell was so hugely indulged. At the same time, the music-hall public withheld full faith in a liberal society whose rhetoric of meliorist incorporation could not disguise the continuing inequities and deprivations of their class experience. Parody safely deflated the swell's more extravagant promises, and one retort to *Champagne Charlie* challenged him directly as a cruel delusion:

> To hear them praise the sparkling wine
> It makes a man severe
> When they know they cannot raise the price
> Of half a pint of beer.[61]

If music hall found its own voice in the swell song there were many who disliked what it had to say. Leybourne was said to 'spurt filth from his mouth', and the lions comiques were generally vilified for their glorification of sex and drink.[62] But the more revealing charges against the halls of this period were those that recognised a more insidious malaise. A writer in *Tinsley's Magazine* of April 1869, who seemed well acquainted with the halls, thought music hall more dangerous now that it had replaced 'vulgarity of the coarsest kind' with 'vulgarity gilded'. He deplored 'its levelling-up theory of democracy . . . and that sham gentility which has become so abnormally prominent among the striplings of the uneducated classes.' Under the tutelage of the stage swell, the 'gent' was becoming a yet more numerous and intrusive discomfiture to polite society.

Business collapses and a flattening out of profit levels disturbed bourgeois confidence in these years, while the extension of the franchise and increases in wages announced a newly advantaged lower class. The democratisation of leisure seemed to threaten social as well as political and economic differentials, as another contemporary noted:

From being machines, fit only for machine work or inert quiescence, the masses are given the liberty of being men – gentlemen indeed, if in that term be applied the possession of leisure, the power of being 'at large' – a coveted attribute of gentility.[63]

The swell, the gent, and 'Arry (*Tinsley's* lumped them all together) now threatened gentility along a wide front. Add to this the charge of effeminacy and the fear that he was an endemic product of the degenerate modern city, and we can appreciate why the swell was castigated as 'that general enemy', to recall Jerrold's phrase, that could not be simply laughed away.[64]

The full resonance of the swell song in popular life during its heyday in the 1860s and 1870s remains elusive. Certainly it captured a wide audience, clearly registering as a hit with the working classes as well as with the young counter-jumpers; it also won its following in the provinces as well as the metropolis. Indeed it has been seen as marking a distinct change in the class consciousness of popular culture, a change away from an anti-aristocratic and populist tone attended by a fall in the intellectual level. Vance and Leybourne are represented as aberrations from an authentic working-class voice, glamorising the aristocracy and blunting class animosities.[65] The schema of which these interpretations form part command respect but they inevitably also oversimplify. Stuart Hall has reminded us that all popular forms combine the bogus and the authentic[66] – in the swell songs the combination is less an amalgam than a dialectic. The swell song was certainly not hostile to the aristocracy, but neither was it an exercise in slavish adulation. As we have seen, it was a knowing vulgarisation, with an ironic and self-conscious regard for the absurdities as well as the plausibilities of the exercise. As a text the swell song is intellectually banal, but as a performance type its levels of engagement are complex and various, at once idealised and realistic, normative and satirical.

If it departs from the true path of class conflict, the swell song nonetheless confronted approved values. A form of bohemianism, it automatically offended the bourgeois, setting play against work, heroic consumption against exemplary abstinence. In a similarly carnivalesque yet less abrupt way that was characteristic of music hall, it played with the prescribed categories of rank and gender. In historical terms, the swell song suggests a half-fantasised, half-actualised search for a style appropriate to an era of popular advance, when occupational sub-cultures were losing their primacy in working-class life, and the more homogenised culture of the late century had yet to cohere. In the lion comique's appropriation of the new formal dress there is a significant displacement of older traditions of holiday colour and display, but the suit is not yet the body's gaoler nor (with the flat cap) the fuliginous and hegemonic uniform of a regimented proletariat.[67]

Though the swell might be a powerful projection of energy, confidence and some defiance, I have suggested the counterpull of a certain folk-wariness, and there are other qualifications to be made if this re-evaluation is not to become too enamoured of Champagne Charlie and what one contemporary called his 'magnificent cheek'. It must be emphasised that the swell triumphalised a form of male behaviour in which women were merely accessories like the cane and the bottle. Moreover, his egalitarian generosity may often have been realised at the direct expense of women, as one victim from the Black country testified:

I married a swell I did . . . when I married him in the morning he had a smart gold watch and chain, and a smart dickey (shirt). But when we came to go to bed at night I'm blessed if he had even a shirt on; and ever since then I've had to keep him by working in the brickyard, and not only keep him, but find him money to drink.[68]

If he could avoid such destructive consequences for himself as well as others, the common man might enjoy himself richly through identification with the music-hall swell. In 1869–70, the Nine Hours movement laid claim to greater leisure time, and its working-class leaders couched their demands in the sober official language of improvement. But the enthusiastic reception afforded George Leybourne on his appearance at benefits in support of the cause bespeaks other projections of popular betterment among the rank and file.[69] Thus it can be argued that amid all the counterfeit trappings of the swell and the showbiz manipulation of the music-hall industry, Champagne Charlie spoke with the authentic voice of his class – 'Yes!'

CHAPTER 6

Music hall and the knowingness of popular culture

Knowingness might be defined as what everybody knows, but some know better than others. At once complicit and discriminatory, this popular mode of expression was frequently noted by middle-class commentators as a distinctive – and objectionable – feature of comic performance in nineteenth-century British music halls. Expanding on the previous examination of the swell song in performance and reception, this essay considers how knowingness functioned as the broader metalanguage of music hall's comic style, providing an important key to a more satisfactory explanation of how it engaged with its public. Treating knowingness as discourse *and* practice enables us to get inside the dynamics of this influential modern cultural form. It suggests too how spoken (and unspoken) language functioned as a prime resource in the 'mobile infinity of tactics' that constituted everyday life.[1]

I

British music hall or variety emerged in the 1830s and 1840s and grew rapidly to dominate the commercialised popular culture of the late nineteenth century. From the 1890s its primacy was challenged by other musical and dramatic forms and by the successive rise of the phonograph, film, radio and, more terminally, television. Even so its influence continued to be considerable. The music hall industry was killed off (though not till the 1950s), but as a style of comic entertainment it made a successful piecemeal transition to the new media, and found continuing expression in something close to its original setting in the working-men's club circuit, as also in the more contrived revivalism of 'Old Tyme' music hall. The term itself is still standard in cultural commentary, and together with suet puddings and red pillar-boxes might be added to Orwell's list of the definitive components of the English national culture.[2]

As such, music hall has generated a huge literature in its celebration, and only recently has this been supplemented by more critical accounts.[3] Since popular culture has found its way on to the scholarly agenda, social historians have been concerned to assess the role of the halls in the cultural formation of class and the politics of modern leisure, and scholars in music history, literature, theatre and cultural studies are subjecting music hall to closer scrutiny as genre and text. Though newer work has begun to look at the wider range of its operation as industry and cultural form, scholarship continues to concentrate primarily on music hall's most distinctive idiom, that of the comic song and its singer.

Here, a major exercise has been the more precise inventory of content – 'What they sang about', as the subtitle of one of the first retrospective surveys of the territory put it.[4] The identification of principal motifs – booze, romantic adventure, marriage and mothers-in-law, dear old pals and seaside holidays, and so on – demonstrates a recurrent emphasis on the domestic and the everyday that supports the most broadly agreed reading of music hall song as a naturalistic mode that both documents and confirms a common way of life. The great popularity of the songs is said to come from the audience's recognition and identification with the routine yet piquant exploits of a comic realism that validates the shared experience of a typically urbanised, class-bound world seen from below.[5]

Discussion of music hall song is inseparable from that of its singers, for the distinctive style of the genre crystallized around individual performers and their acts. Given the apparent verisimilitude of music hall's representations of common life, the appeal of the great stars has often been interpreted in terms of their ability to convey this to their audience in a singularly direct and authentic manner. Thus T.S. Eliot explained Marie Lloyd's success by her 'capacity for expressing the soul of the people'.[6] Today's scholars resist such idealisation, but are still prone to the temptations of 'essentialism' or the acid test of a putative authenticity, preferring, for example, Gus Elen over Albert Chevalier, the sardonic over the sentimental, in the two performers' depictions of the costermonger in the 1890s. In more radical fashion, the Tyneside favourite, Joe Wilson, has been stripped of credentials as an authentic popular hero, for his songs and life-history are said to disclose a self-seeking moraliser distanced from the real working class by his bourgeois ideology.[7]

The demythologising of Joe Wilson is part of the larger preoccupation with music hall's role in advancing or retarding the collective interests of

its public as a subordinate class in a capitalist society. Is this culture 'of'
or 'for' the people? Is music hall song generated from within or supplied
from without, and with what consequences? The general verdict is
pessimistic. G. W. Ross's *Sam Hall*, a revamped traditional ballad sung in
the 1840s as the defiant valediction of a chimney-sweep about to hang, is
taken as exemplifying a combative prelapsarian class politics (though we
may doubt that he really sang 'Fuck you all').[8] Thereafter, commercialised production in the hands of mostly *petit bourgeois* hacks, writing for
professional performers increasingly bent on *embourgeoisement*, feeds the
music hall audience with songs drained of any radical or oppositional
content. In their highly selective realism, the conflict lines of class were
elided and the site of its most direct struggles, the workplace, ignored. In
the most influential account of this dilution of class consciousness,
Gareth Stedman Jones identifies a new flight into escapism in the
celebration of the small pleasures of plebeian life – 'A little of what you
fancy does you good', as Marie Lloyd sang. Thus from the 1880s music
hall songs come to denote what he labels a 'culture of consolation' that
compensates for political and social impotence, a chronic disability
wryly acknowledged in the Chaplinesque 'little man' routines of the
other great contemporary star of music hall's 'golden age', Dan Leno.[9]

In this first flush of scholarly attention there is much that is helpful,
but the 'culture of consolation' tag has achieved the finality of an
epitaph, summing up a prevailing note of political disappointment that
not only obituarises a whole culture but abruptly foreshortens further
critical enquiry. The growing understanding of the complexity of popular cultural forms suggests the likelihood of other explanations for the
capture of one of the world's first mass-entertainment audiences besides
those of market dominance and the play-back of consoling representations of a common way of life. The test of authenticity is a dubious one
where its criteria are formally political, exclusively class-specific and
framed from outside, rather than in terms of the specific determinants of
situation and experience that typify this particular milieu.[10] Music-hall
was both more and less than a class mode of expression and has yet to be
fully understood in terms of its participants' measures of significance
and what its meaning was for them. For this we need to reanimate those
features of music hall still hobbled in cliché – its 'live' form, the 'sheer
talent' of its performers, and their 'magnetic hold' on audiences. Work
on style and performance has advanced markedly, but the text has still
too rarely been made to leave the page, and the actual dynamics of
engagement in the stage form remain understudied.[11]

Though based on an extensive sampling of sources, the essay that follows is still largely speculative and impressionistic. It offers brief accounts of performance style and audience interaction, and relates the articulation of knowingness as popular discourse to the history of music hall development and its circumstantial fit with broader social changes.

II

The solo singer in the pub concert-rooms and cheap theatres that were the proto-music halls of the 1830s to the 1850s necessarily adopted a robust vocal and physical style.[12] The performer had to capture the attention of a large and increasingly anonymous crowd otherwise engaged in the rival attractions of eating, drinking, conversing, gazing, posing, lounging, flirting and promenading. The most effective technique was a cross between singing and shouting accompanied by various forms of stage business and a high degree of physicality, from 'winks and gesticulations', to 'the jerk (of the body) at the beginning of each line, in true street style'.[13] Extravagant or eccentric stage dress often completed the boldness of effect needed to commandeer audience attention in this milieu. Performance was thus heavily accented or presentational, in the sense that it was projected right out at the audience. Though this was in contrast with a more stolid traditional or 'folk' style where the song was left to tell its own story, yet it had its own lengthy historical antecedents. As the contemporary comment suggests, pub-based performances from this era drew on the well-practised techniques of the street ballad singer, whose craft of some centuries persisted among the hawkers or chaunters still contesting the hubbub of the modern street in their assertive appeals to a less than captive audience.[14]

Relatively new to popular song performance and one of the more distinctive marks of the emerging music hall mode was the growing practice of appearing 'in character'. By this convention, the singer impersonated the (increasingly first person) subject of the song more fully by assuming his or her typical dress and manner. Though the concern for the broad effect was still there, this was realism of a more convincing materiality than that offered in the 'true to life' claims of the street ballad singer, while marking a further departure from traditional folk style. There is a considerable correspondence here with the closely observed comic naturalism pioneered on the theatrical stage in the first half of the century. To a degree, the music hall followed the theatre, whose writings and stagings became yet more markedly naturalistic from the middle years of the century with the domesticated settings of the box set.[15] But music hall naturalism rarely extended to the stage set and was almost exclusively vested in the individual performer. There was, moreover, a distinct divergence from the legitimate stage in the practice of direct address with which it was twinned.

Whatever the increasing degree of artifice, professional room-singers insistently broke through the fictions of their impersonations with an ad lib gagging commentary between verses known as 'patter' or the 'spoken'. Mostly extemporised, this direct address of the audience (also practised in the crossover routines of the low comedian in the theatre) represented a further assimilation of English street style and the typical exchanges of life on the street, those of the 'cad' or horse omnibus conductor touting for custom, of the butcher or mountebank shouting his wares, or the ritual contests of abuse known as 'flytings' that still survived in the North. An ancient feature of popular culture, the direct address of the early music hall is a more complex and engaging operation than yet generally allowed.[16] In breaking role, the performer becomes most obviously accessible to the audience as himself or herself. Yet far from destroying the song character to whom the performer returns, the characterisation may be strengthened through the revelation of the self that is invested in the role. This is a more privileged implication in the act of performance than that of the theatre, where the audience is privy to their performance as auditor/spectator who overhears the action or looks through the 'fourth wall' of the conventional stage set. In the music hall, the shifts in and out of role and self, artifice and autobiography allowed the audience to see, as it were, the joins in the performance. In the hands of the inept this was no doubt disastrous, but properly executed it secured a distinctive relationship with the audience by initiating them into the mysteries of the performer's craft and giving them a consequent sense of select inclusion. The content of a song or act was of course also important, but its resonance with an audience was inseparable from the manner of its performance, whose language, in the broadest sense, signalled a common yet inside knowledge of what was really going on. It was this particular province of language use and meaning that we comprehend as discourse, that contemporary commentators termed 'knowing'.[17]

It was through knowingness that the skilled performer mobilised the latent collective identity of an audience. The basic appeal of music hall is said to lie in its affirmation of a newly urbanised people settling into a common way of life, yet awareness of this shared experience had to be activated anew at every performance among the so many and various aggregations that were the specific audiences within this extensive public. Indeed, to use the term 'audience' in this context begs the question, for it presupposes a degree of focused attention that could rarely have been the case in a large city hall whose volatile assembly might be better designated as a crowd, out of which the performer had to construct an audience. Even in those halls with a particularly stable and socially homogeneous attendance, the acknowledgment of a common ground had to be summoned up or signified beyond the obvious givens of place, occasion, appearance and a core constituency of *habitués*. Althusser's concept of 'interpellation' is suggestive here as the form of ideological address or hailing that recruits individuals into a particular subject-role or identity.[18] In some such way, the performer's knowingness activates the corporate subjectivity of the crowd, and calls an audience into place. In music hall this was a rapidly shifting exercise that cast its audience variously or sectionally as men, women, husbands, lodgers, costers, swells, citizens, working men, Britons, and so on, but arguably the underlying subject position that informed them all was that of those 'in the know'.[19]

At the same time, this interpellation is not just the calling into position of a particular subjectivity, but is more in the nature of a transaction or co-production.[20] Where a performance takes, the crowd/audience registers recognition and identification, certainly, but it also asserts its own collective authorship/authority in the performance. This response is obviously not just conjured out of nowhere. As with any audience, there may be a considerable predisposition to give attention, according to previous acquaintance with the performer, word-of-mouth endorsement or the bait of publicity, yet these predispositions still have to be exploited. In this, however, the music hall performer could count on the active engagement of an audience well practised not only in being hailed but in hailing back, for the language of the street and market-place that informed the exchanges with the audience was very much one of give as well as take. Consumers were used to answering back, for more generally the negotiations of buyer and seller were still relatively unconstrained by the fixed practice of modern retailing; indeed, in one of the more typical transactions of working-class life, that of the pawnshop, it was the customers who made most of the patter.[21]

Yet the language of such exchanges was likely to be more compact and elliptical as the pattern of encounter in a period of accelerated urbanisation grew more fleeting and discontinuous. Symptomatic of this was the rise of the catch-phrase, pronounced by one commentator in 1841 as a typical manifestation of the 'popular follies of great cities' and 'the madness of crowds': 'every street corner', he declared, 'was noisy with it, every wall was chalked with it'.[22] Catchphrases were generated by the songs and dialogue of the popular theatre, and the pub concert-room or singing saloon was soon caught up in their circulation. Thus a song from the late 1830s which tells of a concert-room romance, *Don't Tell My Mother, She Don't Know I'm Out!* (figure 10),[23] would have played off or may have directly inspired the contemporary shouted enquiry 'Does your mother know you're out?' Unlike the folk proverb, the catchphrase often floats free from more obvious referents and depends for its meaning on an extra-textual knowledge.[24] As such, it was prime material for the more allusive and abbreviated social dialect from which the comic song was constructed. Also significant for this new formation was a marked shift in structure from the narrative to the situational. The more leisurely story-line of the ballad gives way to an episodic emphasis which exploits some social predicament in a quick succession of scenes or actions whose common import is punched home in a tag-line or chorus. The new mode of comic song works therefore less as a story than as an accumulation of short jokes with a reiterated punch-line, which in turn might be recycled as a catchphrase. Like the catchphrase, the music hall dealt in a new form of vocal shorthand, whose language operated like a cue or flash charge that needed the knowledge that was knowingness to complete its circuitry. When the circuit worked, as contemporary accounts show, the song went off like a rocket.[25]

An example comes in a report in the improving press from 1856 of songs sung 'in character' at a 'low house of amusement':

It is to these flash songs that we take violent objection. By name, they are often the same as we see in music-seller's windows and on our own drawing-room tables; but they are garbled and interpolated here in a manner to defy description. They are sung, or rather roared, with a vehemence that is stunning, and accompanied with spoken passages of the most outrageous character. At the end of every verse the audience takes up the chorus with a zest and vigour which speaks volumes – they sing, they roar, they yell, they scream, they get on their legs and waving dirty hands and ragged hats bellow again till their voices crack. When the song is ended, and the singer withdraws, they encore him with a peal that seems enough to bring the rotting roof on their heads, as with frantic shouts, shrieks and catcalls they drag him back again so that they may gloat once more over the delectable morsel.[26]

Figure 10 'Don't Tell My Mother, She Don't Know I'm Out', from *The London Singer's Magazine*, 1838–9.

Even with allowance for journalistic exaggeration, the emotional temper of the occasion is clearly a long way removed from most Olde Tyme
music hall singsongs. There is the vigorous delivery complete with
'outrageous' interpolations, while the reworking of drawing-room songs
provides a good example of the cultural appropriation typical of the
music hall repertoire. There is another form of appropriation in evidence as well, though that is too inadequate a term to describe what is
going on here: in the chorus singing (a feature characteristic of a night
out at the halls) the passage suggests the more highly charged sense of a
possessive 'claiming', both of the song and the singer, that goes well
beyond the conventional reading of audience recognition and identification.[27]

Further telling evidence of this performative relationship of singer
and audience is provided in Henry Mayhew's mid-century account of a
London penny gaff. Mayhew observed a crush of some two hundred
juveniles respond to the 'comic singer':

putting on a 'knowing look', [he] sang a song, the whole point of which
consisted in the mere utterance of some filthy word at the end of each stanza.
Nothing, however, could have been more successful. The lads stamped their
feet with delight; the girls screamed with enjoyment. Once or twice a young
shrill laugh would anticipate the fun – as if the words were well-known – or the
boys would forestall the point by shouting it out before the proper time. When
the song was ended the house was in a delirium of applause . . . There were
three or four of these songs sung in the course of the evening, each one being
encored, and then changed. One written about 'Pine-apple rock', was the
grand treat of the night, and offered greater scope to the rhyming powers of the
author than any of the others. In this, not a single chance had been missed;
ingenuity had been exerted to its utmost lest an obscene thought should be
passed by, and it was absolutely awful to behold the relish with which the young
ones jumped to the hideous meaning of the words.[28]

Ingenuity indeed, for after 'cock', one muses, what else can there be,
unless the rhyme fell elsewhere? Yet the scene grips the reader, as the
singer gripped his audience. Here the shared knowledge that is
knowingness is that of sexuality, in whose delights the young audience
seem so precociously well-schooled that the singer's 'knowing look'
concentrates their attention instantly. There is immediate closure with
the audience, some of whom run ahead of the singer to detonate the
rhymes that cue the crowd in their response, and the suggestion is that
the words of the songs are recomposed at their prompting. Above all,
there is the potent sense of collusion. Sometimes lyrics themselves could

suggest this, as in the confidential appeal of *Don't Tell My Mother, She Don't Know I'm Out!* (in however declamatory a voice this had to be made). In Mayhew's account, the whole exchange is animated by a sense of complicit mischief that contributes considerably to his own acute discomfiture.

Claiming and collusion provides a sharper sense of the specific operation and intensity of recognition in music hall, yet 'naming the parts doesn't show us what makes the gun go off'.[29] While these and other responses can be discerned separately in performance, as the above accounts suggest, they are telescoped or superimposed upon each other, fusing together dramatically in the case of the successful act. It is knowingness that ignites this effect by pulling the crowd inside a closed yet allusive frame of reference, and implicating them in a select conspiracy of meaning that animates them as a specific audience. This flattering sense of membership is the more so since music hall performance suggested that such privileged status was not so much conferred as *earned* by the audience's own well-tested cultural and social competence.[30]

A few words here about the history of the word 'knowing' itself. The term is first noted in racing talk of the eighteenth century, when a 'knowing one' was supposedly privy to secrets of the turf or other sporting matters. By the turn of the century the term also denoted up-to-date knowledge of what was smart and stylish.[31] Twenty years later, the theatre comedian John Liston was being critically commended for his 'knowing style' in his naturalistic playing of cockney characters. Here it seems to identify a certain quality of conceit, whose accurate rendering gave Hazlitt as much cause for exasperation with the original in the street as it did for his admiration at its portrayal on the stage. To Hazlitt, the knowingness of the cockney was the delusion of someone who, on the contrary, really knew nothing: 'He is . . . a great man only in proxy . . . surcharged with a sort of second-hand, vapid, tingling, troublesome self-importance'.[32] This sense of something both absurd yet troubling was to be repeated down the century by middle-class witnesses confronted with the phenomenon of the comic singer and his audience. Inverted commas became welded to the term, in a defensive distancing of its contemptible presumptions. What most disquieted Mayhew and other witnesses was plainly its rogue sexuality, yet while sexuality continued to constitute much of the insider's knowledge that was knowingness, other competencies fell within its discourse.

For all its often brashly confident tone, knowingness spoke to the need for a new wariness in the more uncertain negotiations of everyday urban

living. Songs from the late 1830s alert the audience to the petty corrup-
tions of the police and tradespeople, the tricks of con men and prostitutes and the increasing difficulty of reading strangers in the flux of
big-city life. Alertness to the unknown other had no doubt always been
part of the urban sensibility (Elizabethan literature on cozening is one
example) but in the second quarter of the nineteenth century there were
more people who had to learn this, and there was more of it to be
learned. In locating the formation of a new urban popular culture in
these years, Louis James finds its most articulate expression in a mass of
cheap literature which set out to comprehend this new life of the towns,
to understand how it *all* worked, 'claiming omniscience' from a stance of
'knowing intimacy'.33 But if urban worldliness now aspired to the
encyclopaedic it had at the same time to be much more finely tuned,
exercised not only as a matter of an extensive literary curiosity, but as a
matter of more compacted, anonymous and fleeting everyday negotiations. To a critical degree, the world that had to be known had both
expanded *and* contracted. Getting by in this milieu required a new set of
responses, recorded here in Hazlitt's contemptuous but revealing picture of the cockney: 'He sees everything near, superficial, little, in hasty
succession. The world turns round, and his head with it, like a round-
about at a fair . . . His senses keep him alive; and he knows, inquires and
cares for nothing further'.34

What Hazlitt condemned as ignorance, music hall applauded as a
necessary form of self-protection and, in its knowing recognition of this,
a cause for self-congratulation of the kind that further irritated Hazlitt in
the cockney. Laughter helped dissipate unease at the inherent hazards
of city life, but knowingness completed its rout. If the repertoire of Sam
Cowell, a leading singer of the period, did indeed depict a world
'overwhelmingly peopled by fools',35 it is almost certain that the manner
of his performance reassured his audience that they were not among
them. Performers, we may surmise, were applauded not just for their
naturalistic re-creation of a shared world, but for their authority in the
actual business of living in that world, an authority perhaps most
potently demonstrated in songs of its many fallible inhabitants. This
persona may have been more a matter of image than of substance, and
certainly there were some notorious casualties among professionals
themselves, yet Mayhew remarked on the obvious and particular intelligence of one tributary source of concert-room talent, the street performer. 'By intelligence', he noted, 'I mean that quickness of perception
which is commonly called "cunning", a readiness of expression, and a

familiarity (more or less) with the topics of the day – the latter picked up probably in public houses'.[36] A cognate of 'knowing', 'cunning' raises associations of the 'cunning man (or woman)', the local wizard-cum-counsellor of the traditional rural community, suggesting not only that this role could in part have been displaced on to the comic singer, but that, in a more atomised modernising world, every urbanite who would cope must learn to be his or her own 'cunning man'.[37] Another related and suggestive usage is the Northern dialect term of 'canny', bestowed typically in celebration of the 'canny lad', among whose many attributes lay a shrewd resourcefulness in reading situations and escaping the meshes of authority.[38] One cannot presume too much from such associations, but the case can be made that the knowingness of early music hall was a largely new idiom, encoded from the dramatically transformed social realities of a critical era in modern urbanisation.[39]

Yet while knowingness was undoubtedly effective in the collective interpellation of its audience, its broader functional value is questionable, for its lessons are never spelled out in its address. Like the joke with its similarly complicit engagement, its particular expressive bloom withers with explanation. What exactly is there to be known in knowingness? Its properties are at once self-evident and arcane. More than with the joke, a better analogy might lie with the confidence trick (against which music hall song offered so many warnings). Through a confident and confiding manner, the performer repeats its flattery of privileged implication – his or her credentials too winning to scrutinise further. But if, by this analogy, the audience are the knowing victims of the performer's benign manipulations, who or what – apart from mother – completes the classic triad of the confidence trick, as the ultimate victim of the conspiracy to defraud.[40] Parents, spouses and the law are, as many songs suggest, there to be outwitted. In a broader sense, however, knowingness as popular discourse works to destabilise the various official knowledges that sought to order common life through their languages of improvement and respectability and the intensifying grid of regulative social disciplines that marked the period. These official languages are represented in various allusions in the songs and their performance, but are also acknowledged in more overt form in the mock sermons and lectures that were juxtaposed with the other comic acts.[41] Knowingness then is not a direct refutation of these languages, to which it remains inescapably subordinate in the larger systems of society; it is rather a countervailing dialogue that sets experience against prescription, and lays claim to an independent competence in the business and enjoyment of living. There is a strong element of self-deception at work here that may have been both acknowledged and compounded by music hall's love of parody and mock self-deprecation, yet knowingness emerges as a distinctive if slippery form of comic pragmatism. In typical knowing style it proclaimed its utility in the masthead of the *Singer's Penny Magazine* (1835–6), which parodied that Whiggish engine of improvement, the Society for the Diffusion of Useful Knowledge, by advertising itself as the organ of the Society for the Diffusion of Useful Mirth.[42]

III

From the 1860s music hall took on the full apparatus of commercialised production together with more elaborate amenities and greatly expanded premises. By the 1880s the big proprietors were laying claim to a greater social and aesthetic respectability by advertising their halls as 'theatres of variety', and the industry entered the period of its maximum prosperity and influence that peaked just before the Great War.[43] While the move out of the pub concert-room produced a great flowering of songs and artists, it also brought new constraints on performance. These were dictated in part by the rationalisation of operations in an increasingly complex institution, but there was also outside pressure from middle-class moral reformers for whom the comic song and its singers were at best 'a public nuisance' and at worst 'the despair of civilization'. Sensitive to the threat to their licences and their heavy investments, managers moved defensively to censor singers and songs, yet the essential circuitry of music hall's performative relationship remained intact, more deeply encoded in the resilient discourse of knowingness. Broader social changes brought shifts in the constituency of both the knowing and the known, but knowingness continued its ironic counterpoint to the language of respectability, even as the latter became more firmly installed in the formal practice of music hall as both business and profession.

From its beginning music hall had been embattled with reform critics, but the particularly hostile attacks on the comic singer in the late 1870s led to a significant increase of in-house controls on performance. In 1879, the foundation year of the Social Purity Association, the Middlesex bench petitioned the Home Secretary for legislation to eliminate indecency from the music hall stage. Though no such legislation was forthcoming, the shock to the industry translated into the new house rules of the 1880s.[44] These proscribed vulgarity in general, listing official figures and institutions that were to be specifically protected from improper allusion, while audiences were invited to report breaches that escaped the manager's notice. In some cases, performance material had to be submitted in advance for vetting. It was, however, the unscripted exchanges across the footlights that caused the most anxiety. Some contracts forbade the performer's direct address of the audience, and audiences themselves were policed by uniformed officials whose duties included the discouragement of chorus singing. Together with limits set on the number of encores, such measures were supposed to maintain the tighter timetabling of acts that was necessitated by artists' multiple engagements, twice-nightly performances and the matching of show times with suburban bus and train schedules, yet they were also aimed at reducing the volatile spontaneity of the music hall experience and its threat to propriety. Impromptu engagement with the customers seemed yet more diminished as halls grew larger and production more theatricalised, for the artist was put further beyond the reach of the audience, a separation signalled most dramatically by the end of the century with the growing practice of darkening the auditorium.

It seems clear, however, that for all the disciplining and distancing of artists and audience, the live connection between the two persisted, and it was in this period that a mature or classic style of comic singing achieved its sharpest and most efficient definition.[45] Though the bulk of the audience became stabilised in fixed seating facing the front and drinking was gradually confined to foyer bars, the audience was still restless by today's standards: 'It was', said Arthur Roberts, 'all uproar, whether they liked you or not'.[46] Yet while some performers still relied on the shouting style and its forceful accessories of dress and manner, this was now done as much to establish a certain type of character – the naturalistic rendering of the boys on a spree – as to commandeer attention, and in general stage presence became less aggressive. Comic technique was still often strongly accented yet more conversational in tone and pace, while performance overall became more economical. Alfred 'The Great' Vance did his share of emphatic body play and robust vocalising with his 'Slap-Bang' song-hits of the late 1860s, but by the 1880s he was noted for a more ingratiating style of address: 'he treats his hearers as old familiar friends, and takes them into his confidence, a process that they like immensely'.[47]

A summation of the style in its heyday comes from an appraisal of Wilkie Bard in 1911 which commended him highly for 'The rigid spareness and economy of his method – a thing of suggestion, of hints and half spoken confidences, rather than of complete statement.' Bard, the review continued, 'has attuned himself to the new middle-class respectability without losing any of his artistic range and freedom.'[48] The prime device lay in the 'things of suggestion', and as controls tightened and actual time on stage contracted it was the compressed code of the *double entendre* and the innuendo that signalled complicity with an audience, investing language, tone and gesture with oblique but knowing conspiracies of meaning.

While there was a long history of ambiguity and innuendo in popular culture, most typically of a sexual import, music hall deployed such devices in ways that were not only new but afforded their audiences more complex gratifications than present accounts allow. Where older song forms had exploited the idioms of a particular trade or region, music hall spoke across a more generalised demotic range, investing orthodox address with its second-level meaning. 'There was', said one observer in the 1880s, 'an unwritten language of vulgarity and obscenity known to music hall audiences, in which vile things can be said that appear perfectly inoffensive in King's English'.[49] In Glasgow in 1875 a committee of protest enlisted shorthand writers and artists to provide an accurate record of 'immoral performances', yet the impact of the offensive acts could not be inferred from the page alone, and witnesses were often bewildered by the audiences' convulsions over apparently pointless exchanges.[50] The knowing language of music hall sexuality was that of standard English, or rather an open modern vernacular, with little recourse to the *grammatica jocosa* that Bakhtin talks of in traditional forms or the 'out-and-out' bawdy that had distressed Mayhew in the mid-century. Music hall did not, therefore, generate an anti-language in the accepted sense of the term, but rather a resignification of everyday language which knowingly corrupted its conventional referentiality and required a certain competency in its decoding.[51]

At the same time, there was a particular eloquence in what was left unsaid. The incompleteness of the performer's delivery left gaps for the audience; for their laughter, of course, but also for what that signalled of their ability to fill the gaps. An LCC inspector's report of 1908 noted that George Robey left his audience 'to fill in the details and there from to draw their own inferences'.[52] Not too demanding an exercise, it may be said, for in semiotic terms music hall song is more a closed than an open text, a highly stylised and familiar genre playing within a limited horizon of audience expectations. But if we accept the claims of modern linguis-

tic scholarship that it is the spaces more than the spoken that denote
norms of urban language use,[53] then we may allow that the suspense
instability of the spaces generated in live performance on the
provided a running opportunity, on both sides of the footlights, fo
kind of tactical surprise that could simultaneously confirm and
found the generic pattern of expectations, and delight an audience
its own palpable sophistication.

The nature of such self-congratulation may be better appreciated by
considering the conditions of popular discourse in other key cultural
sites of the late nineteenth century. Arguably the regulations that sought
to curtail popular expression in the music halls were more severely
employed in the spreading institutional regimes of the later modern
factory, the big commercial office and the state school-room – all
variously obliging their subordinate inmates to speak less or to do so in
standardised forms that echoed the official idioms of their bureaucratic
authority figures.[54] Together with the contractions imposed by urbanisation, these controls would have further reduced popular communication, while concentrating it into yet more cryptic and elliptical
forms. If then, to borrow Bernstein's formulation, the authentic popular
code became perforce more 'restricted',[55] the conditions of its limitations may have made its meanings more highly charged and its *sub rosa*
competencies more satisfying. By engaging and flattering these skills,
music hall performers could continue to reassure an audience that they
were nobody's fool or – more pertinently in this era – no teacher's
dunce, no head-clerk's cipher, no foreman's stooge.

As is well evidenced, music hall delivery was, of course, far from being
only 'a thing of suggestion, of hints and half spoken confidences', for it
could also be almost manically verbose. Significantly, the language in
which it indulged its prolixities was often a parodic echo of the formal
language of officialdom and élite culture. These knowing conceits were
as much enamoured as mocking, expressing a qualified reach for the
power that these codes represented, while ventilating the anxieties that
their use entailed.[56] But if, like the innuendo and ambiguity, this was in
large part another defensive exercise, the appropriation of 'proper'
English was also a form of retaliation in kind against the linguistic
oppressions of the period.

The creative misalliance between the vulgar and the pretentious not
only nonplussed the outsider but aided the counter-attack of those
singers who protested against the slurs on their profession. Arthur
Roberts, whose allegedly indecent performance contributed to the loss

of licence for Evan's music hall in the *annus immoralis* of 1879, retaliated
with *The Highly Respectable Singer.*

> Good gracious, said I, then are songs nowadays
> So shocking to hearer and reader?
> So very much worse than your funny French plays
> And your novels by modest Ouida?[57]

Though performers were much concerned with establishing respectable professional status for their calling, their protestations were often
disingenuous. They still professed to be taken by surprise by audiences
who 'manufactured' their own meaning from texts which they represented as wholly innocent.[58] Proprietors were similarly compromised
between the conflicting pulls of official values and the popular aesthetic, some maintaining that it was the latter rather than the comic
singer that was culpable in a business yielding to demand from an
audience that 'wants dirt'.[59] Certainly audiences did take over and
rework material, and delighted in transgressions of official rectitude.
The determinedly proper Victoria Coffee Music-Hall in London vetted
all acts thoroughly before their appearance, but the popular voice still
broke through:

Yet, in spite of all these precautions, let there come a change such as an encore
verse, such as some slip or stoppage in the stage machinery, and out will come
something, not in the programme and never heard or seen before, which will
bring down a thunder of enjoyment from the audience, and at the same time fill
the manager's box with sorrow and humiliation.[60]

Audiences also continued to claim their traditional performing rights;
even as their participatory role was threatened by the house regulations
of the 1880s, the musical construction of the songs gave greater emphasis to the entry of the chorus and the further thunder of the crowd.[61]
   As in popular humour generally, sexuality was a pervasive motif of
knowingness, yet the presence of prostitutes in the audience made it take
on a particular inflection in the music hall, for they provided a running
subtext to the songs in a manner that tested the competence of all who
presumed to read the urban crowd with any sophistication. The reformers' attack on the halls in 1879 had been directed at the prostitute as
much as the comic singer, the offence of one allegedly compounding
that of the other. In this regard, too, house rules became tighter. Among
London's bigger and more notable halls, the Oxford, for example,
forbade soliciting and denied entry to any unescorted woman 'unless

respectably dressed'.[62] As prostitutes responded with ever more plausible impersonations of respectability, their identification became increasingly difficult, the more so since young middle-class women were making-up and dressing in a fashionable approximation of the *demi-monde*.[63]

Whatever the protestations of proprietors to the contrary, prostitutes were thus enabled to continue their business in the halls, though they canvassed their services more circumspectly. Crucially here, verbal address duplicated the particular register of music hall song, inflecting the mundane and unremarkable with sexual invitation. In a famous case in 1896, a middle-class reformer who protested at the renewal of the Oxford's licence faltered in his accusation of prostitution: of the woman whose approach aroused his suspicions of soliciting, he could report only, but significantly, 'It was not what she said, but the way in which she said it'.[64] Yet these hearings did demonstrate what the reformers failed to prove, that the presence of prostitutes in the audience added an extra sexual resonance to music hall song and the exchange of meaning between performer and audience. Another witness objected in particular to Marie Lloyd's song, *I Asked Johnny Jones, So I Know Now!* Dressed as a schoolgirl, Lloyd (a famously 'knowing' star) nags her parents for enlightenment on a number of curious incidents of a sexual nature that defeat her immediate understanding, including her father being accosted. 'What's that for, eh?', she demands in the tag-line, getting satisfaction only from her canny schoolboy friend, Johnny Jones – ' ". . . so I know now" '. 'During this song', noted the witness, 'the women looked more at the men'. In the same month, a critic from the respectable musical press testing the modern music hall's claim to improvement was distressed not only by the songs that continued to celebrate drink, but by 'objectionable songs . . . that advertise another trade . . . and also serve to foment the atmosphere'.[65]

What obviously gave pleasure in the music hall world was the rich joke that such proceedings afforded at the expense of society's high moralism and its intrusive vigilantes. The mix of denial and connivance with which proprietors and police met the question of prostitutes' admission to the halls suggests how their undoubted presence could be represented as both fact and fiction. Prostitutes were there and yet not there, at once conspicuous and invisible, according to a kind of worldly hypocrisy which acknowledged things as they inevitably (and profitably) were, as well as things as they should be. It was this capacity to operate at the very interface of the Victorian double standard that was central to music halls' cultural and aesthetic strategy and gave knowingness its more than stylistic utility. At the Oxford hearings, the press reported constant laughter from the public gallery at the discomfiture of the reform critics as they failed in their charges of immorality, either in the songs or the traffic of prostitutes. The reform witnesses had read the codes correctly, but failed to translate them into a politically effective language in front of the licensing committee. Thus knowingness confounded knowledge, to the great delight of its initiates.

Which groups in particular could be said to be 'in the know'? The most obvious aspirants were the numerous young people who remained a prominent element in the music hall audience. Mayhew's account suggests how greatly the sexual implications of knowingness were relished by a mixed crowd of working-class adolescents at the mid-century. These may have spoken to the direct experience of a generation credited with a considerable sexual precociousness; thereafter the likelihood is that the engagement of the young was more a function of the needs of ignorance than of affirmation.[66] The tightening controls on the sexual socialisation of the young of all classes through the late Victorian period and beyond increased the need to know or, crucially, to appear to know. This would have been particularly so for the increasing number of young clerks and shopmen whose actual sexual experience was likely to be minimal. Reluctant to resort to prostitutes, they salvaged their masculine pride by identifying with the assertive sexuality of the *lions comiques*, the brashly tumescent generation of comic singers whose swell songs took the halls by storm in the 1860s and 1870s.[67] The sexuality of the swell song was more narcissistic than predatory, yet it was full of intimations of conquest that flattered the audience as knowing accomplices *after* the fact. Such flattery was all the more precious for individuals in a group that was as much a target for parody as it was for validation, for the young 'gent' was as likely to be mocked for his sexual *naïveté* or incipient effeminacy as he was to be congratulated in assumptions of his fully initiated manhood. The need to be identified in the latter role must have been sharpened by the presence of the prostitute as a palpable reminder of the tests of conventional masculine sexuality.

Were women more or less knowing than men? Which ones were which, and in what ways? This is more difficult terrain. It was particularly noted of British women burlesque stars whose imports of *risqué* dance and comedy routines took New York by storm in the 1860s that they were 'aware of their own awarishness'.[68] Among music hall performers, Marie Lloyd certainly appeared to relish the suggestiveness of the situations she sang about, including her keenly observed imitation of soliciting techniques among Regent Street prostitutes,[69] and other reporters besides Mayhew recorded a knowing response to this kind of material from women in the audience. 'Do you think it is only the males who revel in this talk?', asked a Glasgow reform witness rhetorically.[70] One prominent (and well-researched) type of music hall song represented young working women as accomplished social actors with a knowing edge over their gentish suitors.[71] With the increase in public roles for women in the late century, the opportunities for sexual encounter multiplied. If, as the songs suggest, some women knowingly exploited these opportunities, their knowingness may also have functioned in scouting the risks of these ambiguous new freedoms. Knowingness for women may have signalled a defensive competence that gave a different ring to their laughter.[72]

There were other concerns besides sex. For the bachelor subculture in the halls, knowingness also monitored standards of dress and style as a further test of masculine competence. The aspiration here was to nothing less than gentility, personified again by the *lion comique*. Contemporaries described the halls as 'makeshift lounges' and 'modern schools of manners', where 'an immense number of lads . . . learn how to become gentlemen, under the tuition of the Great Dunce, or some such celebrity'. Instruction was 'by means of symbols' – the acting out of genteel behaviour through the striking of poses and the manipulation of the accessories of dress, whose implications were signalled in the music hall shorthand of tone and gesture, which included the knowing wink.[73] The quasi-aristocratic self-assurance of a Champagne Charlie offered a compelling identity to members of a socially indeterminate group with little cultural capital of their own. Yet indication was far from easy, for while the real swells on stage might readily admit the novice into the mysteries of the freemasonry by 'letting him into a thing or two', they pilloried those who were manifestly inept at carrying off their new role, much to the delight of other sections of the audience. Thus knowingness publicly fed off its more fallible aspirants, marking outlines of inclusion and exclusion with some acerbity, perhaps justifying Beerbohm's contention that people went to the halls to feel superior to someone.

Middle-class commentators continued to suspend knowingness in inverted commas as an indication both of contempt and unease. 'Knowingness', objected one witness, was a pathetic form of self-conceit that left its subject in 'suicidal ignorance of his utter meanness and insignificance', yet such dismissals continued relentlessly as though the malaise could never be sufficiently purged.[74] However pathetic the exercise, *petit bourgeois* youth was clearly treading too closely on the heels of the true bourgeois, making a mockery of the apparatus of gentility and of the latter's own aspirations to its exclusive status. At the same time, knowingness might appeal across the class divide to any youngster anxious to pass muster with more worldly seniors. A public school story from the 1890s tells how a new boy, Ashby minor, prepared himself for his school's initiation rites by learning a comic song complete with appropriate actions – 'one eyebrow must be raised and the opposite corner of the mouth turned down', and so on. He is dumbfounded when his performance is greeted with embarrassed silence. Far from ingratiating himself, he has been guilty of showing off, of 'putting on side'.[75] The episode reminds us of the contrary emphasis in genteel discourse on restraint and understatement (different forms of gapping here),[76] while suggesting how wide a currency the more stylised signals of knowingness had gained.[77] Other evidence shows that it was not Ashby minor alone among his class who was enamoured of its distinctive mix of cheek and insouciance.

Since its beginnings, music hall promoters had bid for a more respectable middle-class public. By the 1890s, improved programmes and the industry's colonisation of the suburbs were achieving something of this aim. E. M. Forster took his mother and his aunt to a music hall in 1896, providing an account of his visit for his school magazine – in Latin, a distinctly bourgeois form of knowingness.[78] But the growing middle-class presence of these years was less a tribute to the new immaculacy of the halls than it was evidence of a dominant class learning how to enjoy being in conspiracy against itself. Middle- and upper-class males had long been a rogue element in the music hall audience, as voyeurs and predators. The bourgeois man and wife who now took their reserved seats in the syndicated halls of the ('naughty') nineties were much less self-consciously transgressive in their pleasures, but were learning to savour the collusive but contained mischief of the performer's address, in whose exchanges they too could register the competencies of knowingness. By the turn of the century, music hall's knowingness was fast becoming a second language for *all* classes, as music hall itself became an agreeable national *alter ego*, a manageable low other, and the defenders of moral and cultural purity were drawn to other targets.[79]

IV

Knowingness encoded a reworked popular knowledge in an urban world which, for all the continuing force of custom and often strong sense of community, was increasingly populous, extensive and unknowable. Unlike the discourses studied to date, it was not the conceptually articulated and literate knowledge of the professional or specialist, but the refinement of a strongly oral and pragmatic everyday consciousness. While the comic realism of music hall song gave close attention to the routinized conduct of popular life, it also traded in its recurrent perplexities. The participatory style of performance and its implications of knowingness offered audiences a test of their competence in negotiating these perplexities in a language of their own triumphant devising – 'the quick, clever tact by which one vulgar mind places himself *en rapport* with a number of other vulgar minds', as one witness put it.[80] In this way, knowingness projected a sense of identity and membership as the *earned* return on experience, which engaged more than a simple generic literacy or the recognition in common of a particular way of life. Its potency lay in its capacity both to universalise and select a popular *cognoscenti* in a fluid and variously collective drama of self-affirmation that punctured official knowledges and preserved an independent popular voice. Thus music hall engaged its public in a more complex set of meanings than that proposed in the compensation model – the relish in knowingness suggests strongly that this was a culture of competence more than a culture of consolation.

Yet however authentic the satisfaction for its initiates, it would be quite wrong to triumphalise knowingness. Readings of present-day popular culture have begun to employ the term as a measure of resistance to hegemonic values in the negotiation of a 'creative consumerism' which, with due allowance for historical specificity, suggests considerable continuity in its operation as a popular resource.[81] Yet the counter-discourse of music hall knowingness was limited to the infraction rather than the negation of the dominant power relationships and, as its echo of official idioms demonstrated, it was compromised between challenge and collaboration.[82] (At times it comes close to Gramsci's disabling 'common sense'.)[83] Nor is it very encouraging to assess its operational or street value, once we move beyond the commercial canniness of Hazlitt's cockney, for this could be as much a form of ignorance as of knowledge. By its very presumptions, knowingness disallowed precise instruction, while in the volatile exchanges across the footlights its reassurances could be instantly betrayed, its privileged status collapsed. Nonetheless, its code may have been useful for combatting the more extensive surveillance of employers, policemen, schoolteachers and other officials. In politics, too, the corrosive glee of knowingness may have fuelled the radical populist cause in such confrontations as the Queen Caroline and Tichborne affairs.[84] But its complicit tone could also turn its cutting edge inside out, as in its co-option by the mass press and other self-styled friends of the people, generating what Hoggart later labelled 'scepticism without tension' and the evasion of real issues.[85] Also significantly, from the end of the nineteenth century knowingness and its characteristic interpellations were recruited for the confident, unproblematic voice of modern advertising.[86] Again, however, the point is not just to register further disappointment, but to understand more fully how such disregarded strands of popular discourse work – for and against the interests of their bearers – in the structuring of social action and consciousness.[87]

Not that knowingness is an exclusive province of the popular, for high discourse has an informal or performance element that signifies competence beyond the formal demonstration of its particular knowledges. This refinement of mutual implication seeks to confer an extra gloss of distinction on specialist fractions in the dominant culture, and on bourgeois life in general. The appropriate manner here is one of cultured allusion, of what Pierre Bourdieu notes as 'analogies endlessly pointing to other analogies' which never have to justify themselves by any explicit reference to first principles.[88] As we nod sagely together at the mention of another heavyweight cultural critic we acknowledge our own variant of this higher knowingness, while I exit stage left with no more than the merest suggestion of the comic singer's knowing wink.

CHAPTER 7

The Victorian barmaid as cultural prototype

Sexuality, we are now told, plausibly enough, is everywhere.[1] Yet recent scholarship, for all its advances, has done little to register or interpret this ubiquity. The history of sexuality which sees the nineteenth century as the crucial era in creating its modern sensibility has concentrated on certain areas: the submerged histories of 'deviant' groups; the ideology of written texts; controversies over regulation; and individual cases of that remarkable phenomenon, closet *hetero*sexuality.[2] These emphases on the wilder and more esoteric reaches of sexuality reinforce the construct of separate terrains by focusing on the (unacceptable) public face and the (secretive) private face in civil society. What is missing is an illumination of the 'middle' ground of sexuality, not as another exclusive territory, but as an extensive ensemble of sites, practices and occasions that mediate across the frontiers of the putative public/private divide.[3] Arguably it is here – in such everyday settings as the pub, the expanding apparatus of the service industries, and a commercialised popular culture – that capitalism and its patriarchal managers construct a new form of open yet licit sexuality that I propose to term *parasexuality*, a form whose visual code is known to us as the familiar but largely unexamined phenomenon of glamour.

Parasexuality? The prefix combines two otherwise discrete meanings: first, in the sense of 'almost' or 'beside', denoting a secondary, or modified form of sexuality (cf. paramedic); second, the counter sense of being 'against', denoting a form of protection from, or prevention of sexuality (cf. parachute). However here the function argued is conceived somewhat differently, as an inoculation in which a little sexuality is encouraged as an antidote to its subversive properties. Parasexuality then is sexuality that is deployed but contained, carefully channelled rather than fully discharged; in vulgar terms it might be represented as 'everything but'.

Everything but what? What is the prime form of sexuality for which parasexuality is taken to offer a modification or antidote? The language of discharge bespeaks a fundamentally male or phallocentric concept of sexuality – the hydraulic model – in which sex is a limited but powerful energy system, a spermatic economy whose force must always be either fully released or suppressed, its prime expression being the male orgasm. While the upheaval in sexual politics in our own day has taught us to recognise other less oppressive forms, this was a powerful model of sexuality in nineteenth century Britain and, however rebarbative it may be, it remains on the historical agenda.[4] The objectification of women as spectacle and commodity examined below is now understood as a projection of male hegemony and has been further defined in the pathologies of scopophilia and fetishism; yet while we recognise the saliency of such features in modern capitalism their formation is still underexplored.[5]

Parasexuality identifies a significant historical initiative as a *managed* version of the fraught imperatives of release or suppression in orthodox bourgeois sexuality. Management is an appropriate term in the increasingly rationalised operations of an emergent leisure industry in the nineteenth century, and is taken here to denote not only systematic direction, but also the proper utilisation of resources. In the pub, the music hall and the popular theatre, unlike the home, the courts and legislature, sexuality was a natural resource rather than a natural enemy. Thus while parasexuality was certainly a form of control, it started from a point of acknowledgment and accommodation rather than denial and punishment – in this sense it might be said to reverse Foucault's couplet of regulation as production.

Of course, management of any kind is rarely as efficient a process as the word implies, and this was certainly true of the business of pleasure which was in any case marked by its own distinctive practices. Paradoxically, if unsurprisingly, the normalisation of sexuality that was parasexuality proved to be controversial and was much contested by vigilante groups as a threat to established values. In exploring the limits of normative tolerance a new breed of capitalist cultural managers could therefore be represented as challenging the dominant ideology, yet the impression remains that whatever the charges made against them, these men were interested only in flexing not transgressing such limits. Parasexuality may be understood therefore as an exercise in framed liminality or contained licence that constituted a reworking rather than a dismantling of hegemony.[6] At the same time, the definition of limits was not just an issue between an industry and its critics, but a matter of everyday negotiation among front line participants, whose exchanges constituted an informal process of management that made its own contribution to the repatterning of nineteenth-century sexuality. History is also made by the people in pubs.

And so to the barmaid, a seemingly unproblematical social type, and an unlikely subject for any kind of historical theorising. For the unreconstructed male she is an instant cue for the knowing smile; for the feminist she is the classic token woman.[7] Both perspectives register the barmaid's role with its obvious but safely anchored sexuality as a timelessly familiar feature of the British pub. This essay is concerned to show that the barmaid was not always taken for granted, but has a specific and indeed sensational history of her own in the Victorian era, one of whose important themes is her glamorous embodiment of a distinct form of modernity – parasexuality.

What follows is an attempt to locate this specific strategy of cultural management within the popular discourse of pub sexuality by relating rather than merely juxtaposing the modes of social history and cultural or critical studies. The history of the barmaid is examined first in relation to the modernisation of the Victorian pub. The concept of glamour is then discussed as a preliminary to a reading of contemporary graphic texts and what they suggest of male subjectivities in relationship to the barmaid. In the light of this evidence the essay then situates pub sexuality and its controversies in the material context of female barwork. It concludes with a brief speculative reconnaissance of the barmaid's membership in the larger constituency of young women service workers, notes some further representations of their type, and considers the implications for sexual politics in the critical years of the late Victorian period.

I

The modern barmaid was a product of the transformation of the urban public house from the 1830s, when the tavern was superseded by the so-called gin palace with its dramatic innovations of scale, plan, management and style.[8] The new pub was devised to service the increasing volume of custom in the expanding towns, and to hold its market share in the face of heightened competition in the licensed trade. Many old pubs were little more than the parlours or kitchens of private houses catering to a familiar neighbourhood clientele. In catering to the more numerous, transitory and anonymous urban crowd, the new pubs were much bigger, and sales were made across a bar counter which separated customers from the drink supply and made for a more efficient and secure operation. Capacity was maximised by doing away with chairs and tables which also ensured a more rapid turnover in customers. Any feeling of congestion was relieved by the upward spaciousness of high ceilings and the illusory roominess contrived by the generous use of mirrors and plate glass, for the gin palace sought to attract the new generation of 'perpendicular drinkers' by the lavishness of its amenities. The new pubs needed the barmaid both as staff behind the counters of its enlarged premises and as a further item of allurement among its mirrors and mahogany, its brassware and coloured tile.[9]

There was, of course, nothing new in the employment of women and their attractions in the serving of drink. The older alehouse had commonly been a family enterprise wherein the service of wives and daughters was routinely exploited as an extension of their domestic duties. The alewife who ran the business in the absence of her husband was variously rough or motherly, but dependent upon an outgoing manner as a social stock in trade, while daughters or maidservants often added a fresher allure.[10] What was new about the barmaid of the 1830s was the redefinition of her traditional role brought by changes in the social logistics of the pub. Most importantly, she was now physically separated from the public by the novel device of the bar counter, part of the pub's duplication of the apparatus of the retail shop which formalised selling and began the conversion of its clientele from guests to customers.[11] The bar was now also a boundary or cordon sanitaire which kept the barmaid almost literally out of reach of the customer (or vice versa), and met the publican's new concern for respectability to protect his licence and greater business investment in a time of tighter licensing controls and reform hostility.

Yet if the roaming wanton of the alehouse had now become contained within the closed territory of the serving area, the configuration that secured her separation from the public house made her role there more conspicuous and seductive. The bar counter with its newly sumptuous fittings was the visual as well as transactional focus of the pub-gin palace and provided a framing effect that gave it the dramatic properties of a stage, thus heightening the presence of its attendants as social actors and objects of display. This theatrical aura was amplified by the flaring quality of the new gas lighting and the reflections of the pub's numerous mirrors. Moreover, the new barmaid shared her stage with a concentration of the commodities that the pub sold, suggesting that she herself might be an article for purchase and consumption.

The impact of the barmaid as spectacle was registered in significant terms from her earliest appearance in the new setting. Thus in the 1820s Thompsons, of Holborn Hill, London, was 'particularly noted' for retaining 'four handsome, sprightly and neatly dressed young females, but of modest deportment . . . An opportunity of casting a scrutinising glance at the so-highly spoken of barmaids operated as a spell, and myriads . . . were drawn in thither'.[12] There was renewed attention to the modern barmaid during the Crimean War, when a fashionable pub in the City hired women to make good the loss of men to the services. Such was the reported sensation at their appearance that other houses rapidly copied the practice, while barmaids had also been noted in the 1840s serving behind the refreshment counters of railway stations.[13]

The number of pubs grew steadily from the 1830s, but there was also growth in other forms of catering as well as the railway system; thus music halls, theatres, hotels, restaurants, and exhibitions provided more newly conspicuous jobs in barwork from the third quarter of the century. Of the Oxford music hall that opened in 1861 as the first purpose-built hall in the West End, it was recorded that 'the brightest, most glittering, and most attractive thing about the bars was the barmaids,' and Billy Holland's barmaid contests at various other London venues provided steady publicity in the 1860s and 1870s.[14]

Most renowned of London barmaids were the nine hundred or so employed by Spiers and Pond, pioneers of large-scale commercial catering, with extensive interests that included the sumptuous Criterion in Piccadilly where the barmaids operated in shifts: 'one corps would march out from behind the bars and others would walk in and relieve them like soldiers relieving the sentry.' Kaiser William II was said to have insisted on an incognito trip to a branch of Spiers and Pond on his first London visit, and was delighted by its spectacle of well-drilled pretty women.[15]

Foreigners were particularly impressed by the English barmaid, for her occupation and setting were virtually unique to Britain and the colonies of Australia and New Zealand.[16] English barmaids excited great attention in the English pub-restaurant at the Paris Exhibition in 1867.[17] The story was told of the American visitor to England who, on being asked what had struck him most, replied without hesitation, 'Barmaids!', an exclamation that reformers took to be one of horror.[18] Some of his more enthusiastic countrymen sought to exploit such a novelty by replicating an English bar and its barmaids in New York in the 1890s, but fell foul of legislation prohibiting the employment of women in public saloons.[19] Thus the barmaid attracted controversy and attention both at home and abroad.

As these accounts suggest, much of the impact of the barmaid lay in her enhanced public visibility, her staged openness to the 'scrutinizing glance.' What is significant here is not just, as we now conventionally say, the woman as sex object, but the woman as bearer of *glamour*, arguably a distinctively modern visual property, and central to para-sexuality in its practice of managed arousal.

The most familiar usage of the word is in its description of the Hollywood stars of the 1930s and after – the 'glamour girls' of screen and pin-ups – and a film historian defines glamour in this context as 'alluring charm or fascination, often based on illusion, that transforms or glorifies a person or thing.'[20] Previous usage in the nineteenth century was confined to a poetic vocabulary, as introduced by Sir Walter Scott to denote a magical or fictitious beauty.[21] There is considerable signifi-cance in the word's debut in Scott's novels, for in its application to the world of the past that was the setting for his work, we can identify a further property of glamour, implicit but unacknowledged in other definitions yet crucial to its operation as parasexuality – that of distance. Distance not only sustains and protects the magical property that is commonly recognised in glamour, but also heightens desire through the tension generated by the separation of the glamour object and the beholder, a separation that also functions to limit the expression or consummation of desire. Distance may be secured in a variety of ways: by time and history as in Scott's usage; by putting the loved one up a tower as in the conventions of courtly love; by the traditional device of the stage; more recently by the shop window or the distance inherent in the mechanical representations of photography, film and television; or, by a bar. Thus it is the bar that constitutes the necessary material and symbolic distance that simultaneously heightens and contains the sexual attractiveness of the barmaid and qualifies her as a glamour figure. It may be that something of the enigmatic property of glamour lies in its asexuality, but glamour here is conceived as a dramatically enhanced yet distanced style of sexual representation, display or address, primarily visual in appeal.[22]

II

The operation and meaning of glamour as embodied in the Victorian barmaid can be read from contemporary illustrations. The point of departure, however, is not Victorian Britain, but Paris and the Folies Bergères whose barmaid was immortalised in Manet's famous painting of 1881. This needs acknowledgment not only as probably the most familiar image already in readers' minds (which excuses its non-reproduction here), but as the subject of a suggestive recent interpretation. In general, Manet's picture exemplifies points made previously. Together with the richly rendered fruit and bottles on the counter before her, the barmaid here is plainly on display, her presence dramatised by the reflections of chandeliers and mirrors in what seems a particularly luscious but unproblematic still life. For the art historian T. J. Clark, however, the picture is a tissue of uncertainties, whose formal symmetry disguises disjunctions of planes and surfaces that correspond to the disjunctions of *modernité* – the unsettling mobility, the shifting and elusive nature of identity, the emphasis on externals, the ennui. In Clark's reading of Manet, the emptiness of the barmaid's face is the emptiness of alienation, for she herself is no more than a glamorous article, seller and commodity in one, as 'the whore appraising the client while offering herself for appraisal'.[23] My concern is not to challenge this interpretation, but to use it as a point of reference in reading other graphic texts, to the rear of the artistic avant-garde, that offer more palatable significations of modernity and its subjects.

In figure 11, we are back in London in the confidences of J. Stirling Coyne, who contributed 'The Barmaid', with illustration by Gavarni, to a collection edited by Albert Smith, *Sketches of London Life and Character*, in 1849.[24] Gavarni was a celebrated French illustrator and Bohemian, just then in the middle of an extended trip to London. Smith was a journalist whose book is of a familiar type as a guided tour of the exotic world on or under our own doorstep, an insider's look at London's terra incognita. Coyne was both journalist and dramatist whose specialty was the world of the lower middle and working classes. Coyne's text is a fulsome tribute to the barmaid as priestess of the night amid the gas-lights of the temple of Bacchus; she is 'the modern Hebe, whose champagne is not more intoxicating than her *oeillades*'. What is conveyed is both the intensity of the sexual focus on the barmaid and her immunity from its dangers. Her smiles, her banter, her various marks of favour are, we are assured, 'a mere matter of business with which the heart has nothing to do,' for 'the Barmaid seems to be a kind of moral salamander, living unharmed in the midst of the amorous furnace in which Destiny has placed her'.

In Gavarni's illustration, the barmaid's presence is central and dramatic. The sexual charge is strong but mediated by convention, idealisation and displacement. On the first count, the glamour is softened by the conventional prettiness of the ringlets, the oval face, and rosebud mouth. Although a daughter of the people, the barmaid is rendered in the style of the drawing-room belle, a traditional solution in coming to terms with working-class sexuality. The idealisation comes in the quasi-sanctification of her beauty through the aura of light and its halo effect. Here now is the woman as the ministering angel, a role central to the Victorian conception of the ideal wife. Light also reinforces the written text's assertion of the barmaid's fundamental purity, her resistance to the defilement of the pub as 'the amorous furnace'. This receives further symbolic emphasis in the contrast between her representation and that of her most visible admirer, who wears the soiled working dress of the London coal-heaver. For the rest, the Freudian will note the displaced symbolism of the beer engine: the phallic pump, the spurting tap and the ready receptacle – the hydraulic model indeed. (An admirer of the barmaid heroine in a play of the 1890s noted in particular 'that divine poise of the arm as she draws the handle',[25] and there is also the vulgar legend of the publican's daughter 'who pulled the wrong knob and got stout.')

Arguably, however, the greatest impact of the picture would have come from the privileged access it affords the male beholder, for whom the frustrations of distance have been collapsed.[26] If the bar was the barmaid's stage, then the spectator has here been allowed backstage. The bar – a solid structure indeed – now serves to keep other admirers out, enhancing the sense of privileged inclusion. The woman's turned head and tender expression clearly signal favour, but the basic power of the picture to suggest a personal and private intimacy in a *public* house would seem to depend on its magical suspension of the normal barriers to its fulfilment. It is by antithesis a considerable testimony to the cultural effectiveness of their everyday operation. The commentary also carries the strong presumption that the invisible male observer will be middle class, so that while Coyne emphasises the barmaid's unyielding heart in business hours and records her courtship with a young man of her own class, the picture encourages interest in a cross-class liaison which adds to its sexual charge.

The other contemporary representation of the barmaid at work (figure 12) is significantly later, being the illustration accompanying a contribution on 'Bar and Saloon London' to George Sims' encyclopaedic three volume *Living London*, 1901–3.[27] Sims was a popular

Figure 11   Gavarni, 'The Barmaid', from Alfred Smith (ed.), *Sketches of London Life and Character*, 1849.

Figure 12 'Bar and Saloon London', from George Sims (ed.), *Living London*, 1901–3.

journalist, novelist, and latter-day Bohemian. Since this is now imperial London, the editorial style is correspondingly grander than Smith's, promising a panoramic vision of the world city while emphasising the accuracy as well as the range of the compilation. To this end these volumes rely heavily on the photographic record, and though the scene reproduced here was considered, because of its particular animation, to be more suitably rendered by a drawing, the (anonymous) graphic artist has clearly aimed for a high degree of photographic realism. The written text is unadorned reportage, with none of the Bohemian poetics of Coyne's sensational if cosy exoticism of fifty years previous.

It seems therefore at first acquaintance that the documentary has superseded the artistic mode. Certainly the picture offers us a finely detailed rendition of the pub, its fittings and inmates: the island bar and the compartmentalised division of the drinking area, each with its own distinctive clientele, are well observed and typical of the development of the large urban pub by this date; the debris on the floor, including a cast-off shoe from one of the bar staff further suggests the naturalistic intention of the artist. In such a setting we may conclude that the barmaid herself has become no more than a work-a-day matter of fact.

Yet together with its documentary content, this illustration offers its own mythical interpretation and significant continuities with Gavarni. If the gin-palace glitter is a little muted, the barmaids are nonetheless glamorised in the style of the conventional fin de siècle beauty. More notably, the beholder is again afforded a privileged access to the scene; of course the perspective meets the artist's need for a panoramic comprehensiveness, but he exploits it beyond its necessary visual function. The invisible observer – the male stranger – has again circumvented the bar, and penetrated backstage (Victorian journalists had called the inner reaches of the new pubs the 'penetralia'). He is thus privy to the dramatic incident in the foreground where the barmaid coolly hears out the overtures of the soldier; whereas the soldier must surely be disappointed, the onlooker is encouraged by the complicit glance of favour from the other barmaid, and the admiration of the pot-boy. Thus this 'modern' documentary slice of life has a traditional hero-protagonist and a story-line: the invisible spectator, in echoes of an older genre style, is on the brink of romantic success, to be achieved no doubt at the gratifying expense of a virile rival – 'the wild colonial boy' or Boer War veteran – and played out before an appreciative audience of his own sex, albeit only of one.

So, unlike Manet's barmaid of Clark's reading, the women in these two more popular treatments do not simply return the stare of the beholder, but confer recognition and identity. In this context, the beholder is less the voyeur or predator than the ultimate participant in a flattering drama of opportunity and inclusion in the press and rush of big city life. Should we then say that the vision of the avant garde is disturbing yet probably more accurate, while that of a more popular aesthetic is reassuring yet ultimately deceitful? Maybe; but it should be noted that whatever the element of fantasy and manipulation in the latter, there is a considerable grounding in reality. It is the particular genius loci of the pub, as it was with the popular theatre and music hall, to be an intermediate institution that combines the properties of both public and private domains. Its internal space is in part firmly ordered between the open and closed, but much of it remains negotiable, including that across the bar counter – and from both sides.[28]

Yet the bar as separator remains a crucial feature of the pub as predominantly male territory. It allows flirtation and the rehearsal of sexual exploit, yet also provides an alibi for the novice or the insecure who are relieved of putting their prowess to the test. Moreover, though the pictures we have seen suggest an opportunity for closer encounter, they remain only images, constituting in effect a doubly distanced view of their subject, perhaps confirming the feminist suspicion that sex at a distance is the only completely secure relationship that a modern man can have with a woman.[29]

A further point is that the bar concealed the lower half of the female body with its attendant risks, thus focusing the male gaze on the breasts which became an exaggerated feature of vernacular representations. This may have reinforced associations of maternal nourishment and the oral appeal of drinking.[30] There is some correspondence here with an upward shift in erogenous focus in the conventions of the carte de visite, the personalised photographic miniature that proliferated from the 1860s and became a requisite item in job applications for female bar-workers. Unbeknown to sitters, extra copies of these cards were sometimes sold as early pin-ups.[31]

Of course, the two book illustrations tell us less about the barmaid herself than about a male positioning of her. They do, however, confirm her high visibility – compare the background role assigned to the traditionally dominant figure of mine host the publican in the Sims sketch – and the power of glamour in the force field of a reworked everyday sexuality.

III

Who was the Victorian barmaid? What were the actualities of barwork, and how did they sustain or confound the glamorous images examined above? What else can we learn of sexuality in the sub-culture of the pub and the perceptions of drink sellers, customers and reform critics?[32]

In England the greatest concentration of women barworkers was in London, but they were common enough in the big provincial cities and larger towns. They were much less common in Scotland and Ireland where employment was restricted to big city hotels. (In Scotland, as a type, they were referred to with suspicion as 'London barmaids'). Reliable numbers cannot be established, but in the improved categories of the 1901 census the number of barmaids was returned as 27,707 for England and Wales, of whom 7,632 were employed in London; the licensed trade habitually claimed higher figures, and argued for a count of 100,000 barmaids in England's public houses during the reform agitation of 1907–8.[33] On the most generous arithmetic, the barmaid was a minor calling compared with the nearly one and a half million female domestic servants enumerated in 1901, but her distribution as well as her setting made her a significant minority.

A wide variety of conditions obtained in the licensed trade and its numerous outlets, but by the 1890s if not before a broad distinction was recognised between the 'mere' or 'old-fashioned barmaid', and the 'young lady in the public line of business' or 'modern barmaid'. Recruitment, remuneration, duties and prospects differed accordingly.[34] The first category was a daughter of the working class who started work early as a housemaid in a small working-class pub before graduating to service at the bar. Though not found in the roughest of houses, she was likely to spend her career in working-class pubs and might keep in employment into her late thirties. The second category came from a higher social background, entering the business in the late-teens and passing immediately to work behind the bar in a public house catering predominantly to the upper and middle class. As a saloon or lounge barmaid she could also find employment in theatre, music hall, railway and restaurant bars. From the start she was paid more than her working-class sister, proceeded more quickly to a full wage and had some prospects of advancement to a supervisory post with a big company. In general, however, the career of the saloon barmaid was finished by her mid-twenties.

There were far many more women seeking employment than there were placements. Recruits were said to come from every grade of the working and lower middle class, while the majority of entrants to the London trade enlisted from 'the country'. At all levels of entry, there was a substantial number of women already socialised in the trade as daughters or relatives of publicans. Yet even the publican's daughter, for whom choice was so obviously predetermined by family, seemed anxious to use her insider's knowledge to break away from family. In this she conformed to a common characterisation of newcomers to the trade as free spirits, for while some were undoubtedly outcasts and casualties to start with, the majority were said to be impatient to escape from the monotony of more conventional jobs and locations, and were drawn to barwork as an avenue to the big city and a fuller life. By the 1890s, too, it seems that the trade was drawing more entrants from a higher social class. There are cases of women who preferred bar work to clerking or governessing, occupations which had disappointed in either remuneration or social interest, and Spiers and Pond were said to receive numerous applications from parents in the clergy and professional classes seeking employment for their daughters. With allowance for status inflation and the defensiveness of the trade, there does seem some plausibility, if a dubious exactitude, to the claim that 1,178 of the barmaids working in London in 1892 were the 'daughters of gentlemen'.[35]

In turn of the century London, the basic wage for a barmaid was 8–10s a week. In addition the employer provided board and lodging, though deductions for laundry and breakages (a controversial item) chopped as much as two shillings off, and the maintenance of a smart appearance could be expensive. Extra income from tips was mostly prohibited. A full weekly wage for the experienced saloon barmaid in a thriving pub might reach 15s, though the big London music halls, followed by the theatres, paid more. Wages and terms of work were notably inferior in the provinces, but in general, taking into account the provision of board and lodging, the barmaid's earnings were high compared to other semi-skilled female occupations.[36]

Whatever the sector of the trade, barmaid's work was long and demanding. London pubs were licensed to be open for $123\frac{1}{2}$ hours per week in the 1890s and a barmaid might be on duty for more than a hundred of those, but the most reliable report of the period recorded a standard working day of some 12 hours or so, making up a 70–80 hour week.[37] The day ran from early morning to past midnight with 4 or 5 hours off for meals, dressing and rest. Opening hours were shorter on Sunday, the usual day off for the barmaid; after a year she might take a week's holiday, and up to a month thereafter, in some cases with pay. During working hours a barmaid was habitually on her feet, and though male staff did the heavier work, the physical regimen of the bar was punishing. In addition to serving drink and food – and remaining civil – there was cleaning up after closing time, which could be particularly onerous on Saturday night. At the end of such a demanding schedule, few barmaids can have resembled the refulgent creature of the Gavarni print.

Although the division into old-fashioned and modern or saloon barmaids indicates a clear distinction in status and function, attention to the particular circumstances of barwork suggests a more complex picture. In single handed berths at the cheap end of the market a barmaid was little better than a maid of all work, with dismal food and accommodation, yet it was in the smaller establishments that a barmaid might find herself welcomed as one of the family.[38] The best conditions were found with the big companies, notably Spiers and Pond who were widely respected as model employers. Employees here lived in company dormitories and visitors pronounced them well housed, well fed and well looked after. Yet there were complaints from one branch of bad food on the table and dead rats under the floor, and the paternalist regime could be irksome.[39] A further variable in the trade was the high rate of turnover and mobility among women bar workers. One unavoidable constant was a working environment heavily polluted by gas and tobacco fumes, conditions found at their worst in the underground railway bars.

The sense of the evidence is that the barmaid maintained a considerable degree of self-respect and independence in the often testing conditions of her trade. In working-class pubs, she was low caste even in her own class,[40] but the saloon barmaid had a high regard for her status and considered herself superior to other service workers such as domestics and shopclerks.[41] Though also subordinate and in some cases closely regulated, it was no requirement of her job that she be either deferential, anonymous, or invisible. Indeed on her own territory the barmaid enjoyed a certain authority: 'behind the bar,' said one observer, 'she is the mistress of the situation . . . and an absolute despot.'[42] There was considerable social contact on the job, if much of it was conventionalised and almost exclusively male. In big establishments there was the company of other working women, while in the single-handed berth, which probably accounted for the majority of situations, there was the presence, if not always the support, of the publican's wife. Gossip across the bar provided a bush-telegraph that kept even the solitary barmaid aware of conditions elsewhere in the trade and made her a stubborn defender of her basic terms of employment.[43] The rapid turnover was in part an index to the publican's hunger for fresh faces but may have also been a further expression of the barmaid's confidence in pursuit of her calling.

If the level of earnings and the common requirement of living-in disallowed complete independence, barmaids were reputedly among those best placed to take the traditional avenue to supposed escape and fulfilment, for it was the popular myth that barmaids always married, and almost always married well. Premises in the centre of London afforded a high concentration of wealthy upper class males, and there were many tales of erstwhile barmaids transported by marriage from some West End bar to a suburban mansion. Furthermore, barmaids were said to prosper in marriage; not only were they sociable creatures but, as the myth went, their schooling behind the bar made them shrewd judges of men.[44]

Such a benign account of the barmaid's expectations of living happily ever after was dismissed by a growing lobby of reformers for whom the barmaid constituted a most serious problem of physical and moral welfare. Dating from the mid 1880s, the reform campaign was part of the more general movement for social purity. Its impetus came from various evangelical rescue organisations and branches of the temperance movement. Its membership was predominantly that of churchmen and middle-class women, with the support of a number of politicians, mostly Labour MPs and Progressive members of the London County Council. The reformers were particularly active in London, but there were organised campaigns in other big cities, notably Manchester and Glasgow. The earliest initiatives sought to provide social centres and services for those out of work, or who wished to live off licensed premises, and a series of Parliamentary bills were introduced (unsuccessfully) from 1890 on, calling for a reduction in hours and the improvement of working conditions.[45] The campaign then moved to call for an end to the employment of women in the bar, and recorded some success in the Licensing Act of 1904, which gave Justices of the Peace discretionary power to forbid such employment in granting new licences. A new licensing bill in 1908 required the phased but ultimately total prohibition of barwork for women (other than members of the publican's family), but the measure failed.[46]

Though the references are obscure, barmaids were reported to have gone on strike in 1889, and they made further attempts to organise themselves in the early 1890s,[47] but in a trade that was difficult to unionise, most active worker participation there was supported the employers' counter attack against the reformers and their demand for the elimination of the barmaid. In this highly controversial issue, the reform proposals of the 1908 bill were also contested by the radical suffragists, Esther Roper and Eva Gore-Booth, who rallied support from the trade in their Manchester-based Barmaids' Political Defence League, which defended the women's right to work.[48]

In their attack on 'the Moloch of the drink trade', reformers cast the barmaid as the physical victim of a sweated industry, but they were often more exercised by her plight as a moral casualty, fatally vulnerable to drink, seduction and worse. Drink was the very raison d'etre of the barmaid's occupation, but formal constraints upon her personal consumption were well advertised by the trade. House regulations commonly forbade treating by customers, and the larger businesses often demanded abstinence during working hours. Private opinion in the trade varied considerably on the extent of the barmaid's temperance or otherwise, but two of them interviewed by the Parliamentary investigator Eliza Orme in 1892 maintained that 'the variety and amusement of the life lessens the propensity to drink.'[49] For reformers, however, the bar automatically constituted a permanent temptation; they remained convinced that regulations were habitually set at nought by surreptitious drinking to counter fatigue, and quoted rising insurance premiums as evidence of general intemperance in a trade they pronounced more hazardous than that of filemakers and lead workers.[50] In reform logic, drink also inevitably increased the moral risks of bar work by softening resistance to seduction.

Reformers conceded that the women drawn to bar work were not themselves necessarily of a low character, but maintained that the pub environment was inevitably corrupting. In their view, 'the variety and amusement' of bar life meant the inescapable sexualisation of social encounter; accordingly, the 'banter' and 'chaff' of conventional account translated in reform terms to 'bad language . . . [that] tends to the insidious weakening of the barrier of modest and maidenly shame in which her [the barmaid's] strength resides.'[51] Reformers were convinced of the publican's sexual as well as economic exploitation of young women. For evidence they referred to the advertisements for vacancies in the trade which targeted the under-20s and commonly called for photographs (the carte de visite) of applicants. The reform conclusion was that the barmaid 'is employed by the publican as a decoy for men, and her very existence depends on her ability to attract.'52 When her novelty as the siren of the bar wore off, she was likely to be dismissed, and numerous personal testimonies to prison chaplains and police court missionaries were adduced to demonstrate how easy was the subsequent descent to prostitution.53

As it managed the flow of drink, the trade also managed the flow of sexuality, though this was territory harder to police. Some house rules expressly forbade the shaking of hands across the bar as part of a general prohibition on physical contact between server and customer, and reform investigators found the relative broadness of bar counters worth report.54 Dress was also formally regulated. By the 1890s 'except in very small houses the rule is universal that barmaids. . .must wear black dresses. . .and a large apron of the same material'. With this occupational uniform went white collars and cuffs, but no further relief or distraction was allowed, and employers proscribed false hair and busts.55 It was and has remained a truism in the trade that the plain rather than the showy barmaid was the better choice. In any case, where trade was habitually brisk there was little time for dalliance. A French visitor in the 1860s who noted the prettiness of English barmaids suggested that they were 'protected from all human seductions behind the imposing serenity and the Olympian majesty of business.'56 Thus the ritualisation of the task as well as its busyness may have reinforced the sexual controls of pub protocol.

Who were typical customers, and what were their likely perceptions of the barmaid and her glamorised sexuality? It was the saloon or lounge barmaid who was most obviously meant to be attractive. Her customers were middle to lower-middle class and, of course, almost exclusively male. Most reports from City and West End premises suggest two broad though overlapping categories of clientele: the habitual 'lounger', from the leisured man about town to the more raffish 'horsey' type; and the 'business man' of varying rank, from the banker down to the clerk and the shopman.57 Whatever the actual provenance of its customers, the saloon preserved the fiction of catering to gentlemen.

It seems plausible enough that the erotic charge for the male habitue derived in part from the piquant inflections of the conventional gentleman-maidservant relationship, restaged away from home in the liminoid space and time of the pub.58 Thus the business-like, even officious manner of the barmaid noted above reversed the normal roles of authority relationships for the middle-class male to whom most women, and certainly those in service, were habitually deferential. It is a commonplace that watching other people work is fascinating, but how much more so would this have been for middle-class males who did so little of it themselves, and for whom the extensive female labour and service that supported their life-style was usually either honorific or invisible? There seems to be little need to argue at length for the attractions of the austere livery of the dress-uniform. Here, practises meant to register distance exercised their own fascination. At the same time enduring associations of the nurturing role of the nanny or nurse-maid could make the barmaid a figure of comfort as well as power, particularly in the case of the older woman who survived in suburban public houses and was plainly valued for her maternal-confessional role.[59]

What the graphic texts also demonstrate is the vital role men ascribed to the barmaid in the bidding for, and bestowal of, recognition. The considerable emotional investment in the winning of the woman's gaze that these attempts signify, strongly suggests the degree of anonymity and competition in the pub crowd that had to be bid against. In consequence men, too, put themselves on display. The hunger for a privileged acknowledgment from the woman behind the bar also suggests a further prize for the male ego, given the intimate terrain of the pub, its eroticised associations of drink and the night, and the fascination the barmaid might hold as the stranger of uncertain background. She was respectable, yes; she was the girl whom a chap might just marry, by Jove; she was also the girl who just might. . .without one having to marry her – perhaps the typical male reading of parasexuality. It may be then that together with perhaps nobler sentiments – there was another male perception at play, half fantasy and half calculation – that of the barmaid as potential mistress or 'kept woman'. Indeed, she may have functioned as a collectively kept woman in the male social psyche. With all these attractions in play, the wonder is not that men had to be lured into pubs, but that they were ever persuaded to leave.

Spokesmen for the licensed trade habitually disclaimed any inten-tions of even the mildest sexual exploitation of women workers. They preferred women over men not because they were 'attractive', but because they were less expensive, less clumsy, less wasteful and less corruptible. Such valued workers were necessarily treated well by their employers, while the presence of women in licensed premises was said to have a civilising influence, an argument made by the barmaids them-selves in defending their occupation against elimination in 1908.[60] The licensed victuallers proclaimed the respectability of their trade, their barmaids, and their customers who, according to one spokesman in 1906 'are the fathers and brothers of other respectable middle class girls.'[61] The trade thus addressed the world from a moving escalator of respectability such that the gaudy temptress of reformers' accounts was always dismissed as a figure from the periphery of the trade or its unimproved past.[62]

Some employers, however, did manifestly stoke the fires of the 'amorous furnace.' 'In many houses in the West End and the City used by clerks, lawyers and shopmen', according to an account of the mid '70s, 'landlords find it greatly to their interest to have handsome, fine, showy, attractive and talkative young ladies behind the bar.' These women were dressed by their employers, served only in peak hours, and were most likely to be trapped as mistresses.[63] Neither adventures nor misadventures were necessarily resolved in marriage – 'men in pubs', observed one commentator tartly, 'are not the marrying kind' – and a combination of low wages and sweet talk undoubtedly led some barmaids into destructive relationships. Muriel Perry, the mistress but never the wife of J. R. Ackerley's businessman father – was seduced by the latter when a barmaid at the Tavistock in Covent Garden in 1909.[64] Whatever the various controls at work, barmaids were women at risk.

In all of this there remains the important but elusive matter of the barmaid's perception of her role and its sexual dimension – the view from behind. There is little direct testimony but the foregoing evidence does strongly suggest that young women were partly drawn to barwork by its promise of excitement, in which sexual opportunity was a strong element as a prelude to marriage. And while employers denied that the barmaid was as a decoy, it was an acknowledged part of her job that she make herself 'agreeable'.[65]

But how did the barmaid comply with this requirement? There is some significant indication that the barmaid protected herself from the beeriness and leeriness of the pub's sexual culture by her own manipulation of its particular parameters of distance and intimacy. George Moore catches this in his characterisation of Lizzie Baker, the Spiers and Pond heroine in *Spring Days: A Realistic Novel* (1888):

Lizzie had her bar manners and her town manners, and she slipped on the former as she would an article of clothing, when she lifted the slab and passed behind. They consisted principally of cordial smiles, personal observations, and a look of vacancy which she assumed when the conversation became coarse. From behind the bar she spoke authoritatively, she was secure, it was different – it was behind the bar; and she spoke with a cheek and a raciness that at other times were quite foreign to her . . . what she heard and said in the bar remained not a moment on her mind, she appeared to accept it all as part of the business of the place.[66]

The crucial function of the bar comes across plainly here, as does Lizzie's modern consciousness of barwork as role-playing, and there is corroborative testimony in the words of some of Miss Orme's barmaid-respondents who ridiculed any idea that they were flattered by the customers' chat: 'If they only knew it,' they said, 'we regard them no more than a set of bottles.'[67]

Parasexuality in the Victorian pub was very much the product of a male agenda and male management, yet its women subjects were accomplished managers too. Certainly the anti-barmaid reformers had a case, for barwork could be squalid drudgery and its rewards disappointing. There were also real dangers of sexual corruption. Yet compared with prostitution, parasexuality was mostly safe sex, and the evidence suggests that in general the Victorian barmaid was not, like Clark's reading of Manet's subject, an alienated whore, but an assertive and competent modernist; there may in fact have been more alienation on the other side of the bar.

IV

Claiming cultural 'firsts' is always likely to be a dubious exercise. It could be argued that there is an earlier and more obvious case than the barmaid of the woman as parasexual and modern glamour object; that is the actress, who made her appearance at the Restoration and functioned as what Tracy Davis terms 'a kind of sexual wage earner.'[68] The actress was a key figure in the promotion of glamour, but the particular novelty of the Victorian barmaid remains in her relative ubiquity and approachability. She was an everyday phenomenon, marginally distant yet more proximate than the actress; it was, as we have seen, in this sense of normality that the barmaid proved so sensational. Yet while the particular circumstances of her employment kept her a controversial figure into the 1914–18 war, she was by then much less singularly conspicuous, for her visual impact had been diminished by the more general glamorisation of women, of which she had been such a notable prototype.[69]

From the last quarter of the nineteenth century, the barmaid's role in this larger process was shared not only with the actress (and from the

'90s, the chorus girl), but with other young women workers from an expanding new service sector whose more numerous incursion into public life brought further dramatic changes to the sexual landscape.[70] At work, at large, and in representation, these women played an important role in the late-century crisis in sexual politics.

While the licensed trade downplayed her sexual role and reformers cast her as the victimised temptress, the barmaid was elsewhere being celebrated as one of a new type of popular heroine. From the 1870s the popular stage conspired with everyday life to sing the praises not only of the barmaid but of her sister workers in telegraph offices, department stores and multiple teashops. This new group, too, held court from behind a counter, though their adventures were also set in the street, the omnibus and the various new leisure resorts of the big city. In music hall song they are adept manipulators of the class marginal 'gent',[71] but in the 1890s a new stage genre offered a more idealised representation of these young working women as partners in male exploit and more exalted cross-class romances.

This was musical comedy, a lavish and fashionably popular entertainment whose dramatists, as noted at the opening of *The New Barmaid* in 1896, were 'working steadily through the list of female occupations.'[72] As the titles of its hit productions testify, musical comedy celebrated its heroines in the rhetoric of the 'girl': *The Gaiety Girl* (from the chorus), *The Shop Girl*, and *The Earl and the Girl*, pointing to the typical musical comedy resolution (and some dramatic examples from real life) of the society marriage. Max Beerbohm caught the essentials of the genre. 'All the classes mingle on the easiest terms. Everyone wants everyone else to have a good time and tries to make everything easy and simple all round. This good time, as I need hardly say, is of a wholly sexual order. And yet everyone from the highest to the lowest is thoroughly good.' It portrayed 'an innocent libertinism', at which, he concluded, 'all the Tory in me rejoices'.[73]

What, more generally, might Beerbohm have been applauding? We may speculate that the blooming of musical comedy represents a reassuring response to several contemporary challenges to male domination and sexual identity. Thus the cosmetic gloss on cross-class relationships shifted attention away from the 'Maiden Tribute' case of 1885 and the exposé of upper class males as vicious predators on working-class girls. Presumably too, musical comedy's sunny heterosexuality helped to dispel the unease brought by Oscar Wilde's conviction in 1895. The parasexual construct of the 'girl' evoked a more agreeable romantic companion than the 'new woman' who made her troublesome debut in the nineties, and in general it provided a defensive counter-image to the emergent challenge of feminism signalled in the campaign against the Contagious Diseases Acts and the demands of young professional women in the period.[74] Though the musical comedy heroine was a spirited character, she was no threat to male primacy.

At the same time, the glamorous fantasy of the musical comedy girl was derived from the palpable social reality of a numerous new group of woman who did not fit the exclusive categories of madonna or magdalen. Out of hours, away from the social markers of the workplace, the class and status of the new working woman were harder to read. The young aristocratic protagonist in Moore's *Spring Days* first meets his barmaid-lover at the theatre as one of two girls he cannot readily place: 'They were evidently not prostitutes, and they did not seem to be quite ladies.' An account from 1880 noted 'Strange Women' abroad, 'neither ladies nor common,' whom, it concluded, were 'respectable women copying the dress and manners of 'unfortunates' for mere excitement; but they don't want gentlemen to go too far.'[75]

This phenomenon may have contributed a more unspecified disquiet to the protests of the more conservative middle-class women who addressed the barmaid problem and other social purity issues. The dilemmas of identification reduced the defences of respectability for women in general, while the expanded field of licit sexual encounter increased the threat to class endogamy at a time when the independence of the 'new woman' would have been thought to reduce the pool of eligible young middle-class females. Suddenly, it must have seemed, other young women were everywhere, and the reformers were fearful for the integrity of their class as well as their sex.

The barmaid and the pub were thus part of a larger nexus of people and institutions that stood athwart the public/private line and provided the social space within which a more democratised, heterosocial world of sex and sociability was being constituted, a world that is still inadequately mapped by historians.[76] It is on this distinctive terrain that the less august branches of capitalism converted sexuality from anathema to resource, from resource to commodity, in the development of a modern sexualised consumerism.

Parasexuality, with its safely sensational pattern of stimulation and containment, was a significant mode of cultural management in the construction of this new regime and the sexualisation of everyday life. It is plain from its operation and such self-serving fictions as Beerbohm's 'innocent libertinism', that it worked primarily to valorise male pleasures. Yet the making of this world was undertaken not just by a cadre of male managers – who were neither wholly in control nor always trying to be so – but by the members of this cultural complex at large, in a self-conscious and mutual (if structurally and ideologically asymmetrical) working out of new modes of relationship between men and women.[77]

In a society where the collective licence of carnival had been largely outlawed, and ritualised practices such as 'bundling' (pre-modern parasexuality with its equivalent of a bar) had lapsed, determination of the informal rules and boundaries of sexual encounter was now pursued in a more fragmented and inchmeal manner, in the individual transactions of a continuously recomposing leisure crowd – London after work, reported Sims, had become 'one vast Lovers' Walk'.[78] Thus the mechanistic formula of parasexuality that positioned the barmaid in the Victorian pub dissolved in practice into a more popular discourse, the elasticity of whose rules was scrutinised in a vernacular 'knowingness' that informs music-hall song and other popular idioms.[79]

If it is to have any further utility, parasexuality may best serve not as another reified term in the often dismal maze of critspeak, but as an exploratory concept in the examination of other examples and dimensions of this process.[80] Glamour, and the sexual stimulation produced by looking (scopophilia) plainly gave a new emphasis to the visual element in the changing sexual economy, but the reformers' concern with what pub people termed 'banter' or 'chaff' points to the complementary significance of language and spoken codes, which could be as potent yet as contradictory and unstable as the gaze. The rules against physical contact between barmaid and customer is a reminder that through its very repression, touch took on a new expressive charge, witness the furtive but enraptured holding of hands across the bar depicted in some illustrations. The historical reanimation of this popular discourse in all its sensory dynamics – talking and touching as well as looking ('glotto-' and 'frottophilia'?) – would seem a necessary exercise in charting experience along the moving social frontier that was the sexualisation of everyday life, and in understanding its implications for the sexual politics of gender.

CHAPTER 8

Musical comedy and the rhetoric of the girl, 1892–1914

Musical comedy – the forerunner of today's stage and film musical – has received scant scholarly attention as a significant cultural form. Recollections of its spectacular debut in the 1890s talk of it only in idealised terms as 'the theatre of enchantment', set in a world of jingling hansoms, champagne suppers and velvet nights. Today's theatre historians remain preoccupied with the social problem plays of the era in the New Drama of Wilde, Ibsen, and Shaw, while their attention to the popular stage focuses on melodrama rather than the upstart new genre. Nor do recent cultural histories of the period have much to say, one noting only that musical comedy was indeed 'wildly popular . . . [but] breathtakingly vacuous'.[1]

Perhaps this is all musical comedy deserves – sentimental indulgence, critical disparagement, or silence. (The last two responses are memorably wedded in Kenneth Tynan's review of *The Sound of Music* – 'The Case for Trappism'.[2]) Yet the Hollywood musical, as a latterday variant of musical comedy, has received serious critical scrutiny in film studies, and cultural studies have generally shown how familiar and apparently unproblematical forms can reveal much of social and ideological significance.[3] Certainly some contemporaries thought the new genre was significant. 'This is the real New Drama', wrote William Archer in 1894, later calculating that its popularity outstripped all other theatre forms, including melodrama. It was, he said, 'a form to be reckoned with, a form that has come to stay'. 'One day', he maintained, its history 'will form a curious study'.[4]

The study on offer here speaks as yet to a selective curiosity. Though there is plainly need for a comprehensive history of musical comedy (including its two-way traffic across the Atlantic), my concern is with its representations of gender and sexuality as embodied in the girl-heroine who featured so heavily in its productions, from her collective role as newly modernised chorus girl to that of the female lead starring as the young working woman adventuring in the big city. At the same time, I want to put this in the context of everyday life in the period, get behind the present dismissive evaluations, and begin to explain rather than merely register the enormous popularity of this new genre.[5]

But first, it will be helpful to review the received account of musical comedy and its provenance.[6] As a popular compound of song, dance, and romantic narrative, the genre is said to derive primarily from the Victorian (English) burlesque, an eclectic form based on the parody of some well-known historic episode, legend, play, or book.[7] Written in verse and set to existing melodies, burlesque was a costume drama, featuring transvestite roles for women, actresses in tights, and a numerous female corps de ballet. Over the period, burlesque's characteristic element of often erudite pastiche yielded increasingly to topical allusions, and it was by virtue of its more direct attention to contemporary life that musical comedy came to supplant the older form. While still a confection of song, dance, and romantic story-line (very loosely constructed), the new genre was written in everyday speech, and played in everyday settings. Burlesque's love affair with the pun gave way to the pursuit of the catchphrase, and each of the new shows came with an original musical score aimed at generating its own self-referential hit songs. Where burlesque had been enamoured of the grotesque and the eccentric, the new production style was lavish and spectacular, its sophistications punctuated only by the ribaldry of comic turns imported from the music hall. If its manners were modern, musical comedy's use of the vernacular was nonetheless very selective, constituting a distinctly stylised form of naturalism. Thus its resort to modern dress heavily favoured high fashion, as part of its intense glamorisation of women, both as stars and members of a reconfigured dance chorus.

By most accounts, the first show in the new style was *In Town*, staged by George Edwardes at the Prince of Wales Theatre in London in 1892. A stopgap production, it was so successful that Edwardes commissioned a more considered follow-up of his ad hoc invention. This was *A Gaiety Girl*, written by Sidney Jones and Owen Hall, the first work to be termed 'musical comedy', and the definitive hit of the new form. Running from 1893 to 1896, the show celebrated the modern chorus girl and her most famous home. Musical comedy and the Gaiety Theatre became synonymous, and contributed mightily to the theatre boom of the 1890s and the consolidation of the West End as the prime site for theatre-going and the big night out. The success of long-run productions on the London stage was duplicated by touring companies in the provinces and abroad, notably in America. To export was added import, when the first indigenous American musical, *The Belle of New York*, played in London in 1898. There was also a trade in light opera, brought in from the continent and served up under the new label.

At the centre of this highly profitable phenomenon stood the legendary George Edwardes – businessman, theatre and music hall manager, and impresario. Learning his trade at the Savoy (a reminder of musical comedy's further debt to Gilbert and Sullivan), Edwardes took over the managership of the Gaiety from John Hollingshead in 1886 while it was still a burlesque and variety house. After the successful introduction of musical comedy, he remained in charge of this 'theatre of enchantment', together with its satellites (notably Daly's), and the touring companies. Musical comedy was a collaborative form, but its writers and composers have received little acknowledgment compared to that awarded George Edwardes, 'the Guv'nor'. Was it his ghost, his mother, or a former mistress who wrote his entry in the *Oxford Companion to the Theatre*, with its congratulatory note of a man at once magical, businesslike, and benign?

He had an extraordinary flair for knowing what the public wanted and spared no cost in providing it, with a meticulous care for detail. He was rewarded by crowded houses and the trust and affection of the public and the profession alike.[8]

This was the man most responsible for the exaltation of the woman as girl. The girl who was celebrated in an endless string of show titles: *A Gaiety Girl, The Sunshine Girl, The Shop Girl, The Girl Behind the Counter, The Girl from Kays, The Girl in the Taxi*, etc. The girl who was naughty but nice . . .

There are several categories within which the musical comedy girl can be understood – as working woman, stage persona, public image, and private person – though they constantly intersect and elide. I concentrate here on the first two.

As working women, both actresses and chorus girls in musical comedy seem to have enjoyed higher status and higher salaries than was general within their profession. Certainly the musical comedy chorus played a more prominent role than the conventional female stage auxiliary, and enjoyed something of a collective star status. This was notably so for that model of the new order, the Gaiety Girls, which had its own internal differential, paying its tallest and most imposing members – the Big Eight – three to four times more than the regular chorus.[9]

The experience of the Gaiety Girls, however, also demonstrates the social cost of such rewards in their submission to close male managerial control under George Edwardes. Edwardes employed tutors to teach his girls both stage and social skills – song and dance, but also speech, carriage, and dress. Thus groomed and instructed, the girls became ladies and were encouraged to frequent fashionable restaurants and parade themselves at Ascot. Their off-stage conduct was closely monitored. Head waiters reported back to the Guv'nor on the girls and their escorts, and in a stage take-off of Edwardes, his double was made to say '(Cunningly) I see you all far oftener than you suspect.'[10] All-too-short stage careers could be more abruptly foreshortened: if his girls grew too fat or too thin, became pregnant or ceased to smile, they were sacked. In his youth Edwardes had narrowly failed to qualify as an army officer, remarking later 'That's why I'm commanding regiments of chorus singers instead of soldiers.' The Guv'nor's military alter ego was masked by the more manipulative style of the chivalrous chauvinist. He could be generous with presents, solicitous in his attentions, and adept at smothering dissent with a mix of concern and implicit threats: 'You look tired and ill . . . you are not taking care . . . (handing out pills) . . . now you mustn't lose your looks . . .'[11] Variously Svengali, martinet, snooper and sugar daddy, George Edwardes is a more complex and darker figure than standard accounts allow, alerting us to the often hazardous off-stage sexual politics that went with the relatively advantaged position of women working in this sector.

Edwardes's extensive investments as a businessman invite an industrial as well as a military analogy for the stage operations of musical comedy and its working relationships. Thus the general phenomenon of the modern chorus line can be read as duplicating the more intensified and routinised production regimes of the late Victorian factory. Compared to the eccentric or balletic styles of dance in burlesque and music hall, the musical comedy chorus was more mechanical, performing repetitious, standardised operations in a more closely supervised workplace. Its members were among a numerous, interchangeable, and readily replaceable category of semi-skilled workers, employed in long production runs in a large-scale culture industry of global scope. The Gaiety Girls may be the exception here, since they were reported to pose as much as dance, emphasising perhaps a superior, metropolitan sophistication, but the model of the modern production line fits well for the Manchester-based Tiller Girls, whose troupes staffed Edwardes's touring companies and were employed world wide.

The original troupe was founded in 1890 by John Tiller, the favoured nephew of a rich cotton manufacturer.[12] 'Mr John' thought the Gaiety Girls undisciplined compared to his own, who were graduates of stern instruction in the Tiller Method. A man of explosive temper, his autocratic discipline extended to the off-stage life of his predominantly working-class charges. They recalled him as 'very strict but kind' and talked, a little wryly, of being 'Tillerised' by the system, a fitting echo of contemporary industrialists who advocated 'Taylorising' factory production according to the teachings of F.W. Taylor, the American pioneer of scientific management. Thus older paternalist modes of authority combined with the newer patterns of industrial production, while the military ideal of well-drilled preparedness reflected the additional priorities of an imperial age. 'In matters of discipline', says the male shopwalker inspecting the finger nails of his assistants in *The Shop Girl* (1894), 'General Wolseley and myself entertain views precisely the same.'[13]

The correspondence of life in the chorus line with that of the modern workers was most obvious in *The Sunshine Girl* (1912), set in a soap factory plainly based on the Lever Brothers' model industrial plant on Merseyside, where the chorus sings 'You've got to get a move on / Your ways you must improve on.' The *Sketch*, a London newspaper, delighted in reproducing a photograph from New York showing a lady of the chorus punching a time-clock to register her arrival at the theatre (figure 13).[14] In revealing such features of operation to the public and their continuity with life outside the theatre, the press reinforced the message of women under control and grounded the theatrical dream world in the new routines of modernity.

The musical comedy girl was not only a worker in her own profession, but was commonly cast as a worker on stage. Dramatists drew their typical heroines from young working women in the burgeoning new service sector of the economy, those who held court from behind a counter in telegraph offices, bars, teashops and, most prominently, department stores. The writer for *The Shop Girl* (1894) claimed to have spent long hours in research in Whiteley's and the Army and Navy, to meet what he discerned as the new public appetite for 'the local and the real . . . the life of today'.[15] The large shop or department store would indeed have been familiar to metropolitan and big city audiences. Many of them may have gone straight from shopping to the show – *This Way Madam* (1913) at the Queen's Theatre was set in an almost exact replica of the Swan and Edgar store that was its next-door neighbour on

Figure 13   'The chorus girl as disciplined modern worker', *Sketch*, 13 January 1909.

London's Regent Street. Others in the audience would have known department stores and similar settings as workers in the labour-intensive retail industry. Not that the social realism of the new genre was much concerned with the oppressive actualities of shop work, with its long hours, petty subordinations, and austere living-in conditions.[16] Rather, the department store recommended itself to writers as a locus of everyday life that was already highly theatricalised by its emphasis on glamour and display. Here too was a new social space that facilitated romantic encounter, for the transactions of shopping allowed and yet regularised a relatively easy and unmediated public exchange between the sexes and the classes that elsewhere might have seemed either lowering or impertinent. Certainly the shop was a less hazardous or compromising site than the street.[17]

The setting of the store also emphasised the pleasures of shopping and consumption in an avidly consumerist era.[18] Indeed, there was a direct link between stage and commerce as musical comedy was recruited to the promotional battles between the big stores slugging it out for domination of London's West End. The heroine of *Our Miss Gibbs, or the Girl at the Stores* (1909) staffs the counter at 'Garrods', a luxurious replica of the Knightsbridge Harrods which was locked into a shopping war with the new Selfridge's, the Americanised upstart on Oxford Street. Shopping at 'Garrods' was said to be 'Paradise', but one which was open to all, for musical comedy often featured a 'shop-till-you-drop' number where the working girl broke out from behind the counter to claim her other identity as the lady consumer:

> In an out and round about,
> Hardly ever stopping,
> Buying this and buying that and leaving me to pay –
> Won't you come out shopping, shopping, shopping for the day?

Women so bent on consumption were expensive, but shopping in turn consumed them, absorbing energies that might otherwise be put to more threatening ends. In Sidney Grundy's didactic hit play on the straight stage, *The New Woman* (1894), three angry feminists pass from attacks on 'Man the Betrayer' to teatime chatter about dresses on sale in Peter Robinson's and other London stores. If at times somewhat alarmingly open-ended, shopping was nonetheless a form of control in a well-controlled setting.

Of course, the shop girl – any girl – might be sprung from the worthy routine of her working life through romance and marriage to a rich,

well-born male, a motif much beloved of the period and celebrated in
another hit *The Earl and Girl* (1903).[19] Musical comedy sometimes played
safe in the traditional convention of the heroine who qualifies for the
honour through the discovery of her own genteel birth, lost but now
recovered. Yet its more typical apotheosis of the working girl represents
marriage above her station as the due reward for her own inherent
virtues. Thus she surmounts the barriers of class by a natural gentility
which, though it may require a little pardonable artifice, is available to
all. As the chorus sings in *A Gaiety Girl*, 'everyone's a lady who behaves
herself as such'. The show girls maintain this proposition in the face of
the hauteur of the young titled women with whom they now compete
for male attention, concluding triumphantly: 'We would rather be ladies
by nature / Than mere Upper Ten nomenclature'.

Musical comedy was thus both highly caste conscious yet staunchly
egalitarian, maintaining its soundly democratic principles by the simple
exclusion of all those who were most obviously unequal. Few prolet-
arians appear on its stage, in an era when 75 to 80 per cent of the
population came from the manual labouring class. In the factory setting
of *The Sunshine Girl*, choruses of workmen and working girls sing briskly
about the labour that goes into a bar of soap – 'the toilin' work, the
boilin' work . . . the killin' work, the grillin' work' – but the heroine
works in the perfume department. In other settings where working
people feature as a class, they are also suitably sanitised. As Max
Beerbohm noted of 'Gaietyland', 'the mingling of the classes was on the
easiest of terms . . . [with] never a crude word or gesture'. There was, he
observed, 'nothing to choose between the classes, for all the characters
are refined, though not', he added, 'in the least like in actual life . . . they
have a school, a higher school of their own'.[20] Thus musical comedy's
claim to social realism seems pitched in the idiom of a highly contrived
bourgeois populism, in which, with few exceptions, the ordinary and
everyday are irreducibly middle class, a flattering state of self-election
for us all. But then, as one of its everyday charming characters puts it, in
a rare surfacing of the subtext: 'It is stupid to be poor.'

It is also stupid to be ugly. Thus in musical comedy, the working girl –
its ordinary girl – was also invariably pretty. While this was a traditional
prerequisite of the heroines of popular stage romance, musical comedy
glamorised its women in a more calculated and spectacular fashion,
juxtaposing and interfusing the ordinary and the extraordinary to construct its erotic milieu. 'The first sensation', of *The Shop Girl* (1896), wrote
one reviewer, was the entry of its 'stage beauties in such costume as they

might wear in the street'; in the second act, however, the old Gaiety traditions asserted themselves with 'shapely women in a frou frou of scant but delicate drapery'.[21] To judge from the playscript, the latter were girls from the Frivolity Theatre (echoes of *Ally Sloper's Half Holiday*), introduced into the store's charity bazaar as the occasion for a show within a show, their actress role sanctioning their burlesque semi-nudity. But both sets of women, shop assistants and actresses, were glamorously lit and presented, their very separate social identities elided in their common representation as women on show – 'show girls', everyone of them, to use a coinage of the era. Seaside settings gave further cause for show in glamorous un-dress, as with *The Girl from Kays* (1902) whose chorus paraded 'in red and orange bathing garb'.[22] It became common to musical-comedy formula to shift the second act away from such enclosed settings as the store to a freer milieu, such as the seaside or the exhibition or fairground, exploiting the sense of greater licence in dress and behaviour.[23]

Thus musical comedy's stock in trade was, as Beerbohm further noted, 'of a wholly sexual order'. Yet we may well fail to register fully its more intensely eroticised stage discourse, unless we understand the disarming rhetoric within which its female bearer was positioned. This was the rhetoric of the musical-comedy woman as girl, which framed its subject as 'naughty but nice', or, in another formulaic phrase, 'not too good and not too bad'. These ambiguous apologetics served both to sensationalise and contain sexual expression in a manageable form – parasexuality – that was central to the musical comedy aesthetic.[24]

The boundaries marking off a disabling excess of goodness were plainest drawn, as in the much-mocked image of the saintly 'Old Fashioned Girl' and 'the extremely maiden aunt', caricatured in *The Shop Girl's* hit song 'Her Golden Hair Was Hanging Down Her Back'. If 'old' was out, so also was too radical a formulation of the new, as in the over-intellectualised and sexually neutered New Woman. Also much too good for the musical comedy girl were the Salvation Army lasses pilloried in several shows. When the shop girls from Kays are invited to an Army meeting to learn 'how to resist temptation', they subvert the occasion by deriding its 'Goody Goody Girls' and proclaiming their own determination to 'Frolic, flirt and spoon'. As another musical comedy lyric maintained, 'It was silly to be chilly'.

It was, of course, in the limits to be set to the opposite pole of freedom and licence that musical comedy was more self-consciously circumspect. Yet here, in language that seems to us ludicrously coy and minimalist, is evidence of that sexual freighting that needs taking more seriously, as in the prime case of 'naughty', the sign that both licensed and contained badness, and gave its arch yet potent imprimatur to the decade that fathered musical comedy. We should listen to Margaret Schlegel in *Howard's End*, 'who hated naughtiness more than sin'.[25] Now defined as 'mildly indecent or titillating', naughty spoke to contemporaries in the language of the brothel and the nursery. A naughty house was nineteenth-century slang for brothel and the word could be part of the prostitute's typical address to her client – 'Who's a naughty boy, then?' – at once an invitation, a challenge, and an indulgent semi-reproach. In combination with the vocabulary of the boy and the girl, the term sanctions sexual adventure as no more than childish mischief, to be understood and condoned by nurse or nanny, fond authorities in the middle-class male psyche nourishing strong fantasies of sexual initiation, emotional dependence, and pleasurable guilt. Within this powerful regressive interpellation of the bawdy and the infantile, the 'girl' could be unproblematically co-opted as the fellow (*sic*) conspirator and play-mate. That the girl in this case was also an actress no doubt fuelled the sense of complicit delinquency, for while much has been made of the increasing respectability of the profession in this period, the actress was still cast as an inherently promiscuous figure in the public eye, not least because the circumstances of her work – on show, nocturnal, co-sexual – echoed those of the prostitute.[26]

It was the prostitute who was the irrevocably naughty girl, ostensibly beyond the respectable outer limits of musical comedy's sexometer, yet her too, too bad-ness suggestively haunts its texts. The shop girl as milliner pursued an occupation that had throughout the century been regarded as a cover for casual prostitution, an association both distanced and acknowledged when one of the girls from Kays observes that her room is situated 'at the virtuous end of Regent Street', the resort of the daytime prostitute. Implications of prostitution or some kind of sexual buccaneering may help to account for the huge success of the hit song 'And Her Golden Hair Was Hanging Down Her Back' that helped *The Shop Girl* to run nearly six hundred performances in 1894–5. It is a conventional enough tale of 'artless Flo', a country girl who comes up to London, learns the way of the world and returns home 'With a naughty little twinkle in her eye'. The tag line, 'And her golden hair was streaming/hanging down her back' sung at the conclusion of each verse, carries a ready message of her freeness of manner, together with symbolic associations of sexual power and, in its goldenness, its translation into money. There were other topical allusions that gave the song its risqué appeal and Archer registered its corrupt underside by describing it as 'better fitted for Hogarth than Hicks' – Seymour Hicks, that is, the popular light comedian who co-authored and sang the song, and enjoyed a long career in musical comedy, advising thus on the necessary style for stage success: 'Your manner must be ever alert, your twinkle perpetual, and your gaiety a thing to be envied.'[27]

Twinkles, of course, came in the eye and, as in the case of Flo, were invariably naughty, if only little. Yet it was this littleness or minimalism that endlessly enlivened and refined the otherwise modest scale within which musical comedy's sexuality was bracketed. Thus a song from *The Sunshine Girl* provided instruction on the tactics of erotic display in cosmetics and dress:

> Just a little touch
> Will often be enough,
> A touch of powder puff
> Will be enough, puff, puff.
> Just a little teeny teeny tiny touch,
> Not a bit too little,
> Not a bit too much.
>
> And above the ankle
> Let a little something show,
> A little frill or so.
> What they see of you
> Will frill them frou and frou
> If it's only just a tiny touch.

The same show offered other modulations of littleness by importing Marie Lloyd's notorious music hall hit, 'Every Little Movement Has a Meaning of Its Own', no doubt with its distinctive code of gesture and body language, for it was in performance as much as its writing that musical comedy exploited the minimal to maximum effect.

Crucial here was the genre's extensive use of 'knowingness', the technique of hints and silences that left the audience to fill in the gaps and complete the circuits of meaning, thus flattering them in the sense of their own informed and superior worldliness. Archer noted 'the common knowingness' that focused on matters of the day and reinforced musical comedy's concern with being 'smart and modern', but also noted how much its attentions were exercised in sexual matters. 'In this playful gambolling on the verge of indecency', observed Archer, 'lies half the art of the 'up to date' librettist.' The other half of the art lay in its performance, particularly in the role of the comedian, a regular feature of musical comedy, and usually an import from the music halls where sexual knowingness was a highly developed second language. Crossover artists from the halls readily broke the frame of dramatic formality with their ad libs and direct address to the audience.[28] This infusion of music-hall style not only gave musical comedy a greater spontaneity and rapport with its audience than other forms of popular or music drama, but more sharply exploited the knowingness specific to the West End. Here theatres co-existed with a sub-rosa world of pornography, prostitution, and assignation that reached right up to the stage door and produced a popular mentality that continued to cast the actress as its ready accomplice.[29]

Knowingness not only sexualised musical comedy as discourse, but elasticated its imagined limits, for in the alchemy of performance a little could be made to signify a lot, not only in a diffuse sense, but in that of the fullest discharge of sexual desire – in male terms, of intercourse and orgasm, the lot. The double message is plainest in the contradictions invested in 'Tararaboomdeay', the greatest hit song of the nineties that commentators saw as emblematic of the era's popular culture.[30] George Edwardes poached the song and its tempestuous singer-dancer, Lottie Collins, for the Gaiety in early 1892. Derived from an American popular song, possibly of brothel origins, 'Tararaboomdeay' was rewritten for Collins, who was an established performer both on the halls and musical comedy stage. The accompanying dance was supposedly of her own devising, though it borrowed from the can-can and corresponded closely to the vernacular skirt dance then popular in America. Significantly, Collins would begin her performance in diffident fashion, building to a frenzied climax of high kicking and whirling petticoats, affording the hopeful glimpses of the red (Liberty's silk) drawers underneath.[31] The erotic abandon of the dance offers an extravagant contrast to the measured qualifications of the lyrics.

> A smart and stylish girl you see,
> The Belle of High Society,
> Fond of fun as fun can be
> When its on the strict QT.
> Not too young and not too old,
> Not too timid, not too bold,
> Though free as air, I'm never rude,
> I'm not too bad, and not too good.
> Tararaboomdeay etc.

The emphasis on discretion and moderation may seem no more than a disarming and disingenuous gesture, lost in the transport of the dance, yet the artist was at pains to articulate the message of the words:

Just as soon as I find myself getting a little too free on a word, I immediately tone myself down on the words that follow. My idea of the song is that it represents a young woman who is really not as bad as she seems to be, but who takes advantage of the absence of her elders to have a harmlessly lively time by herself. You will notice that I throw a good deal of emphasis on the assertion 'I'm not too good and not too bad' and the audience has to accept that.[32]

Even so, the corrective emphasis Collins was at pains to impart to her delivery of the lyrics hardly seems well-served by 'the little knowing shake of the head' reported in her performance, signalling as it did her complicity in a liberal interpretation of the song; a liberality manifest in the abandon of the dance itself which always left her physically and emotionally spent.[33] In many perceptions, no doubt, the language of littleness preserved a saving innocence and moderation, but 'Tararaboomdeay' provided the fullest expression of the genre's persistent metonymy that a little might mean the lot, a message that could thus be knowingly read into the many more muted inflections of its code, signifying a sexual plenty even as they prescribed its proper containment.

How were 'girls' to navigate these tricky waters? The songs suggest that whatever the prescribed limits of sexual expression, these were negotiable. Thus to 'flirt, frolic, and spoon' was not always just a tactic of romantic arousal to the conventional end of landing a man in marriage, but a careful deployment of sexual power in the achievement of a woman's independence that stopped short of marriage or other consummation. This constitutes both an opportunity and a dilemma, as the hit song 'The Bonnet Shop' from *The Girl from Kay's* reveals:

> When a girl of common sense
> Wants to make a competence
> It's a theme for thought intense
> How she is to make it;
> If she happens to prefer
> Starting as a milliner
> There's a bonnet shop for her –
> She has but to take it.
> But what has she to do for it,
> to do for it, to do for it?
> She has to snare a millionaire
> A Christian or a Jew for it,

> To smile and say, 'Perhaps some day,'
> And then of course to stop –
> Oh, it takes a lot before you've got
> your little bonnet shop.
>
> But remember where you are,
> Do not flatter him too far,
> For you cannot trust these money making chaps;
> Take his presents if you will
> But be sure to tell him still
> You may like him with a very big 'perhaps'.

This is sex on the instalment plan with no guarantee on either side of final payment. For the woman it involves a kind of sexual brinkmanship that can be nervously exhausting, suggesting new freedoms yet reinforcing the claims of marriage as the safer career (though marriage did not get a uniformly good press in musical comedy, and as one song proclaimed, 'I fear we shall be naughty/Till we're getting on for forty').

In musical comedy the bidding and dealing in sexual favours echo the speculative transactions of the market and the risks and rewards of the business deal. Thus sex itself is a resource or commodity like the nitrates, the oil, soap or pork that generated the spectacular new wealth of the era. The new business girl – the 'Well Regulated Girl', in the knowing phrase of popular humour[34] – seemed well set to negotiate her share, yet this bold agenda was unsettling both for its actors and society at large, as Pinero's comedy drama of 1912, *The 'Mind the Paint' Girl*, suggests.[35]

Pinero's play was set in the off-stage world of musical comedy. The title is that of the hit song, 'Mind the Paint', that has taken the heroine Lily Paradell from plebeian obscurity to fashionable stardom. Her surname suggests some glamorised brand-name product – 'Paradell Pampers Your Parts!'? – or the lily gilded, and the theme of cosmetic, fetishized and thus distanced beauty is reinforced in the song. This tells of the heroine's house – 'a very charming dwelling' – that stands in for herself and her body as a glossily finished construct that invites approach but denies contact or entry:

> When you pay my house a visit,
> You may scrutinise or quiz it
> But you mustn't touch the paint!
> Brand new paint!
> Once you smear it or you scratch it

It's impossible to match it;
so take care, please, of the paint,
Of the paint!

And I'll cry out for assistance,
Should you fail to keep your distance;
Goodness gracious, mind the paint!
Mind the paint!

Chorus:
Mind the paint! Mind the paint!
A girl is not a sinner, just because she's not a saint!
But my heart shall hold you dearer –
You may come a little nearer –
If you'll only mind the paint!
Mind the paint!

The idea of women's sexuality as an attractive yet carefully controlled commodity is carried through elsewhere in the play. Two girls from the chorus line are shown in negotiation with wealthy admirers over presents of motor cars and trips to the continent. They express their dissatisfaction with the returns to Lionel Roper, an avuncular devotee of Lily who tries to shelter her from undesirable liaisons and, as a City man, also looks after her financial interests. 'It's a shame of you, that's what it is', grumbles one of the girls to Roper; 'You went and put Lily Paradell into rubber and enabled her to make a bit.' Playing off the metaphor of the paint as second skin and protective shield, this could be read as a displaced allusion to the contraceptive, both as further protection and as an accessory to a controlled and profitable intimacy.[36] As it turns out, Lily did handsomely out of rubber, putting the returns into decorating her house. 'Mind the paint! Mind the paint! A girl is not a sinner just because she's not a saint . . .'.

The suggestion of a brokered sexuality is reinforced in Pinero's caricature of George Edwardes as the impresario Carlton Smythe. There are various hints in the text that Smythe – 'with his half-closed eyes' – was something of a pimp and a pander, and contemporaries took the play to be an attack on the musical comedy world. Defenders of 'the Guv'nor' and his interests were sufficiently disturbed to mount a first-night protest.[37]

Yet while the career of George Edwardes demonstrates the male power that controlled musical comedy and its representation of women, the male characters who appeared on his stages were in general a debilitated lot – faceless manikins immobilised in their adoration of the girl and unfitted for any work other than the transactions of the stock market, an ambiguous milieu celebrated as the fount of new fortunes, but sniped at as a less than manly occupation. The male shopwalker in *Our Miss Gibbs* is a Mr. Toplady, suggesting the further failings of effeminacy and worse. Marriage partners for the girl are mostly sturdy chaps, but the enfeeblement of the supporting male cast does echo contemporary anxieties at racial degeneration and the sense of masculinity in crisis. What is less easy to read is the extent to which such representations express the more particular and displaced self-contempt of the writers and composers of musical comedy, as marginalised members of mainstream bourgeois culture engaged in a profitable yet professionally déclassé work. The prolific librettist Adrian Ross used this pseudonym to disguise his identity as a one-time Fellow of King's, author of a history of the Merovingian dynasty, and a serious poet. Among other writers was the young P. G. Wodehouse, who wrote endlessly about witless young Englishmen, but chose to do so from his preferred new home in America.

There is space here for only the briefest attention to the other two categories under which the musical-comedy girl can be read, those of public image and private life. Certainly, leading female players were the subject of heavy media attention. The genre itself played up the importance of publicity and self-advertisement, as with Mrs. Farquahar, the maverick widow in *Our Miss Gibbs*, who sings of 'Paragraphs and Pictures' and the need to make the Sunday papers. The chorus in *A Gaiety Girl* proclaimed their pictorial potential: 'Don't we look extremely fetching/Subjects fit for artists' sketching.' This was a nice reminder of Dudley Hardy's striking posters for the show which covered the front of the theatre and, together with his programme illustrations, achieved their own celebrity. Bold in line and colour, Hardy's images of the girl were widely employed in other advertisements, denoting the close association of commerce and art in which musical comedy was an unabashed partner.[38] Together with regular press reviews of the plays, there was increasing use of the featured interview with the star, and a clutch of glossy weeklies devoted to the stage provided illustrations of productions and players. Fashion columns gave special attention to costume, discussing not only specially designed couturier gowns but the dresses that could be had ready-made in listed department stores. Boxes of chocolates and other confectionary bore prominent pictures of the musical comedy girl. More extensive visual currency came with the picture postcard, most opportunely freed from its original General Post Office monopoly in 1894 (a year after the opening of *A Gaiety Girl*). This cheap popular medium featured tinted photos of actress stars 'looking soulful under rose covered trellises'.[39] In sub-rosa counterpoint to these sentimentalised images were other pictures of 'so-called chorus girls . . . in a wide range of publications', that Archer denounced as 'a canker of the commonwealth' and 'the journalistic counterpart of the comedian's leer'.[40] Journalistic knowingness no doubt added spice to speculative items of chat about actresses' private lives. Interviews were invariably respectful, though a slightly mocking hyperbole and extensive use of reported speech also suggests a mix of resentment and condescension on the part of (male) interviewers unable or unwilling to see much beyond predictable responses to predictable questions about stage careers (wonderful), motorcars (wonderful), and marriages (more mutedly wonderful). Yet we may conjecture that the overall tone of reverent confidentiality gave readers still new to the formula a sense of privileged access to the star, thus adding significantly to her other multiple projections as actress and musical comedy girl.

These then were some of the factors that helped make this new theatrical form 'wildly popular'. But wildly popular with whom? One authority speaks of musical comedy as 'a polite and highly fashionable form of entertainment' which suggests a predominantly middle-class audience.[41] This was certainly an important element, but the centre of gravity probably lay further down the social scale. At the Duke of York's Theatre one Saturday night in 1896, Archer judged the 'great majority' of his fellow patrons to be 'young men and women who worked hard for their living at the desk or behind the counter . . . the people to whom this sort of thing was really addressed'. 'We were simply good, honest, respectable, kindly lower middle class lads and lasses [i.e. boys and girls], enjoying an entertainment exactly suited to our taste and comprehension.'[42] The stage-door johnny lying in wait for the female star was most often represented as a besotted member of the upper classes, but came from a surprising social range – it was the Sultan of Zanzibar who tried to buy Madge Saunders, but it was a rubbish collector who spent his life savings following Violet Lloyd all over the country.[43] Women performers also commanded a substantial following among their own sex, witness the millgirls devoted to Mabel Russell and the servant girls who wrote to Ada Reeve.[44] With its extensive provincial hinterland and wide media exposure, musical comedy commanded an audience that made it broadly as well as wildly popular.[45] It was indeed a bourgeois construct, but one whose middlebrow formula spoke to a new mass market.

What might be said of the further social impact of musical comedy and its reception in popular and gender consciousness? Certainly it spoke specifically to male desires in its representation of women. Its more intense techniques of glamorisation enhanced the mystique of the woman as object of the male gaze, as star, and secular goddess. At the same time its naturalised stage settings and action collapsed the allure of the distant and spectacular into the routines of a stylised but familiar version of everyday life, encouraging hopes of access in its plausible mix of the fantastic and the mundane. The rhetoric of the girl worked further wonders, generating a welcome androgyny that converted the girl into the playmate or one of the boys, transforming the stilted exchanges of conventional social address between the sexes into the chummy discourse of men relaxing with other men. Through the running allusions to the actress behind the stage persona and her implication in the freely imagined world of assignations and quasi-prostitution, the easy address of boy and girl could generate fantasies of consummation and promiscuity in a licensed naughtiness that elasticated while it did not quite break the bounds of respectability. One telling male testimony to this effect was that of Beerbohm, who talked of the Gaiety's 'innocent libertinism', speaking perhaps less as the critic than as a man who had himself been heavily girl-struck in his younger years.[46]

What was the appeal of musical comedy for women and how might it have affected their lives and relationships with men? Women's adulation of women-as-stars suggests a ready response to newly fashioned consumerist ideals of feminine beauty and success which reinvigorated traditional motifs of social mobility and happiness. In playing out its eroticised urban fairy-tale, musical comedy cast women as active and competent adventurers, which delighted them as an audience, for on Archer's evidence they were as flattered as the men in assuming the worldly identity conferred by knowingness.[47]

At the same time, the new genre privileged rewards over risks in its reassurance that you can have your cake and eat it – in this case, that a woman can entertain desire without inviting disgrace – while encouraging a greater sexual competitiveness in women's bid for men's favour. All of this can be read as a male construction of femininity – reactionary men defining their own ideal New Woman – yet however compromised, musical comedy did canvass more enterprising roles for women and may well have contributed to their growing cultural assertiveness as registered in other contemporary evidence.

Novels of the 1890s, for example, suggest that while jobs in offices and shops were invariably represented as stifling and narrow for men, for women they were more often seen as a means of escape from the even more restrictive confines of domestic bondage.[48] Although both in its own internal regime and its writing, musical comedy reproduced the subordination of women that prevailed in the shops and stores it favoured for its setting, the prominence of shop girls and other women workers as its spirited heroines may have reinforced women's appreciation of such occupations as avenues of freedom and opportunity. In New York young working women of the period were exploiting one of its favourite tropes to turn the tables on men, by being naughty but not particularly nice – *and* getting away with it, though there is nothing as yet to tie this phenomenon to the parallel success of musical comedy in America.[49] That such exploits only seemed realisable through modes of dress and self-presentation that spoke to male ideals and the further subjections of consumerism, may make any claim for advance inadmissible. Yet within a generation the evidence of oral history suggests how London working women came to use the greater range of cheap consumer goods in ways that not only followed the promptings of popular fashion and femininity, but realised a more independent sense of self.[50] Although a blithely manipulative mode, musical comedy may have stimulated such new imaginative gains for women in a more overtly sexualised identity that was no longer merely hostage to the designs of men.

CHAPTER 9

Breaking the sound barrier

This last piece is more in an older tradition of the essay as, literally, an attempt or trial exploration, rather than the finished product of sustained and systematic research. But rather than an eccentric postscript it does, I think, make a fitting coda to a body of work concerned with performance in the inherently noisy milieu of popular culture. Indeed, it seems almost obligatory (and appropriately knowing) to invert the famous envoi of another, if unlikely, music hall devotee and end not with a whimper but a bang.

It was Roland Barthes who said 'I want a history of looking', and historians have certainly obliged him in recent years. As befits a hyper-visual modern world we have all been seeing and looking with ever greater intensity and sophistication, while the other senses have been ignored. Some repair of this deficiency is already under way. Thus Corbin[1] has provided a pungent account of the role of smell in nineteenth-century France as a crucial index of social difference and strategies of control. His compatriot, Attali, has urged the recovery of another sensory dimension in his book on the political economy of music which he entitles *Noise*. I understand music as a select distillation of sound outside the category of what is examined here as noise, but join with Attali in his criticism of Western knowledge for its soundlessness. 'For twenty five centuries', he maintains, . . . it has failed to understand that the world is not for the beholding, it is for the hearing.' We must, therefore, 'learn to judge a society more by its sounds . . . than by its statistics'.[2] The Canadian composer and scholar, Schafer, has done important pioneer work in recovering some of the sounds of the past and providing the rudiments of a sonography or analytic of the sonic environment, and there is an emerging anthropology of sensory experience in all its overlapping dimensions.[3] But history and critical thought in general can, it seems, do no more than continue to look only at looking – and lament at what it sees, for vision is apprehended as the prime medium of official regulation, commercial enthralment and masculine hegemony.[4]

This essay beats the drum for noise as a significant chunk of the soundscape with determinate and resistant powers and thresholds. It begins with an elementary definition and inventory of noise, gives some consideration to its changing presence in modern history, and takes a more particular look/listen at its incidence in Victorian society. I conclude with the usual earnest injunction to historians and others to make good this glaring/blaring deficiency in their reconstruction and understanding of their own and other cultures.

I

By noise I mean a broad yet imprecise category of sounds that register variously as excessive, incoherent, confused, inarticulate or degenerate – the insistent pejorative comes with the word itself which derives from the Latin nausea, originally meaning sea-sickness. In technical terms noise can be distinguished from other sounds by its lack of any exact or discrete pitch, its lack of what musicologists identify as tone.[5] In communication theory, noise is the general villain, denoting anything that interferes with an intended signal.[6] In social terms its various properties are perhaps best summarised as disorderly. Thus to echo Mary Douglas on dirt as 'matter out of place', we might call noise 'sound out of place'. In any hierarchy of sounds it comes bottom, the vertical opposite of the most articulate and intelligible of sounds, those of speech and language and their aesthetic translation into music. In the official record such expressions 'make sense', whereas noise is nonsense. As such it may provoke a variety of responses from amusement to exasperation, from indulgence to repression, according to shifting thresholds of tolerance. Though noise is a more common feature of the soundscape than the refinements of tone, we have no natural defences to keep it out – evolution has not yet provided us with built-in earlids. As the modern world gets louder we build up other resistances. Noise therefore rarely claims our full attention until it reaches the status of nuisance or worse, and our perception of its varying gradients and inflections has been blunted.

It will be obvious enough that social noise is a matter of subjective definition. Thus for some the most elevated of sounds may abruptly degenerate. Philippe Ariès (the historian) was a devout Catholic who took to wearing earplugs during Mass so as not to be disturbed by all the 'nonsense' introduced by the Second Vatican council. More generally, as the Tower of Babel reminds us, any language can become mere noise or nonsense as one tongue among many, while for the supercilious English it is the language of the other as much as his or her manners that condemns all foreigners as noisy. Conversely, noise that is nuisance to some may be a resource and a delight to others. The clamorous 'enthusiasm' that drew hostile criticism of the first Methodists was for them a 'joyful noise' to render to the Lord, as it was later for the Salvation Army. The experience of noise may thus also differ markedly between producer and receiver.

If noise is not always a nuisance, neither is it always loud or excessive. There are soft and beguiling noises: the rustling of leaves, the swish of silks, the murmur of academic approval; or a medley of low-level sounds which dissolve into what we term, unproblematically, background noise. Noise that may be highly vexatious may register little in decibels, as in the insistent cough or sniff in a library. Yet noise that leaves its mark in history is generally more eruptive, if still not always unwelcome. In this regard I briefly list three socially defined types of noise: noise as merriment; noise as embarrassment; noise as terror.

The most obvious expression of noise as merriment is laughter, a fundamental human sound and action with a great range of inflections and valencies, but one most instinctively discharged as joy. As such, ancient authors identified laughter as a gift from the gods, a form of healing and a spiritual privilege that registered human superiority over the animals. (Indeed, in truly blessed individuals, more frequently women, laughter can be reported as attaining tone or musicality.) For today's social historian, however, laughter is likely to reverberate more forcefully and significantly in the early modern period, following Bakhtin's reconstruction of carnival and the rampant physicality of folk pleasures. For Bakhtin, laughter was a regenerative and liberating noise, a dramatic bodily effusion that challenged the repressive seriousness of official authority.[7] As he argues, laughter and the folk humour that was its stimulus were reintegrated into formal literary culture in the works of Rabelais and other Renaissance writers as a universal sign of the human condition, before again suffering devaluation as profane, vulgar and ill-mannered. In the seventeenth-century Sir Thomas Browne commended laughter as that 'sweet contraction of the muscles of the face and pleasant agitation of the vocal organs'; by the following century, Lord Chesterfield found 'nothing so illiberal and so illbred as audible laughter . . . not to mention the disagreeable noise that it makes and the shocking distortion of the face it occasions'.[8] In the early twentieth century, another philosophic voice, that of Fred Karno of Karno's army, show-man, entrepreneur, and discoverer of Charlie Chaplin, expressed his contempt for the mass pleasures he purveyed by defining laughter curtly as 'noise from a hole'.[9]

We are here nicely poised between merriment and embarrassment, for Karno's sneer conflates laughter with the lowest of bodily noises, the fart. In the determinedly orificial culture that constituted the grotesque realism of Bakhtin's early modern folk, the fart was no doubt a ready element in the battery of noises deployed in carnivalesque merriment. Indeed, in an account of seasonal feasts in Romans in southern France in the late sixteenth century it was incorporated (excorporated?) as a ritualised signal for the advent of spring, when some prodigally flatulent townsman donned a bearskin and broke out of the forest to utter the Great Fart of Dehibernation.[10] With the tightening of body protocols in modern life, the humorous licence of the fart gained from the corre-spondingly greater sense of transgressive glee, as illustrated in T. E. Lawrence's record of life in an RAF training depot in the 1920s:

and so hot are our bellies that you will not wait three minutes in this hut of fifty-four men without hearing a loud spirtle of wind from someone. 'The cry of an imprisoned fart', they call it: our surest humour, which may break the tension even of an Armistice two minutes [silence]. The very sergeants shake with laughter when one leaps out roundly.[11]

Breaking wind or its simulation remained a powerful critical sanction of the crowd, euphemized as 'blowing a raspberry'; ('raspberry tart', rhym-ing slang for a disapproving fart-like noise, theatrical slang of the late nineteenth century, as Partridge notes with his customary efficiency).[12] In a most bizarre manifestation, the flatus became sublimated as a stage act in the performances of Joseph Pujol, Le Pétomane, a major star of the *fin de siècle* Paris music hall, whose modulated (and odorless) emissions enabled him to give a variety of comic and musical impres-sions, restaging the battle of Austerlitz and blowing out a candle at two feet. Bourgeois audiences went into convulsions of delight.[13] Yet in aristocratic or court culture such looseness had long since been unpar-donable. John Aubrey noted that Edward de Vere, 17th Earl of Oxford, when first presented at court, 'making of his low obeisance to queen Elizabeth, happened to let a fart, at which he was so abashed and ashamed that he went to travell, seven yeares', incurring expenses that exhausted the fortune of his line. Here, indeed, was sound embarrass-ingly and ruinously out of place.

Not only can noise embarrass, it can terrify. 'Terror arrives first through the ear', reported J. B. Priestley,[14] observing the behaviour of the newborn, but mindful too of his service in France in the First World War when incessant artillery barrages pulverised the nerves of men in the trenches . . . hell on earth to match the confusion and uproar of Pandemonium in the biblical and Miltonic hell. German dive bombers in the Second World War were fitted with devices to maximise the noise of their descent upon a hapless enemy. 'White noise', a high pitched disorienting electronic sound, was used by British security forces in Northern Ireland in the internment period of the early 1970s for interrogation of suspects. And long before machine-made noise, the battlefield had resounded to the war cry as warriors sought simultaneously to steel themselves and terrify their foes. Human noise remains as a terror tactic in modern high-tech armies, though the instability of man-made noise can make its execution an uncertain exercise. Conscripts who underwent infantry training in Britain's National Service army will recall the occasional high comedy of bayonet practice as big civilian lads in khaki would lunge at the straw-filled dummy standing in for the foe, emitting only the merest squeak in place of the requisite blood-curdling scream. In contrast the apocalyptic noise of the Last Trump, will, we are assured, be conclusively terrifying.

But noise has often constituted a popular counter-terror and form of symbolic violence as a rudimentary and readily mobilised resource of the crowd. The licence of carnival can be converted into riot when the 'many-headed monster' gives voice in the tumult of the mob. Below the crescendo of protest and rebellion lie many other modulations of popular noise in the protean forms of 'rough music' as examined by E. P. Thompson for the eighteenth century. Rough music, 'a rude cacophony, with or without more elaborate ritual' was variously deployed to intimidate, shame or ridicule enemies of the people and offenders against traditional values. It could, claims Thompson, be 'a kind of "street theatre" . . . a conscious antiphony' that mocked the ceremonials of the state and local notables.[15] Directed at newly-weds or hapless cuckolds its strident sounds could dissolve into good humour with the gift of drink money. For other targets – overbearing officials, blacklegs, sex offenders and racial interlopers – appeasement could not be bought and the clamour of community hostility drove victims to flight or suicide in this replay of ancient rituals that drove out evil spirits by their noise.

Rough music was excessive, repetitive and sustained noise, combining high spirits with a sadistic edge. Laughter, shouts, chanted obscenities and animal noises – *katzenmusik* in its continental manifestations – these were supplemented with home-made percussion from the beating of pots and pans and the rattle of stones in kettles, together with many other similarly improvised sounds.[16] Tools of a trade might also serve, as in the relatively benign ceremony of 'ringing in' which marked rites of passage in engineering workshops in mid-Victorian England. Rough music was even tuned to a nicety by butcher's men who ground their cleavers to produce a peal of bell-like notes when struck against marrow-bones in a wedding serenade.[17] But whatever the ritual envelope within which rough music was contained, to outsiders it remained the sound of disorder.

The potential for disturbance and disorder in noise is eloquently registered in its significant absence, for silence frequently denotes not only its opposite but its suppression by countervailing powers, while as the extensive list of well-worn modifiers – stony, pregnant, knowing, eery, hushed, forbidding, deathly – demonstrates, silence is highly qualitative and rarely empty. The dialectics of noise and silence have long patterned domestic politics and the socialisation of the young. 'Children', according to the Victorian injunction, 'should be seen but not heard'. In a more manipulative mode, the Greek male exalted muteness in his mate: 'Silence', Sophocles piously intoned, 'is a woman's glory.' In the Roman household, peace and stability were further secured by the *silentiarius*, a slave whose job it was to regulate the noise of other slaves, while Julius Caesar introduced some of the earliest anti-noise legislation.[18]

Silence, we might say, is the sound of authority – generational, patriarchal and formidably inscribed in the regimes of church and state. As reverence not untinged with fear, it was the necessary tribute to the Christian god, institutionalised in Christian monastic orders as the condition of piety and learning. The mix of surveillance and silence that policed the Victorian child was replicated in the forbidding disciplines of the penitentiary. Bedlam – the noise of derangement – was quarantined in the asylum as a further exercise in what Foucault called the political technology of the body. (He planned to write an archaeology of silence.)[19] 'Silence in court!' is still the command that exacts deference before the law while hearing is the traditional medium of obedience, the word itself derived from the Latin to obey. Yet silence is not necessarily an absence of sounds, but rather an act. As such it can also register disengagement, evasion and resistance, a resource of the 'secret people' of history and a cloak for mischief and conspiracy in a muted struggle for the sign; its power to frustrate authority in the most authoritarian of regimes is recognised in the punishable offence categorised by the British Army as 'dumb insolence'.

But neither noise nor silence can be wholly defined in isolation, for the other senses manifestly overlap in the generation and reception of sound, colluding or colliding, reinforcing or confusing. Sound itself is, of course, palpable, impacting physically on the body as vibration. Studies with newborns reveal that babies will both look at and try to grab a sound in a darkened room.[20] Sound may be felt distinctly as a compelling rhythm or an intrusive shock. In non-Western cultures this may be co-opted as part of a perceptual synthesis to induce a heightened consciousness. Thus the ritual drum beat of the Huicholes of Mexico produces blotches on the skin and reinforces the hallucinatory effect of peyote.[21] Modern drug users seek a similar conjunction in more private ways, but artists and cultural entrepreneurs have also long sought an aesthetic syncretism. Baudelaire's theory of *correspondances* from the mid-nineteenth century made explicit this ancient literary quest for an effective mix of sensations, and was carried further by the Symbolist poets and the Dadaists. The latter – who explored the aesthetics of noise as 'bruitism' – also experimented with what they termed 'op-tophonetics'.[22] Wagner's music dramas were perhaps the most grandiose formal exercises in synaesthetics, but sound was also used to reinforce sight in a range of popular modes that constituted an emergent age of spectacle. Victorian fairy plays combined ingenious sound effects with the release of perfumes to enhance the sense of the magical. By the 1950s three-dimensional movies were to make cinematic action almost tangible. Bob Hope joked that soon the movie would be projected on to your choc ice so that you could suck it, the kind of effect more plausibly articulated in Aldous Huxley's utopian satire *Brave New World* (1932), where the masses are enthralled by Saturday night visits to the 'feelies'.

The inherent promiscuity of the senses recurs in everyday as well as literary or artistic language. We report 'chilling sights' and 'hard looks'; voices variously grate or caress, while the eyes of lovers conventionally reach out to touch or devour the adored other. The visible becomes audible in dramatic ways. Dr. Johnson noted the imaginative victory of the blind man who conceived of scarlet as 'the clangour of the trumpet'; the repressed intensity of mental pain is caught graphically and unforgettably in Edouard Munch's picture, *The Scream*.

In all of this, noise is a common compound signifier, most often of excess or vulgarity. Colours are represented across all the senses, but register most forcibly in terms of noise, as in 'a riot of colour' or 'screeching yellow'. The social translation is plainest in charges of vulgarity in dress, even though this may well be the desired effect, as with the Edwardian music hall performer Kate Carney, of whom it was reported 'She wears such loud dresses, you can't hear the busses go by'. At the other end of the scale, a patrician *homme d'affaires* in Kingsley Amis's *The Russian Girl* (1994) is impeccably attired in 'an almost inaudibly wonderful greyish suit'. In passing we may note that intellectuals can be perceived as redundantly or offensively audible in what they do, if not in how they dress; thus Stuart Hall records wryly that much theoretical talk might be more appropriately termed theoretical noise.[23]

II

The foregoing account suggests certain categories and dimensions under which a general history and critique of noise might be attempted. Perception and response are largely subjective and culturally determined, affected by specific temporal and locational proprieties. Important too is the changing function of hearing and sound within the combinations and hierarchies that pattern sensory perception as a whole in the sense ratio of any particular era or culture. Changes in means, type and volume in the production of noise and other sensations constitute another significant related factor.

The early-modern period in the West was an era of crucial shifts in the sensorium. Though now under some reconsideration[24] the generally accepted account maintains that pre-modern societies were predominantly phonocentric, privileging sound over the other senses in a world of mostly oral-aural communication. The advent of typographic print in the fifteenth century gave a dramatic new saliency to visual perception. Lucien Febvre, one of the few historians to attend to sensory perceptions in the mentalities of the past, declared the sixteenth century 'the age of the ear', even as the ear was being increasingly displaced by the eye. In the following century Descartes declared war on the senses in general, rescuing only sight as necessary for science and technology. His pursuit of a new cerebral purity would greatly restrict intellectual interest in sensory consciousness and affect.[25]

Though the democratisation of print did much to erode the caste-like status of the scholar-administrators who had previously enjoyed exclusive control over the visual word and its scribal transmission, literacy remained a prime index of social distinction and the 'great tradition' that marked off gentle from common-folk. Beyond literacy lay the higher achievement of a literary sensibility, as another social marker and prime component of a sophisticated code of upper-class manners, and it was through print that aspirant gentlefolk took instruction in the proper conduct of all the senses, their bodily deployment and containment.

A key text in this regard was the courtly bestseller, *On Civility in Children*, written by Erasmus in 1530 and dedicated to a prince's son.[26] It encouraged new standards in outward bodily propriety, urging improvement in eating, cleaning and blowing practices. 'The sound of farting', declared Erasmus, 'is horrible . . . especially of those who stand on elevated ground'. Yet as classical epigrams warned, to suppress wind was dangerous. Erasmus solved the contest between ancient medicine and modern manners by suggesting that a cough might hide the embarrassing noise. Rising thresholds of social shame and bodily delicacy soon disallowed this subterfuge and fear of farting in public was to cause acute psychic and physiological distress among the Victorian bourgeoisie. What had been to Erasmus a healthy if disconcerting solecism was now pathologised as 'the green disease'. Good manners and civility also required that the blowing of the nose be muted, while slurping, lip-smacking and snorting during eating were proscribed in the earliest of conduct manuals as boorish, rustic and disgusting. Readings of the body in Renaissance drama suggest that the mouth, long suspect in the Christian ascetic tradition as the gaping hole that demanded to be filled, was now stigmatised as the anus in the face whose noises were vulgar effusions that required new forms of civil custody.[27]

The control and selection of sound was articulated in other ways in the definition of genteel identity. An admissible sound, music, was now reformed as an aesthetic value, its purified sounds purposefully addressed to a silent concert audience in an assertion of bourgeois autonomy.[28] Unwelcome sounds were separated out. The bourgeoisie followed the nobility in the partition of domestic space and the construction of private inner rooms away from the clamour of petitioners, attendants and servants. Some permissible upper-class noises were redistributed on gender lines. In the 1750s, Lord Lyttelton instructed his architect to provide 'a room of separation between the eating room and the drawing room, to hinder the ladies from the noise and talk of the men when left to their bottle'.[29] Thus the hallooing of the hunting field might still find a licensed echo in an eighteenth-century dining room, though meetings of the sexes dictated a more restrained tone. Elegance extended outwards as well as in, with private grounds duplicating the secure and subdued enclosures of the private house, a noble ideal miniaturised in innumerable Victorian suburban villas and back-gardens, hopeful invocations of rural peace and strongholds against the sounds of the city.

Of course, the countryside had its own disturbing sounds. Early humanists disdained it precisely because of its 'agitation and noise'.[30] By the eighteenth century such disturbances had dissolved in the wishful conceits of a revived pastoralism; conversely, as with thunder, they might be exalted as part of the awesome panoply of the sublime in the Romantics' new worship of an elemental nature. But it was the accumulating sounds of the modern city that now most clamantly registered as noise and nuisance and worse.

Thus Southey, who applauded the sublime in nature, was appalled by the infernal tumult of metal manufacture in industrial Birmingham – 'the noise is beyond description' – while his fellow Lake poet, Wordsworth, was transfixed by 'the deafening din' of London's streets. With its historically exceptional size, London had long since attracted anti-urban jeremiads: Pope, writing from his garden retreat in Twickenham in the 1720s, had characterised the capital as a new Babel. London soon became less the exception than the prime exemplar of an accelerated urbanisation, generating images that resonated with the common experience of a modernising world. The city as noise-maker recurs in Dickens as the brute bearer of challenge and anxiety. It is a 'monster roaring in the distance', signalling 'the rising clash and roar of the day's struggle'.[31]

The monstrous roar of the big city came from the simple but overwhelming fact of its great concentration of people, people now more frequently on the move, engaged in new forms of work and leisure, and dependent on new technologies.[32] It was the street that bore the human overflow and its competing voices, including still the traditional cries of itinerant street sellers and balladeers. Wheeled and horse-drawn transport increased: metal rims and hooves pounded on stone sets, accompanied by the incessant crack of the whip and shouts of the drivers, aggravations to the ear that contributed greatly to the *weltschmerz* of Arthur Schopenhauer. Residents on London's main thoroughfares complained that traffic drowned their dinnertime conversation.[33] From the 1840s the railway train added its hoots and rattles to the mêlée. The most haunting and sentimental of sounds for the many migrants and exiles of this world, they were a considerable irritation to Thoreau as a short-haul migrant at Walden Pond.[34] By the end of the century the motor car had added its lacerating note to the sounds of modernity, described by Robert Musil as a kind of sonic shrapnel: 'a wiry noise, with single barbs projecting, sharp edges running along it and submerging again and clear notes splintering off – flying and scattering'.35

Urban noise was a major challenge to poets and writers struggling to realise a modernist aesthetic. For some it could be naturalised in the relatively benign mode of the urban pastoral. For others it remained intractable, its nervous staccato rhythms at odds with the harmonious regularities of conventional forms. Proust seemed both enamoured and repelled: his narrator likened Paris street noises to a morning symphony, but the author himself retreated to the insulation of his famous cork-lined room. Baudelaire was the key figure who strove rather to integrate the dissonances of the modern city with the poetic voice in his new genre of the prose poem, an uneasy exercise whose tensions and disfigurements became a constitutive element in aesthetic modernism.36 Similar fraught negotiations between traditional principles of harmony and metre and the dissonances of modern experience made a more sensational impact in avant-garde concert music, climaxing in the riotous reception of Stravinsky's *Rite of Spring* in Paris in 1913. In vernacular music, jazz exploited noise as musical shock and met with similar resistance, its sounds further stigmatized as those of an unacceptable modernity returned to barbarism at the hands and voices of the low Other, a racial as well as a class threat.37

In addition to the new traffic, other forms of mechanisation assaulted modern ears. Dickens complained at 'the shrill, screaming, ceaseless whirr' of the speculative builder's circular saw; he could hear 'the innocent planks screaming as the merciless teeth eat into their very marrow'.38 The factory concentrated the noise of machinery, obliterating the song and sociability of traditional craft production and adding to the sensory deprivation that Marx claimed had animalised and alienated the industrial proletariat. Factory noise increased over the century as mechanisation expanded and the tempo of production accelerated, punctuated by the alarms of steam whistles, hooters and sirens summoning and dismissing workers. 'Isn't the noise of the machines awful?' was the question put to a young factory worker at the start of the twentieth century. 'Yes', he replied, 'not so much when they are going on as when they stop'.39

Together with mass production came mass entertainment. Greater numbers amplified the noise of public leisure in the great cities. At the Crystal Palace in the late 1880s George Gissing recorded the uneasy juxtaposition of two cultures as the sounds of modern improvement from massed choirs and orchestra competed with the noise of older carnivalesque pleasures in the bars and tearooms: 'This great review of the People' dissolved in an 'imbecile joviality' incessant with 'hee-hawing laughter . . . the yell, the cat-call, the ear-rending whistle'.[40] From another perspective it was modernity that was the villain as its mechanised leisure forms displaced the authentic popular voice and its self-made pleasures. A Communard returning to Paris from exile in 1913 was appalled by the invasive proliferation of gramophones:

vomitoria . . . which spewed out a mishmash of cafe-concert songs, brass bands and the lavender water of the opera-comique like so much liquid manure . . . silence raped by the most tyrannical of noises . . . Yet another result of excessive mechanisation. After getting rid of the human arm, it's now subjugating the human voice![41]

The gramophone was not suppressed, but attempts were made to control other noises in the nineteenth-century city. In England the new police moved on the street traders and charged ballad singers and other itinerant musicians with vagrancy. In Haussmann's Paris, street traders were among the poor and marginal classes banished from the rebuilt city centre and their cries were thus lost. To reduce noise, main thor-oughfares in both cities were finished in macadam or asphalt though the improved surfaces encouraged greater traffic which, in now familiar fashion, cancelled out the gains. Straw was laid down outside hospitals and the homes of the sick to muffle the din.

But amid the growing clamour the dominance of visual perception was steadily reinforced. The new urban milieu was comprehended in primarily visual terms through the metaphors of mapping and reading the city, while the relationships of its anonymous inhabitants were, as Simmel noted, monitored more by the eye than the ear.[42] From the mid-century, the modern consumer was constructed and enthralled by spectacle and display in the new optics of the exhibition and department store, a voluntarily self-regulating citizen, subject to novel powers of surveillance in both seeing and being seen, 'the ineluctable modality of the visual', as Joyce recorded of modern Dublin.[43] At the same time other sensations were subordinated: obtrusive smells receded as the city and the body were deodorised, while modern manners reduced contact by touch among the multiplying crowd.

Plainly, however, the stimuli of sound and noise grew; what remains much less clear is their relative saliency. Members of modern societies are said to be limited in their differentiation among sounds in consequence of the dulling effect of their environment and a pre-emptive sensitivity to the visual. Perhaps Simmel was correct in claiming that the central struggle for the new city dweller was 'to remain audible even to himself', absorbed in an inner consciousness that was the refuge of the besieged modern subject. Yet it can be argued that physical and psychic survival in the city demanded a more finely tuned and active alertness to its many layers of sound. In the 1890s pedestrians complained against the bicycle as a 'noiseless vehicle', unlike other traffic in giving no warning of approach. It may be instructive here to extend to hearing Benjamin's proposition that distraction has superseded contemplation as the habitual state of modern visual reception. Thus we may understand modern street noise as a montage of sounds with shocklike juxtapositions of dissimilars and constant dissolves met and mastered by a newly developed sonic subconscious.[44]

III

Before concluding I want to listen a little closer to noise in Victorian England as an index of identity and difference, their interactions and contests. What we hear amid its many and various inflections is a continuing struggle between refinement and vulgarity. Freedom from noise became a defining characteristic of the English bourgeoisie, as much a mark of their nationality as their class. Observing their aversion to living in the heart of cities compared to their continental peers, the architect E. T. Hall noted in 1901: 'In England the mistress of the house and family generally like to have the opportunity of being quiet: "a quiet evening at home" is what one constantly hears . . .'.[45] Quietness came with the privacy and seclusion of the suburban house and garden, yet this was far from always secure. In side-by-sides there were complaints at neighbours' daughters whose exercises on the piano – 'that formidable instrument' – carried through thin party walls.[46]

Much more disturbing was the threat of invasion by the noise-makers in person, a perennial anxiety now fixated on the modern proletarian crowd as the embodiment of mass culture in an advancing democracy. In the 1860s Matthew Arnold demonised a newly enfranchised populace as 'marching where it likes, meeting where it likes, bawling what it likes, breaking what it likes'. Other commentaries conflated noise with mobility and destruction. Thus the novelist Ouida deplored the excursion trains that vomited forth . . . throngs of millhands, cads and their flames . . . tawdry, noisy, drunken . . . tearing through woods and fields like swarms of devastating locusts . . . yelling loathsome creatures . . . exact emblems of the vulgarity of the age . . . vulgarity very likely to live and multiply and increase in power and extent.[47]

C. F. G. Masterman, Liberal politician and reformer, spoke for the middle-class elector in characterising 'Democracy' as first and foremost 'loud-voiced', a truculent proletarian figure whose cry of havoc might yet bring apocalypse to the suburbs, 'surging up the little pleasant pathways, tearing down the railings, trampling the little garden; the "letting in of the jungle" upon the patch of fertile ground redeemed from the wilderness'.[48]

It was the city street rather than the garden which remained the front line in the contest over noise and the alleged struggle between civilisation and barbarism. Here in the mid-century, the eccentric polymath Charles Babbage conducted a strenuous campaign to purge London of itinerant musicians, their numbers greatly increased by an influx of foreigners (a further offensive feature). Setting himself up as the champion of intellectual labour against the mindless mob – 'no man having a brain ever listened to street musicians' – Babbage strove to enlist police and Parliament against this 'torture', more blackmail than entertainment, and 'an additional 25% income tax on brain workers'. A Commons bill of 1864 supported by a petition of other prominent writers and intellectuals proved too feeble to protect the empurpled Babbage from his serenaders, and crowds gathered outside his house to enjoy his gratifying irascibility. There were plenty of Londoners who delighted in street music as music, but here it was perceived and delivered as noise, a popular demonstration whose function as extortion and calculated nuisance qualify it as a latter-day charivari, a variation on rough music 'in conscious antiphony' to the protests of a class superior and his challenge to the freedoms of the people.[49] In his essay 'Civilisation', John Stuart Mill attributed the advance of society's refinements to the 'keeping as far as possible out of sight, not only actual pain, but all that can be offensive or disagreeable to the most sensitive person'.[50] While nineteenth-century civilisation was increasingly effective in quarantining distressing sights, it was plainly less successful in its acoustic policing, a reminder of the more intrusive properties of noise as sound: it goes round corners; it goes over as well as through walls; it surrounds and envelops and is not easily localised.

Noise as resource and resistance could be deployed in house and home as well as the street. Servants countered the submissiveness of their role with offstage laughter and slammed doors; significantly, the climax of Ibsen's *A Doll's House* comes from the sound of a heavy door slamming shut, as Nora walks out on her husband. Other resonant domestic noises include those of the working-class mother in a London tenement who rattled the plates at Sunday dinnertime whether she had food or not for her family – to convince other tenants that she had.[51]

Working-class life and culture were inherently and inescapably noisier, at work, at home and in a generally more congested environment. A middle-class passer-by alarmed at the raised voices issuing from a working-class pub asked his companion if murder was going on. 'No', answered the more worldly of the two, 'only an argument'. Responses to a culture in which you had to raise your voice to be heard included the solitary hobby or the autodidact's pursuit of nature, but there remained a positive relish for noise of a distinctly emphatic kind (a parallel perhaps to the popular appetite for strong tastes – pickles and 'rusty' bacon – that provided stimulus amidst a dietary monotony). Thus virtuoso step-dancing was among the most popular of entertainments in Victorian pubs and music halls, judged and applauded for the precise tattoo of steel shod feet on a cellar door:

> He jumps, and his heels knack and rattle,
> At turns of the music so sweet;
> He makes such a thundering brattle,
> The floor seems afraid of his feet.[52]

If noise was part of the general envelope of popular sociability, it came also with discernible gradients and inflections. In his work on theatre audiences in Birmingham in the middle years of the century, Doug Reid usefully identifies three categories.[53] First, there is 'normal noise' arising from the theatre's function as a social centre (phatic as opposed to emphatic). Secondly, there is 'ritual noise, marking the course or significance of the evening', the pattern of applause or censure, most insistently articulated in the orchestrated interventions of the claque. Finally, suggests Reid, there is 'the objectionable noise of disorder and deliberate disturbance' denoting the riotous breakdown rather than the ritual punctuation of the performance. (Buford's observer-participant account of English soccer thugs suggests similarly distinct registers.)[54] All such reverberations had long been part of audience behaviour among all classes, but its persistence among Birmingham's artisans into the mid-Victorian era was a hold-out against a broadly mounted campaign to make the theatre and other popular assemblies respectable. The theatre claque that had practised with the complicity of managements was redefined as a nuisance and outlawed, together with other demonstrative behaviour. Music halls were also closely policed, but popular practice was such that at the close of the century they could still be characterised as 'insurrections of noise', an impression confirmed by those on stage: as the performer Arthur Roberts recalled, 'It was all uproar whether they liked you or not.' He noted too that when music hall artists were first called upon to perform in private drawing rooms before the Prince of Wales and other affluent patrons, they were greatly unnerved by the respectful silence that greeted their appearance.[55]

Noise or its suppression reinforced the differences of gender as well as class. Bravura noise-making was an essential signal of masculine identity for much of this era. From a theatre in Cincinnati in the 1830s Frances Trollope reported 'every man seemed to think his reputation as a citizen depended on the noise he made'.[56] The swell songs that were the first big hits of the British music hall in the 1860s and 1870s triumphalised noise: 'A noise all night, in bed all day, and swimming in champagne!'; 'Come on boys, let's make a noise!'[57] Such loudness can be erotically exciting; 'sophomore boys', concludes Ackerman from a later sample, 'are all decibels and testosterone'.[58] Noise-making continued to be the sign of male release, particularly among the young, though now more likely to conflict with tighter disciplines on public behaviour and norms of manly restraint prescribed by respectability.[59]

Socialised as the quieter if not silent sex, women were likely to be more aurally alert than men.[60] Noise unsexed women, witness the derogatory labelling of feminists who protested in public against the Contagious Diseases Acts in the 1860s as 'the shrieking sisterhood' with its associations of hysteria as a uniquely female pathology.[61] There was more tolerance on the popular stage, though its noisy women could threaten a disquiet greater than that normally licensed and contained as entertainment, particularly as gender politics grew more fraught. In the 1890s the singer-dancer Lottie Collins achieved huge success with 'Tararaboomdeay!', a song that proved to be the hit of the century. The daughter of a step-dancer, Collins styled herself 'The Girl on the Ran Dan Dan', an historic onomatopoeia from the vocabulary of rough music. The song, accompanied by a frenziedly erotic dance, was delivered with explosive emphasis on the title word; 'its blatancy and penetrating shrillness', said a contemporary historian, was 'the voice of the crowd asserting itself'.[62] Consonant with the social psychology of the day, bourgeois fear of the crowd was now suffused with the male fear of woman, the creature of extremes who expressed herself in crescendo.[63]

IV

Babel, pandemonium, bedlam – noise has not had a good press. Nor do we need to turn to history to be reminded that it continues to disturb us physically and socially. Too much unwanted noise is known to raise blood pressure, increase stress and lower the immune system, yet in North America noise pollution is doubling every decade and ten per cent of the population has some form of hearing impairment. Fifty-five per cent of the industrial workforce in Western countries are exposed to levels of noise that threaten damage to hearing.[64] Muzak, or piped background music, is an insidious irritant to many, while the astounding power of electronic amplification boosts entertainment noise still higher. The decibel reading of a discotheque or rock concert is in the same range as a nearby thunderclap, as a latterday equivalent of the music hall crowd answer the call to 'Shout, Shout, Let It All Out!'. Dick Hebdige characterised punk rock as noise to specify its challenge to the symbolic order and what Althusser termed 'the teeth gritting harmony' of the ruling ideology.[65] Miniaturised technology spreads other contemporary 'insurrections of noise' throughout public space; not just the ghettoblaster but the overflow from the Walkman's individual earphones becomes a kind of sonic exhibitionism that forces others to listen to what should be private and undisclosed. (For today's young, it seems, silence is leaden rather than golden, while the noise they generate is for them as much insulation as intrusion.) Meanwhile, the ritual noises inside the soccer stadium (as latterly the cricket field) provide a forceful echo of the claqueurs of Victorian popular theatre, accompanied in some cases by the violent takeover of the streets.

Such disturbances are likely to bring out the Babbage that lurks within all of us engaged in the mostly silent and anguished exercise of thinking and writing. Indeed, the language of noise still does conspicuous duty in denoting intrusions into scholarly endeavour, witness Stuart Hall's striking description of the impact of feminism on the Birmingham Centre: 'It broke in, made an unseemly noise, seized the time, crapped on the table of cultural studies'.[66] Yet noise is a specific historic phenomenon that can signify more than outrage. It is an expressive and communicative resource that registers collective and individual identities, including those of nation, race and ethnicity which I have been unable to consider here; it is a ready form of social energy with the power to appropriate, reconfigure or transgress boundaries; it converts space into territory, often against the social odds.

Historians habitually invoke the 'sights and sounds' of an era as necessary objects of their enquiry, but the latter rarely receive more than lip service. Of course, if we are to listen as well as look to any real effect we must learn how to listen more acutely as well as how to reconstruct the listener in history and identify its more reliable earwitnesses.[67] We must attend not only to noise but to the whole range of sounds that enliven the past and contribute to its changing sensory orders. There are obvious methodological difficulties to such a project. But there is a viable technical language in the making,[68] and it is not inconceivable that the electronics of virtual reality may yet provide us with a reconstructed soundtrack to accompany our learned effusions, together with the scratch and smell panels and other undreamed of devices that would truly enable historians and others to 'come to their senses'. What I offer for the present is a modest call to attention, a well mannered shout to echo what James Joyce called 'the black crack of noise in the street'.

Notes

INTRODUCTION SOCIAL HISTORY, CULTURAL STUDIES AND THE CAD

1 Patrick Joyce, 'The end of social history?', *Social History*, 20 (January 1995), pp. 73–91. This follows a number of other contributions to the journal on the state of the discipline. See also Adrian Wilson (ed.), *Rethinking Social History: English Society 1570–1920 and Its Interpretation* (Manchester University Press, 1993).

2 From among several accounts of the 'cultural turn', see Richard Johnson, 'Culture and the historians' in J. Clarke, C. Critcher and R. Johnson (eds), *Working Class Culture: Studies in History and Theory* (London, 1979), pp. 41–74; Stuart Hall, 'The emergence of Cultural Studies and the crisis of the Humanities', *October*, 53 (Summer 1990), pp. 17–23. See also Patrick Brantlinger, *Crusoe's Footprints: Cultural Studies in Britain and America* (London, 1992).

3 Tony Bennett, 'Popular Culture and "the turn to Gramsci"' in Bennett, C. Mercer and J. Woollacott (eds), *Popular Culture and Social Relations* (Milton Keynes, 1986), xi–xix; Gareth Stedman Jones, *Languages of Class: Studies in English Working Class History* (Cambridge University Press, 1983). For an exemplary critical overview of these and other developments, see Raphael Samuel, 'Reading the signs', *History Workshop Journal*, 32 (Autumn 1991), pp. 88–109, and 33 (Spring 1992), pp. 220–51; helpful for this period is Christopher Kent, 'Victorian social history: post Thompson, post Foucault, postmodern', *Victorian Studies*, 40 (Autumn 1996), pp. 97–133.

4 Joyce, 'End of social history?', *Democratic Subjects: The Self and the Social in Nineteenth Century England* (Cambridge, 1994), p. 6.

5 Geoff Eley, 'Playing it safe. Or: how is social history represented? The new *Cambridge Social History of Britain*', *History Workshop Journal*, 35 (Spring 1993), pp. 206–20.

6 Kelly Boyd and Rohan McWilliam, 'Historical perspectives on class and culture: conference report', *Social History*, 20 (January 1995), pp. 93–100.

7 Peter Bailey, *Leisure and Class in Victorian England* (2nd edn, London, 1987).

8 E.g., F. M. L. Thompson, 'Town and city', in Thompson (ed.), *Cambridge Social History of Britain*, 3 vols (Cambridge University Press, 1990), vol. 1, pp. 1–86.

9 Judith R. Walkowitz, *City of Dreadful Delight: Narratives of Sexual Danger in Late Victorian London* (London, 1992). For similar treatments of the nineteenth-century city from literary scholars, see Christopher Prendergast, *Paris and the Nineteenth Century* (Oxford, 1992) and Deborah Epstein Nord, *Walking the Victorian Streets: Women, Representation and the City* (Ithaca, 1995). David Harvey, *The Condition of Postmodernity* (Oxford, 1991) draws on the classic essays by Baudelaire and Simmel on contemporary city life in his typology of modernity. Such conditions were not exclusive to the great capital cities, see below, Chapter 6.

10 Bailey, 'Jazz at the Spirella: Coming of age in Coventry in the 1950s', in Becky Conekin, Frank Mort and Chris Waters (eds), *Moments of Modernity?: Reconstructing Britain, 1945–1964* (London, 1998).

11 Bernice Martin, *A Sociology of Contemporary Cultural Change* (Oxford, 1981); Richard Hoggart, *The Uses of Literacy* (Harmondsworth, 1958); Michel de Certeau, *The Practice of Everyday Life* (Berkeley, 1988).

1 THE VICTORIAN MIDDLE CLASS AND THE PROBLEM OF LEISURE

1 'Philosophy of Amusement', *Meliora: Quarterly Review of the Social Sciences*, 6 (1864), pp. 193–210.

2 Stanley Parker, 'The sociology of leisure: progress and problems', *British Journal of Sociology*, 26 (1975), pp. 91–107. For the current sociology of leisure, see Chris Rojek, *Decentring Leisure: Rethinking Leisure Theory* (London, 1995). For the broader history of leisure in this period, see Peter Bailey, *Leisure and Class in Victorian England* (2nd edn, London, 1987), and for a review of the historiography, see Bailey, 'Leisure, culture and the historian: Reviewing the first generation of leisure historiography in Britain', *Leisure Studies*, 8 (1989), pp. 107–27.

3 Peter Borsay, *The English Urban Renaissance: Culture and Society in the Provincial Town* (Oxford, 1989).

4 James Clegg (ed.), *Autobiography of a Lancashire Lawyer* (Bolton, 1883), pp. 23–125.

5 Walter Besant, 'The amusements of the people', *Contemporary Review*, 45 (March 1884), pp. 342–53. For recollections of childhood in the thirties and forties, see Alfred G. Gardiner, *Life of Sir William Harcourt* (London, 1923), I, p. 10: 'Our earliest life was made for all of us very monotonous, and no variety or amusements of any kind were provided . . . we never had a holiday.'

6 For the Ashworths, see Rhodes Boyson, *The Ashworth Cotton Enterprise* (Oxford, 1970), p. 39. General improvements in the middle-class standard of living and the increasing range of satisfactions it allowed are charted in J. A. Banks, *Prosperity and Parenthood: A Study of Family Planning Among the Victorian Middle Classes* (London, 1954).

7 Henry Mayhew, 'The Cockaynes in Paris', in *Shops and Companies of London and the Trades and Manufactories of Great Britain* (London, 1865), I, pp. 81–4.

8 T. H. S. Escott, 'A foreign resident', *Society in London* (London, 1886), pp. 166–7.

9 Ralph H. Mottram, *Portrait of an Unknown Victorian* (London, 1936), pp. 120, 125. See also Edwin Hodder, *Life of Samuel Morley* (London, 1887), pp. 430–43.

10 'Our rising generation', *Saturday Review*, 26 March 1864, pp. 375–6. See also 'Our modern youth', *Fraser's Magazine*, 68 (1863), pp. 115–20.

11 *Daily Telegraph*, 8–21 January 1869. See also, Banks, *Prosperity and Parenthood*, pp. 195–196.

12 Providing one was not in search of diversion on a Sunday - Hippolyte Taine found himself ready for suicide after his first Sabbath in London – there was no gainsaying the vitality of the metropolis as an entertainment centre; witness the tributes of the theatre manager Stephen Fiske, *English Photographs by an American* (London, 1869), pp. 127–8.

13 T. H. S. Escott, *Social Transformations of the Victorian Age* (London, 1897), p. 14.

14 See Bailey, *Leisure and Class*, Chapter 3.

15 Anthony Trollope, *The New Zealander* (Oxford, 1972), pp. 150–70.

16 Byron Farwell, *Burton: A Biography of Sir Richard Francis Burton* (New York, 1963), p. 249.

17 *The Times*, 8 October 1861, p. 6. In the forties, the paper's retention of the antique form, holydays, was out of conviction that the Church should resume its benevolent role in popular recreation; by the sixties, however, the usage was heavily ironic.

18 'Holiday Plans', *Saturday Review*, 16 June 1866, pp. 714–15. See also, 'Happy Holidays', *Saturday Review*, 7 April 1877, pp. 411–12.

19 Leonore Davidoff, *The Best Circles: Women & Society in Victorian England* (Totowa, New Jersey, 1973), pp. 42–6.

20 Matthew Browne, *Views and Opinions* (London, 1866), p. 280.

21 James Ewing Ritchie, *Days and Nights in London* (London, 1880), pp. 182–95; Ouida [Marie Louise de la Ramée], *Views and Opinions* (London, 1895), pp. 333–4. See also, Harold Perkin, 'The "social tone" of Victorian Seaside Resorts in the North West,' *Northern History*, 11 (1976 for 1975), pp. 180–94.

22 Matthew Arnold, *Culture and Anarchy* (Cambridge, 1966), p. 105.

23 For the sense of reduced opportunity in middle-class life and the economic background, see Banks, *Prosperity and Parenthood*, pp. 12–14, 129. For improvements in working-class wages and the increase in social (and more visible) drinking which contributed to middle-class ire, see A. E. Dingle, 'Drink and Working-Class Standards in Britain, 1870–1914', *Economic History Review*, n.s., 25 (November 1972), pp. 608–21.

24 *The Times*, 14 April 1873, p. 7. See also, 'On strike and on spree', *Meliora: Quarterly Review of the Social Sciences*, 9 (1866), pp. 323–33; W. R. Greg, 'The proletariat on a false scent', *Quarterly Review*, 123 (January 1872), pp. 251–94.

25 J. Keningale Cook, 'The labourer's leisure', *Dublin University Magazine*, 22 (1877), pp. 174–92.

26 Walter Besant, 'The people's palace', in *As We Are and As We May Be* (London, 1903), p. 55.

27 Nels Anderson, *Dimensions of Work: The Sociology of a Work Culture* (New York,

1964), p. 90. See also Alasdair Clayre, *Work and Play: Ideas and Experience of Work and Leisure* (London, 1974), pp. 43–4.

28 For the Puritan roots of this suspicion, see Michael Walzer, *The Revolution of the Saints: A Study in the Origins of Radical Politics* (New York, 1972), pp. 199–231; for a long-standing hostility to plebeian leisure, see Robert W. Malcolmson, *Popular Recreations in English Society, 1700–1850* (Cambridge, 1973), pp. 5–12.

29 In 1871 there was an outcry against the pigeon shooting at the fashionable Hurlingham Club; see *The Times*, 21 June 1871, p. 9 and Henry Haweis, *Thoughts For the Times* (London, 1872), p. 300. 'With some illustrious exceptions there is not enough real education among our upper classes, or we should not find them gawping over sports that the middle class have long abandoned as brutal and undignified.'

30 Bailey, *Leisure and Class*.

31 William C. Lake, 'Leisure time', in John E. Kempe (ed.), *The Use and Abuse of the World* (London, 1873), I, pp. 39–56.

32 George Dawson, 'The morals of travelling' (1876) in *Everyday Counsels* (London, 1888), pp. 124–39.

33 James Ewing Ritchie, *The Night Side of London* (London, 1857), pp. 132–8.

34 Robert W. Dale, 'Amusements', *Good Words*, 8 (1867), pp. 329–335. See also James Baldwin Brown, *The Gregarious Follies of Fashion: An Address to the Younger Generation* (London, 1876).

35 Greville J. Chester, *The Young Man at Rest and at Play* (Sheffield, 1860).

36 Samuel Earnshaw, *The Tradition of the Elders* (Sheffield, 1860). Sheffield was also the home of one of the most militant clerical opponents of the theatre, Thomas Best; see his *Love of Pleasure* (Sheffield, 1862).

37 John Morley, 'The capacity for pleasure' in *Studies in Conduct* (London, 1867), pp. 1–10. Morley thought that considerations of time, cost, and professional ambition operated as a more forceful limitation than religion: 'Just as we have ceased to believe that pleasure is fatal to salvation people start up to persuade us that it is fatal to getting on in the world.'

38 'What attitudes should Christian Churches take in relation to amusements', *Congregationalist*, 8 (July-August 1879), pp. 543–56, 650–65. This question was also debated on several occasions at the annual Anglican Church Congress. For reports of these particular sessions see *The Times*, 11 October 1873, p. 7 (Bath); 14 October 1871; p. 6 (Nottingham); 11 October 1877, p. 11 (Croydon); 4 October 1878, p. 11 (Sheffield); 2 October 1880, p. 9 (Leicester). See also the report of an Anglican conference on temperance which considered the matter, in 'Amusement', *All The Year Round*, 16 (1876), pp. 133–136.

39 Kempe, *Use and Abuse*, 1, p. 57.

40 John E. Clarke, *Plain Papers on the Social Economy* (London, 1858); Reverend Harry Jones, 'Recreation', *Good Words*, 22 (1881), pp. 43–9.

41 W. H. Miller, *The Culture of Pleasure* (London, 1872), pp. 64–5.

42 In a sermon 'Sports and Pastimes', in Kempe, *Use and Abuse*, 1, pp. 57–74, Archbishop Thomson expressed the fear that the Church was losing contact

with culture at every level. The Church did talk about generating its own recreations, but the Nonconformists seemed more active in this direction, see Kenneth Young, *Chapel: Joyous Days and Prayerful Nights* (London, 1972).

43 Haweis, *Thoughts for the Times*, p. 288. This was not, as elsewhere it might have been a veiled allusion to prostitution or sexuality. Haweis echoed other clergymen in noting how often he was 'in collision' with the public on the issue of leisure.

44 Haweis, 'Music and Morals', *Contemporary Review*, 16 (1870), pp. 89–101.

45 Peter W. Clayden, 'Off for the Holidays: the rationale of recreation', *Cornhill Magazine* 16 (September 1867), pp. 315–22. The annual vacation, perhaps because it took up such a conspicuous slab of time, seemed to call for some special justification. See also, J. W. Kaye, 'On Holidays', *Cornhill Magazine*, 2 (August 1860), pp. 242–251: 'Holidays and How to Keep Them', *Leisure Hour*, 6 July 1872; 'Happy Holidays', *Saturday Review*, 7 April 1877, pp. 411–12. Leslie Stephen, 'Vacations', *Cornhill Magazine*, 20 (August 1869), pp. 205–14, was exceptional in his advocacy of 'the negative pleasure of indolence'.

46 The dictum is quoted, for example, in William B. Jerrold, *London: A Pilgrimage* (London, 1872), p. 162. For other examples of the periodicals' treatment of leisure and its rationale, see 'The Philosophy of Amusement', *Meliora: Quarterly Review of the Social Sciences*; W. Lucas Collins, 'Our Amusements', *Blackwood's Magazine*, 100 (1866), pp. 698–712; 'Amusements', *Bow Bells*, n.s., 4 (21 February 1866), p. 83: 'Leisure', *Saturday Review*, 23 March 1867, pp. 360–61; 'Pleasure Taking', *Saturday Review*, 4 June 1870, pp. 729–30; George J. Romanes, 'Recreation', *Nineteenth Century*, 6 (September 1879), pp. 401–424; Herbert Spencer, 'The Gospel of Recreation', *Popular Science Monthly*, 20 (1882), pp. 354–59; James Paget, 'Recreation', *Nineteenth Century*, 14 (December 1883), pp. 977–88. There is a further sampling in Kathleen Blake, *Play, Games and Sport: The Literary Works of Lewis Carroll* (Ithaca, 1974), pp. 180–212.

47 Many of the diversions of high society were also represented as a duty, if on different grounds; see Davidoff, pp. 39–40, 57. For the increasing justification of holidays on medicinal grounds, see Banks, pp. 94–5, and L. M. Hubbard, *Where to Spend a Holiday* (London, 1887).

48 For a sardonic cartoon treatment drawn from the pages of *Fun*, see James F. Sullivan, *The British Workingman by One Who Does Not Believe in Him* (London, 1878).

49 'Happy Holidays', *Saturday Review*, 7 April 1877, pp. 411–12.

50 William F. Rae, *The Business of Travel* (London, 1891). See also, comments on hotel architecture in M. Bence-Jones, 'Lavish Hospitality and Fun: Scarborough III', *Country Life*, 155 (2 May 1974), pp. 1062–5.

51 Escott, *Social Transformations*, p. 197. On this new common ground, accomplishment in sport became a potential social escalator for the middle-class schoolboy; see 'Sports and Studies', *Saturday Review*, 30 August 1873, pp. 268. The *Saturday Review* noted the increased operation of the more general

phenomenon of social emulation in the 'eager attempts of persons to wedge themselves into a slightly higher stratum of the social formation by seizing on the favourite amusement of that higher level' ('Pathos of Pleasure Seeking', 29 August 1874, p. 271). For the Hurlingham episode, see note 29. See also John Lowerson, *Sport and the English Middle Classes 1870–1914* (Manchester, 1993); P.H. Hansen, 'Albert Smith, the Alpine Club, and the Invention of Mountaineering in Mid-Victorian Britain, *Journal of British Studies*, 34 (1995), pp. 300–24.

52 Cynthia L. White, *Women's Magazines, 1693–1968* (London, 1970), pp. 75–6.

53 Alphonse Esquiros, *The English at Home* (London, 1861–3), II, pp. 52–63, noted 'this tendency of the English to form groups through the attractions of certain pleasures', and argued their importance in reconciling the competing needs of self and society. For the function of voluntary associations in the formation of class identity, see R. J. Morris, *Class, Sect and Party: The Making of the British Middle Class, Leeds 1820–1850* (Manchester, 1990).

54 Asa Briggs, *Mass Entertainment: The Origins of a Modern Industry* (Adelaide, 1960); Charles Wilson, 'Economy and society in Late-Victorian Britain', *Economic History Review*, 18 (August 1965), pp. 183–98.

55 For a note of their sighting in considerable numbers in the Isle of Wight in the late seventies, see Henry James, *English Hours* (London, 1905), p. 232.

56 *The Times*, 8 October 1886, p. 10. Among the new generation of prosperous and respectable Methodists who emerged in the nineties, the religious act itself was interpreted as a form of entertainment. See Robert Currie, *Methodism Divided: A Study in the Sociology of Ecumenicalism* (London, 1968), pp. 131–138.

57 Grant Allen, 'The New Hedonism', *Fortnightly Review*, 55 (March 1894), pp. 377–392.

58 William E. H. Lecky, *The Map of Life* (London, 1899), p. 64.

59 Charles F. G. Masterman, *The Condition of England* (London, 1909), p. 15.

60 For some more recent examples, see Lowerson, *Sport and the English Middle Classes*; Morris, *Class, Sect and Party*; Leonore Davidoff and Catherine Hall, *Family Fortunes: Men and Women of the English Middle Class 1780–1850* (London, 1987); Janet Wolff and John Seed, (eds.), *The Culture of Capital: Art, Power and the Nineteenth Century Middle Class* (Manchester, 1988).

2 A ROLE ANALYSIS OF WORKING-CLASS RESPECTABILITY

1 G. Best, *Mid-Victorian Britain, 1851–1875* (London, 1971), pp. 256–63.

2 B. Harrison, *Drink and the Victorians: The Temperance Question in England, 1815–1872* (London, 1971), pp. 24–5, 195, 366–7, 394–5. See also, T. W. Laqueur, *Religion and Respectability: Sunday Schools and Working-Class Culture, 1780–1850* (New Haven, 1976).

3 T. R. Tholfsen, *Working-Class Radicalism in Mid-Victorian England* (London, 1976), pp. 17–18, 216–21. See also his article, 'The intellectual origins of mid-Victorian stability'. *Political Science Quarterly*, 86 (1971), pp. 57–91. Thol-

fsen defines respectability in a limited and almost pathological sense as the narrowly emulative sub-bourgeois mentality that followed from an uncritical subordination to middle-class values, but his radical working man epitomises the contrary element in working class social consciousness. His usage echoes Engels, for whom respectability connoted submission and pusillanimity. It was, wrote the latter, 'the most repulsive thing' and 'bred into the bones of the workers'. Engels to Sorge, 7 December 1889, in *Marx-Engels on Britain* (Moscow, 1953), pp. 522–3. For subsequent attention to the function of respectability see F. M. L. Thompson, *The Rise of Respectable Society: A Social History of Victorian Britain 1830–1900* (London, 1988).

4 G. Crossick, 'The Labour aristocracy and its values: a study of mid-Victorian Kentish London', *Victorian Studies*, 19 (March 1976), pp. 301–328; C. Reid, 'Middle-class values and working-class culture in nineteenth-century Sheffield: the pursuit of respectability', in S. Pollard and C. Holmes, (eds.), *Essays in the Economic and Social History of South Yorkshire* (Sheffield 1976), pp. 275–95. For a somewhat later period, see R. Q. Gray, 'Styles of Life, the "Labour Aristocracy" and Class Relations in Later Nineteenth Century Edinburgh', *International Review of Social History*, 18 (1973), pp. 428–52. See also his 'The Labour aristocracy in the Victorian class structure', in F. Parkin (ed.), *The Social Analysis of Class Structure* (London, 1974), pp. 19–38 and *The Labour Aristocracy in Victorian Edinburgh* (Oxford, 1976), ch. 7. For a running debate on the issue of a labour aristocracy see the contributions of H. F. Moorhouse, Alastair Reid, and Gregor McLennan in *Social History*, 3 (1978), pp. 61–82, 347–61; 4 (1979), pp. 481–93; 6, (1981), pp. 71–81, 229–33 respectively.

5 Tholfsen's characterisation of the mid-Victorian city as 'a stable culture in a state of inner tension' is apt; see his *Working-Class Radicalism*, p. 11. For such tension at its most explosive, see R. Price, 'The other face of respectability', *Past and Present*, no. 66 (February 1975), pp. 110–32.

6 Fitzjames Stephen, 'Anti-Respectability', *Cornhill Magazine* 8 (September 1863), pp. 282–93. G. M. Young, *Portrait of an Age* (Oxford, 1936), p. 25, catches the right tone: 'Respectability was at once a select status and a universal motive. Like Roman citizenship, it could be indefinitely extended, and every extension fortified the state.'

7 From an address to the TUC, in 1871, recorded in *Occasional Papers of the Working Men's Club and Institute Union*, no. 20 (January 1872).

8 Such were the staple observations of the 'then and now' genre in social commentary, e.g. J. M. Ludlow and L. Jones, *Progress of the Working Class, 1832–1867* (London, 1867), and J. Kay-Shuttleworth, 'The laws of social progress, as illustrated in the history of the manual Labour Class in England', in *Thoughts and Suggestions on Certain Social Problems* (London, 1873), pp. 3–39.

9 Bolton Chronicle, 18 March 1871. See also evidence from Liverpool in 'Street Ruffianism', *Porcupine*, 11 November 1865, J. E. Ritchie, *Days and Nights in London* (London, 1880), pp. 49–50; C. Keene, *Our People* (London, 1881), p. 155.

10 Most historians of mid-Victorian England have their favourite horror stories of the roughs on the rampage, e.g., Best, *Mid-Victorian Britain*, p. 203: G. Kitson Clark, *The Making of Victorian England* (London, 1962), p. 62.

11 See above, n.5. For other relevant studies see L. L. Shiman, 'The Band of Hope Movement: respectable recreation for working-class children', *Victorian Studies*, 18 (September 1973), pp. 49–74, and 'The Birstall Temperance Society', *Yorkshire Archaeological Journal*, 46 (1974), pp. 128–39. See also, R. J. Morris, 'The history of self-help', *New Society*, (3 December 1979), on the Woodhouse temperance community in Leeds, and R. Moore, *Pit Men, Preachers and Politics: The Effects of Methodism in a Durham Mining Community* (Cambridge, 1974), pp. 140–55. Among the late Victorian and Edwardian working-class social and cultural distinctions weakened somewhat, and the line between respectables and non-respectables conformed less exactly to the craft and income differentials between the skilled artisans and the rest. See Gray, *Labour Aristocracy*, p. 120, and cf. S. Meacham, *A Life Apart: The English Working Class, 1890–1914* (London, 1977), pp. 26–9.

12 E.g., F. M. Leventhal, *Respectable Radical: George Howell and Victorian Working-Class Politics* (Cambridge, Mass., 1971); B. Harrison and P. Hollis, 'Chartism, Liberalism and the life of Robert Lowery', *English Historical Review*, 82 (July 1967), pp. 503–35.

13 Robert Park, 'The city: suggestions for the investigation of human behaviour in the urban environment', and Louis Wirth 'Urbanism as a way of life', reprinted in Richard Sennett (ed.), *Classic Essays on the Culture of Cities* (New York, 1969), pp. 91–130, 143–64. For the urbanisation of consciousness as part of the more general process of modernisation, see P. L. Berger, B. Berger, and H. Kellner, *The Homeless Mind: Modernisation and Consciousness* (Harmondsworth, 1974), pp. 62–77.

14 H. Gerth and C. Wright Mills, *Character and Social Structure* (New York, 1964), p. 120. In general I have adopted the concept of role employed by these authors: 'technically, the concept "role" refers to (1) units of conduct which by their recurrence stand out as regularities and (2) which are oriented in the conduct of other actors', pp. 10–11. See also, M. Banton, *Roles: An Introduction to the Study of Social Relations* (London, 1965).

15 On observability, see the important article by R. K. Merton, 'The Role-Set: problems in sociological theory', *British Journal of Sociology*, 8 (1957), pp. 112–20. See also Gerth and Mills, *Character and Social Structure*, pp. 122–24; R. Frankenberg, *Communities in Britain: Social Life in Town and Country* (Harmondsworth, 1966), pp. 240–2.

16 W. L. Sargant, *Economy of the Labouring Classes* (London, 1857), p. 353.

17 W. C. Lake in J. E. Kempe, (ed.), *The Use and Abuse of the World* (London, 1873–5), I, pp. 39–56. On the greater independence of leisure roles, see Banton, pp. 33–34 and A. Southall, 'An operational theory of role', *Human Relations* 7 (February 1959), pp. 17–34.

18 Thomas Wright in A. Halliday (ed.), *The Savage Club Papers* (London, 1868), pp. 214–30.

19 The phrase was used by an early champion of rational recreation, R. A. Slaney, MP, in evidence to the Select Committee of the House of Commons on Public Walks, *Parliamentary Papers*, 15 (1833), p. 9, and the theme found common expression among reformers, e.g. S. W. Jevons, 'Methods of social reform: amusements of the people', *Contemporary Reviews* (1878), pp. 499–513.

20 *Bolton Chronicle*, 14 July 1866 and 26 May 1877. See also P. H. J. H. Gosden, *The Friendly Societies in England, 1815–1875* (Manchester, 1961).

21 See the comments of Shaw and William Morris on lecturing engagements at clubs, quoted in J. Taylor, *From Self-Help to Glamour: The Working Man's Club, 1860–1972* (Oxford, 1972), p. 59, and F. Rogers, *Labour Life and Literature: Some Movements of Sixty Years* (London, 1913), pp. 96–7.

22 G. Stedman Jones, 'Working-class culture and working-class politics in London, 1870–1900: notes on the remaking of a working class', *Journal of Social History*, 7 (1974), pp. 476ff.

23 R. Roberts, *The Classic Slum: Salford Life in the First Quarter of the Century* (Harmondsworth, 1973), pp. 22–4.

24 Jones, 'Working-Class Culture', pp. 471–2.

25 Peter Bailey, *Leisure and Class in Victorian England* (London, 1987), pp. 83–4.

26 Report of a Wesleyan Sunday School Convention, *Bolton Chronicle*, 8 April 1876.

27 Members of the Christ Church football club in Bolton deserted their patron, Rev. J. F. Wright, four years after he had formed the club; they walked out of a meeting in the church school rooms, crossed the road to the Gladstone Hotel and reconstituted themselves the Bolton Wanderers. P. M. Young, *Bolton Wanderers* (London, 1961), p. 19.

28 This capability would seem to be part of a general expressive repertoire – consider the impersonations of Mayhew's beggars – though a case has been made that the dramaturgical resources of today's working class are severely limited by early socialisation patterns, see J. Ford *et al.*, 'Functional Autonomy, Role Distance and Social Class', *British Journal of Sociology* 18 (December 1967), pp. 370–81.

29 E. Goffman, 'Role Distance', in *Encounters: Two Studies in the Sociology of Interaction* (Harmondsworth, 1972), pp. 75–134.

30 *Ibid.*, p. 101.

31 So well have I taken Young's advice to heart that this phrase has been resonating in my skull for years: unfortunately the vibrations have shaken it loose from the anchorage of an exact reference. May I offer, with apologies, that it is recorded somewhere in J. M. Knapp (ed.), *The Universities and the Social Problem* (London, 1895).

32 'Our Working People and How They Live', *Good Words* 2 (1870), pp. 246–55.

33 M. Wolff and C. Fox, 'Pictures from the Magazines', in H. J. Dyos and M. Wolff (eds.), *The Victorian City*, 2 vols., (London, 1973), vol. II, pp. 559–82.

34 See the illustrations 7 and 9 in Best, *Mid-Victorian Britain*, following p. 142.

35 J. Keningale Cook, 'The labourer's leisure', *Dublin University Magazine*, 90 (1877), pp. 174–92; T. Heywood, *A Memoir of Sir Benjamin Heywoood* (Manchester, 1863), p. 201.

36 L. Bayliss, *The Old Vic* (London, 1926), pp. 267–8.

37 *Club and Institute Journal*, July 1875–February 1878.

38 J. B. Brown, *First Principles of Ecclesiastical Truth* (London, 1871), p. 278.

39 See also, J. K. Walton, 'Residential amenity, respectable morality, and the rise of the entertainment industry: the case of Blackpool, 1860–1914', *Literature and History*, 1 (March 1975), pp. 62–78.

40 Servants practised a wide range of disruptive tactics behind the increasingly ill-fitting mask of occupational deference, to the considerable disquiet of their employers. See L. Davidoff, 'Mastered for life: servant and wife in Victorian and Edwardian England', *Journal of Social History*, 7 (1974), pp. 406–28; P. Branca, *Silent Sisterhood: Middle-Class Women in the Victorian Home* (London, 1975), pp. 30–4, 56, 57; T. McBride, *The Domestic Revolution: The Modernisation of Household Service in England and France, 1820–1920* (London, 1976), pp. 25, 109, 120. Similar forms of worker resistance and unpredictability in other fields of employment deserve attention.

41 L. James, *Print and the People, 1819–1851* (London, 1976), p. 80, points out that the use of reductionist dichotomies – town and country, moral and immoral – had already become a basic literary technique by the 1840s and a central mental structure for organising experience in the modern city.

42 Ritchie, *The Night Side of London* (London, 1857), pp. 132–8. For the tension created by the claims of two incompatible ideals of urban living; individual privacy and public accountability – see D. Olsen, 'Victorian London: specialisation, segregation, and privacy', *Victorian Studies*, 17 (March 1974), pp. 265–78.

43 For the nature and extent of middle-class fears on this count, see Jones, *Outcast London: A Study in the Relationships Between Classes in Victorian Society* (Oxford, 1971). Working-class respectability may have been to the new self-regarding middle class patriciate what plebeian deference had once been to the squirearchy. For a suggestive study of deference as a form of social interaction, see Howard Newby, 'The Deferential Dialectic', *Comparative Studies in Society and History*, 7 (1975), pp. 139–64.

44 G. Gissing, *The Nether World* (London, 1903), p. 69.

45 Herbert J. Gans, 'Urbanism and suburbanism as ways of life: a re-evaluation of definitions', in A. M. Rose (ed.), *Human Behaviour and Social Processes* (London, 1962), pp. 625–48.

46 David Cannadine, 'Victorian cities: how different?', *Social History*, 2, (January 1977), pp. 457–82. See also, Olsen. For historians who have used the Chicago School's work to define the urban context in Victorian England, see Jones, *Outcast London*, and H. E. Meller, *Leisure and the Changing City, 1870–1914* (London, 1976).

47 See A. Poole, *Gissing in Context* (London, 1975), pp. 31–59; L. S. Saposnik, *Robert Louis Stevenson* (London, 1974), pp. 88–101.

48 See Derek Hudson, *Munby, Man of Two Worlds: The Life and Diaries of Arthur J. Munby, 1828–1910* (London, 1972). See also J. R. Ackerley, *My Father and Myself* (New York, 1975), for an Edwardian double life.

49 Raphael Samuel, ' "Quarry Roughs": Life in Headington Quarry, 1860–1920: an essay in oral history', in Samuel (ed.), *Village Life and Labour* (London, 1975), p. 242.

50 Cf. E. P. Thompson, 'Patrician society, plebeian culture', *Journal of Social History*, 7 (Summer, 1974), pp. 382–405, for the dramaturgy of class encounter in the previous century.

51 T. Burns, 'Leisure in industrial society', in M. A. Smith, S. Parker, and C. Smith, *Leisure and Society in Britain* (London, 1973), pp. 50–53. See also, D. Wrong, 'The oversocialised conception of man', *American Sociological Review*, 26 (April 1961), pp. 183–193, and Goffman on 'inner autonomy' in 'The nature of deference and demeanour', in *Interaction Ritual* (Harmondsworth, 1972), p. 58. Michel Crozier, *The World of the Office Worker* (Chicago, 1971), pp. 212–13 is also suggestive on this point: 'The multiplicity of alienations possible, and the incoherence which naturally emerges as a result, tend to liberate the individual. The more the choices offered allow him a diversity of combinations, the more easily he can escape the determinism of his group, of his condition, and even of his society.' For a wider examination of the various tactics employed by modern man to counter or subvert the oppressive reality of daily life, see S. Cohen and L. Taylor, *Escape Attempts: The Theory and Practice of Resistance to Everyday Life* (1978; Harmondsworth, 1992).

3 'ALLY SLOPER'S HALF-HOLIDAY': COMIC ART IN THE 1880S

1 For the publishing history, see D. Gifford, *Victorian Comics* (London, 1976), who attempted its revival in the same year, following similar unsuccessful exercises by others in the 1920s and 1940s.

2 H.G. Wells, *Tono-Bungay* (London, 1909), p. 35; E. R. Pennell, 'The modern comic newspaper: the evolution of a popular type', *Contemporary Review*, vol. 50 (October 1886), pp. 509–23; A. Anderson, *The Man Who Was H. M. Bateman*, (London, 1982), p. 10. David Kunzle, *The History of the Comic Strip: The Nineteenth Century*, (Berkeley, 1990), has since pronounced Ally Sloper 'Europe's first really enduring serialised comic strip and cartoon character'.

3 An almost full run of *Ally Sloper's Half-Holiday* can be consulted at the Newspaper Division of the British Library, Colindale, and there is some related ephemera at Bloomsbury. For a selection of the cartoons, see W. G. Baxter, *Fifty Sloper Cartoons* (London, 1888).

4 See Peter Bailey, *Leisure and Class in Victorian England* (2nd edn., London, 1987).

5 'The characteristic tensions being produced were not so much, perhaps, between class and class as between the individual and the mass, and between the individual's inner life and his outward behaviour.' H. J. Dyos and D. A. Reeder, 'Slums and suburbs', in Dyos and M. Wolff, *The Victorian City*, (London, 1973), vol. 2, p. 360, speaking of Victorian London.

6 See G. Stedman Jones, 'Working-class culture and working-class politics in London 1870–1900', *Journal of Social History*, 7 (Summer 1974), pp. 460–508. S. Hall, 'Notes on Deconstructing the Popular' in R. Samuel (ed.), *People's History and Socialist Theory*, (London, 1981), pp. 227–40, reinforces the idea of a crucial break in the eighties. For the press in particular see R. Williams, *The Long Revolution* (Harmondsworth, 1965), pp. 225–9 and 'Press and popular culture in historical perspective' in G. Boyce, J. Curran and P. Wingate, (eds.), *Newspaper History from the Seventeenth Century to the Present Day*, (London, 1978), pp. 41–50.

7 For significant engagement with such questions, see P. Joyce, *Visions of the People: Industrial England and the Question of Class, 1840–1914* (Cambridge, 1991).

8 The great age of graphic satire from Hogarth to Cruikshank has attracted significant attention, see M. D. George, *Hogarth to Cruikshank: Social Change in Graphic Satire* (London, 1962); R. Paulson, *Popular and Polite Art in the Age of Hogarth and Fielding*, (London, 1979). On the comic strip in particular, the magisterial authority is Kunzle, *The Early Comic Strip: Narrative Strips and Picture Stories in the European Broadsheet, c. 1450–1825* (Berkeley, 1973) and *The History of the Comic Strip: The Nineteenth Century* (Berkeley, 1990). See also M. Wolff and C. Fox, 'Pictures from the magazines', in Dyos and Wolff, vol. 2, pp. 559–82; T. M. Kemnitz, 'Matt Morgan of *Tomahawk* and English Cartooning, 1867–1870', *Victorian Studies*, vol. 19, (September 1975), pp. 5–34; L. James, *Print and the People*, (London, 1976), (and his 'Cruickshank and Early Victorian Caricature', *History Workshop*, no. 6, (Autumn 1978), pp. 107–20). On the importance of art for the historian, see R. Samuel, 'Art, Politics and Ideology', in the same issue, pp. 101–6 and N. Green and F. Mort, 'Visual representations and cultural politics', *Block*, no. 7 (1982), pp. 59–68.

9 G. Simmel, 'The sociology of the senses: visual interaction', in R. E. Park and E. W. Burgess (eds), *Introduction to the Science of Sociology*, (Chicago, 1921), pp. 356–361.

10 Kunzle, *Comic Strip*, pp. 316–22. For other treatments of the comic press of the period see B. Hillier, *Cartoons and Caricatures* (London, 1970); J. Geipel, *The Cartoon: A Short History of Graphic Comedy and Satire* (London, 1972); G. Perry and A. Aldridge, *The Penguin Book of Comics* (Harmondsworth, 1975); D. Gifford, *Victorian Comics* (London, 1976); V. Neuburg, *Popular Literature: A History and a Guide*, (Harmonsworth, 1977). But a full account of *ASHH*'s cultural descent would need to consider the influence of papers like *Day's Doings* in the 1870s which pioneered pictorial glamour. In the matter of editorial style and address to a similar audience, the *Half-Holiday*'s most obvious progenitor is *The Town*, 1837–42, see D. J. Gray, 'Early Victorian scandalous journalism: Renton Nicholson's *The Town*', in J. Shattock and M. Wolff (eds), *The Victorian Periodicals Press: Samplings and Soundings* (Leicester, 1982), pp. 317–48.

11 *Buxton Advertiser*, 16 June 1888; F. R. Boase, *Modern English Biography*, (London, 1965 reprint). Baxter was succeeded by W. F. Thomas who kept closely to his predecessor's image of Sloper.

12 Kunzle, 'Marie Duval and Ally Sloper', *History Workshop*, no. 21 (Spring 1986), pp. 133–40.

13 W. Tinsley, *Random Recollections of an Old Publisher* (London, 1900), vol. 1, pp. 267–8; Boase, *English Biography*; letter from Charles Ross Jr. to *Sunday Express*, 16 April 1950. I am grateful to Victor Neuburg for letting me read a photocopy of the latter's unpublished MS, 'Brief Notes on Ally Sloper', (1951), in which he records his father's annoyance at Dalziel's presumption as self-styled founder of the *Half-Holiday*.

14 G. and E. Dalziel, *The Brothers Dalziel* (London, 1901), pp. 272–328; F. G. Roe, *Victorian Corners* (London, 1968), pp. 82–7.

15 C. Kent, 'The idea of Bohemia in Mid-Victorian England', *Queen's Quarterly*, vol. 53, Autumn 1973, pp. 360–9; R. G. G. Price, *A History of Punch* (London, 1957), p. 20.

16 A. J. Mayer, 'The lower middle class as historical problem', *Journal of Modern History*, vol. 54, September 1975, pp. 417–18. See also, F. Thompson, *Lark Rise to Candleford*, (Harmondsworth, 1973), p. 535: 'They (the lower middle class) had not sufficient sense of humour to originate it, but borrowed it from music hall turns and comic papers'. Cf. G. Crossick (ed.), *The Lower Middle Class in Britain* (London, 1977), which offers some necessary qualifications to the conventional passive-pathetic typology of this group.

17 E. G. Salmon, 'What the working classes read', *Nineteenth Century*, vol. 20, July 1886, pp. 108–17.

18 Hillier, p. 61; M. Summers, *The Galanty Show: An Autobiography* (London, 1980), pp. 42–43; conversation with Fred Roe, 28 June 1980; Ross, Jr., 'Brief Notes', thought middle and upper class readers were more loyal to the paper when cheaper rivals proliferated in the nineties.

19 Letters to *Daily Telegraph*, 18 December 1965 and 3 January 1966 recalling Sloper's popularity.

20 Evidence for circulation figures is very scarce and invariably unreliable for this period; advertising lists habitually used peak figures as if they were averages or spoke of the number of 'readers' rather than the copies sold, according to A. Lee, *Origins of the Popular Press* (London, 1976), p. 178. Sales of *ASHH* were probably of the same order as those of the other mass penny weeklies of the 1880s, Newnes' *Tit Bits* and Harmondsworth's *Answers*, see R. D. Altick, *The English Common Reader: A Social History of the Mass Reading Public, 1800–1900*, (Chicago, 1957), appendix C, pp. 391–6.

21 P. J. Keating, *The Working Classes in Victorian Fiction*, (London, 1971), pp. 13–18; James, *Print and the People*, pp. 145–51.

22 Mrs. Sloper's choice of tipple is significant. Though beer was a vulgar drink, there would have been a certain social cachet to Bass Ale, for the pale, sparkling, lighter-bodied ale was preferred by the upper classes and was just reaching the popular market where it challenged the primacy of darker, more heavy-bodied beers. Bass was the first really national brewer and the red triangle was the first trade mark to be registered under the Act of 1875.

See B. Spiller, *Victorian Public Houses* (Newton Abbott, 1972), pp. 24, 71. For Sloper's taste in drink, see below, n. 31.

23 E. Moers, *The Dandy: Brummell to Beerbohm* (London, 1960), p. 215: A. Smith, *The Natural History of the Gent* (London, 1847), p. 2. For the heavy swell on the halls, see below, chapter 5.

24 Stedman Jones, 'The "Cockney" and the Nation, 1780–1988' in D. Feldman and Jones (eds) *Metropolis London: Histories and Representations since 1800* (London, 1989), pp. 272–324.

25 Pennell, is good on stock comic types. See also, A. Nicoll, *Masks, Mimes and Miracles: Studies in Popular Theatre* (London, 1931); E. Welsford, *The Fool: His Social and Literary History* (London, 1935); J.F. Wilson, 'Comic Papers of the Victorian Era', *Sell's Dictionary of the World's Press* (London, 1902), pp. 67–8; J. Greig, introduction to C. Veth, *Comic Art in England* (London, 1930); Roe.

26 Kunzle, *Comic Strip: Nineteenth Century* p. 319 on the impact of Baxter's makeover.

27 Ross pioneered the new style, see his *Wicked London: A Good Guide* (London, 1881) where he plays host to the grandsons of the original Tom and Jerry who have rather a disappointing time of it in the new tourist's London. For the antithesis between East and West Ends, see Keating, and Stedman Jones, *Outcast London* (London, 1971). Battersea was built up from the 1850s and was a mixed district, including model houses for workers and a fashionable enclave. To readers of the period its main associations may have been Clapham Junction with its suburban rail network, and Battersea Dogs' Home – Sloper lived opposite the latter.

28 For a more restrained version of Gladstone democratised, see the painting by John Morgan from 1885, *One of the People – Gladstone in an Omnibus*, reproduced in C. Wood, *Victorian Panorama: Paintings of Victorian Life* (London, 1976), p. 218.

29 Roe, *Victorian Corners.*

30 For the authentic dismay of the tyro at first being encased in a dress suit, see A. Bennett, *The Card*, (Harmondsworth, 1975), pp. 13–15: 'he had innocently thought that you had only to order a dress suit and there you were. He now knew that a dress suit is merely the beginning of anxiety: Shirt! Collar! Tie! Studs! Cuff-links! Gloves! Handkerchief!'

31 For much of its history, gin had been stigmatised as the most vulgar and ruinous of drinks but its status was beginning to improve from the 1870s with the introduction of unsweetened or London dry gin which was considered a healthier and more refined drink, see J. Watney, *Mother's Ruin: A History of Gin*, (London, 1976), pp. 70–1. As with his wife's bottle of Bass, Sloper's choice in drink suggests a certain sophistication.

32 H. Taine, *Notes on England* (London, 1872), pp. 37–44. False noses were part of the traditional Derby Day dress. Sloper's version of the great popular festival almost certainly played off associations with Frith's *Derby Day*, and his other set pieces probably carried echoes of well known paintings from high art.

33 A similar suggestion is coded in the name of Tootsie's best friend (and frequent consort of her father), the actress Tottie Goodenough. Tottie was eighties slang for a high class prostitute, while the surname suggests a plausible imitation of respectability. Tootsie eventually succumbed to convention in 1903 when she married Lord Bob to become the Countess of Wandsworth, the fulfillment of the romantic motif of the earl and the girl so beloved of contemporary showbiz. On these themes see also chapter 8.

34 F. Willis, *London General* (London, 1953), pp. 98–195.

35 R. Ellman, *James Joyce* (New York, 1959), p. 716.

36 R. Church, *Over The Bridge* (London, 1955), p. 221.

37 On uncle figures see P. Willmott, *Adolescent Boys of East London* (London, 1966), pp. 72–3 and V. W. Garratt, *A Man in the Street* (London, 1946); at the other end of society, see M. Green, *Children of the Sun: A Narrative of Decadence in England after 1918* (London, 1976), p. 76.

38 The swell or toff – from immaculate to dilapidated – remained a common type in music hall and film into the interwar years. But Sloper's own potency was abruptly deflated by the Great War. In his wartime cartoons he is much diminished and marginalised as a superannuated voyeur, watching the sexual exploits of servicemen on leave from the sidelines. Since the young were showing themselves to be well-able to die, so they were allowed to demonstrate their ready knowledge of how to live.

39 Cf. Jones, 'Working Class', p. 497.

40 Ally Sloper still lives in the comic one-man show performed in his name by Chris Harris of the Bristol Old Vic, an appropriately outrageous impersonation prompted in part by this essay.

4 BUSINESS AND GOOD FELLOWSHIP IN THE LONDON MUSIC HALL

1 *Era*, 5 December 1869. On Holland himself, see *Era*, 13 December 1890 and 4 January 1896; *Blackpool Gazette*, 3 December 1895. (Place of publication is London unless stated otherwise.)

2 D. Kift, *The Victorian Music Hall: Culture, Class and Conflict* (Cambridge, 1996), pp. 1–15, provides the most up to date review of music hall history and historiography, as well as the first booklength scholarly treatment, which includes substantial attention to the provinces; see also, P. Bailey, 'Making sense of music hall' in Bailey (ed.), *Music Hall: The Business of Pleasure*, (Milton Keynes, 1986), the introduction to a collection of scholarly essays and the companion volume to J. S. Bratton (ed.), *Music Hall: Performance and Style*, (Milton Keynes, 1986). Other more recent work includes D. Russell, 'Varieties of life: the making of the Edwardian music hall' in M. R. Booth and J. H. Kaplan, *The Edwardian Theatre: Essays on Performance and the Stage*, (Cambridge, 1996), pp. 61–85, and A. Crowhurst, 'London's "Music Hall War": trade unionism in an Edwardian service industry', *London Journal*, vol. 2, no. 21, 1996, pp. 149–63. For an invaluable bibliography, see L. Senelick, D. Cheshire and U. Schneider (eds), *British Music Hall, 1840–1923: A Bibliography and Guide to Sources* (Hamden, 1981).

3 Morton dominates the record with the 'official' biography by his brother William and H. C. Newton, *Sixty Years Stage Service* (London, 1905). H. Scott, *The Early Doors* (Wakefield, 1977), pp. 220–5, offers correctives on the Morton myth, and useful notes on other leading London managers. L. Senelick *et al.*, *British Music Hall* (Hamden, 1981), provides some bibliographical references, but there are no entries for managers in R. Busby, *British Music Hall: An Illustrated Who's Who* (1976). The best source remains the trade press, from which most of the material for this piece was drawn, though it cannot all be referenced here. Kift, *Victorian Music Hall*, provides some considerable rehabilitation of provincial proprietors, as does A. J. Crowhurst, 'The Music Hall, 1885–1922: the emergence of a national entertainment industry in Britain', (Ph.D thesis, Cambridge, 1992), a sustained examination of management practices and the social and economic geography of the halls. See also, Crowhurst, 'Oswald Stoll: a music hall pioneer', *Theatre Notebook*, 49, 1995, pp. 149–53, and J. Crump, 'Provincial music hall: promoters and public in Leicester, 1863–1929', in Bratton (ed.), *Music Hall*, pp. 53–72.

4 *Era*, 25 February 1866.

5 *Entr'acte*, 13 June 1874.

6 Besant and J. Rice, *Ready Money Mortiboy*, 1872, vol. 2, pp. 159–66, 260–76. I owe this reference to Anna Davin.

7 *Musician and Music Hall Times*, 19 July 1862.

8 *Era*, 5 July 1866; 31 March 1872.

9 *Music Hall and Theatre Review*, 28 February 1908. For the concept of 'the big man' in anthropology and its application here, see P. Bailey, 'Custom, capital and culture in the Victorian music hall', in R. Storch (ed.), *Popular Culture and Custom in Nineteenth Century England* (1982), p. 192.

10 *Era*, 13 December 1890.

11 See H. Powdermaker, *The Dream Factory: An Anthropologist Looks at Movie Making* (Boston, 1950), pp. 92–7.

12 There is no satisfactory history of London music hall for the period. C. D. Stuart and A. J. Park, *The Variety Stage: A History of the Music Halls* (1895), Chapters 4–6, records the heightened activity of the 1860s but probably underestimates the industry's continuing vigour in the 1870s. D. Howard, *London Theatres and Music Halls, 1850–1950* (1970), is an invaluable source and reference book. My figures leave out the smaller pub concert rooms.

13 *Entr'acte*, 12 July 1879 and 24 January 1880; *Era*, 14 September 1879.

14 Select Committee on Theatrical Licences, *Parliamentary Papers*, House of Commons, vol. 16, no. 373, 1866, app. 3, p. 313.

15 *Entr'acte*, 9 October 1880. Morton mortgaged his premises to Combe and Delafield for £600 in 1854; see J. Earl and J. Stanton, *The Canterbury Hall and Theatre of Varieties* (Cambridge, 1982), p. 15. By this time, breweries owned or helped in the mortgage of more than half of London's pubs as well as being an important source of investment capital in other businesses, including the theatre. Hard data for involvement in the halls is scarce.

16 Holland started in partnership with his publican uncle, Morton joined with his solicitor brother-in-law. A number of early directors were surgeons or officers, no doubt prolonging their student or cadet enthusiasms.

17 B. H. Harrison, *Drink and the Victorians* (1971), p. 250. For Payne, see Crowhurst, 'Music Hall'.

18 'One of the Old Brigade', *London in the Sixties* (1908), p. 78.

19 *Entr'acte*, 9 October 1880; 'The Music Hall Business', *St. James Gazette*, 10 February 1885.

20 *Era*, 20 June, 1 August 1869; 3 February 1870.

21 *Ibid.*, 7 March 1875; 12 September 1869.

22 *Music Hall and Theatre Review*, 28 February 1908.

23 *Era*, 5 December 1869. For the performers' perspective, see L. Rutherford, 'Managers in a small way: the professionalisation of variety artistes, 1860–1914', in Bailey (ed.), *Music Hall*, pp. 93–117.

24 *Entr'acte*, 24 September 1870.

25 *Era*, 24 and 31 March, 7 April 1867; W. J. Boardman, *Vaudeville Days* (1935), pp. 117–18.

26 *Era*, 23 August 1874.

27 'The cost of amusing the public', *London Society*, vol. 1 (1862), pp. 193–8.

28 Proprietors experimented with mechanical turnstiles in the 1870s, to eradicate the peculations of the money and check takers.

29 *Entr'acte*, 18 December 1880.

30 *Figaro*, 22 April 1874, provides a good account of the in-crowd, though it provoked an action for libel.

31 For background, see T. St V. Troubridge, *The Benefit System in the British Theatre* (1967). See also E. Dutton Cook, *A Book of the Play* (1876), vol. 2, pp. 123–46; C. W. Scott, 'Charity on crutches', *Era Almanack* (1877).

32 *Era*, 20 October 1883; 7 November 1885.

33 *Entr'acte*, 9 April 1870.

34 Mrs Poole was one of the few women music hall proprietors, having taken over on her husband's death. Wives often played a major role in a business which routinely exploited family, though some proprietors withdrew their womenfolk in classic bourgeois manner and the widow's succession was less common in music hall than in the licensed trade.

35 *Era*, 16 February 1862.

36 *Ibid.*, 25 August 1872.

37 *Ibid.*, 10 June 1877; 25 November 1866; 11 November 1860.

38 See, for example, A. Rosman and P. C. Rubel, *Feasting With Mine Enemy: Rank and Exchange among North West Coast Societies* (New York, 1971); R. Firth, *Symbols Public and Private* (1973), pp. 368–402.

39 *Entr'acte*, 8 May 1875, thought £30 a good return for the established artist.

40 *Ibid.*, 6 December 1873.

41 *Era*, 24 April 1875.

42 *Entr'acte*, 16 December 1873; 8 May 1875.

43 *Era*, 16 February 1862.

44 For a general commendation of music hall's service to the working-class community, see Select Committee on Theatres, *Parliamentary Papers* (1892), 18, q. 5177.

45 For the crucial changes in the 1880s, see Bailey, 'Custom, capital and culture', pp. 191–3.

46 See Crump, 'Provincial music hall'.

47 *Era*, 2 August 1902.

48 For renewed complaints in the profession, see *Performer Annual* (1908); *Stage Year Book* (1909), pp. 71–2.

49 *Eastern Argus*, 20 October 1894; 19 October 1895.

50 *Era*, 26 April 1902; 21 February 1903. For the parallel persistence of traditional styles of authority in industry see H. Newby, 'Paternalism and capitalism' in R. Scase (ed.), *Industrial Society: Class, Cleavage and Control* (1977), pp. 59–73; P. Joyce, *Work, Society and Politics: The Culture of the Factory in Later Victorian England* (1980), chapter 5.

51 The quote is from O. Ramsoy, 'Friendship', *International Encyclopaedia of Social Science* (New York, 1968). See also G. A. Allan, *A Sociology of Friendship and Kinship* (1979), and the suggestive essay by G. Simmel, 'The sociology of sociability' (what he calls 'the art or play form of association'), *American Journal of Sociology*, November 1949, pp. 254–61. T. Zeldin, *France, 1848–1945: Intellect, Taste and Anxiety* (Cambridge, 1977), pp. 651–6, speaks of the need for a history of sociability; see also R. Holt, *Sport and Society in Modern France* (1981), pp. 150–68. There are, of course, distinctions to be made between friendship and sociability.

52 E. P. Thompson, *The Making of the English Working Class* (New York, 1963), pp. 417–29; T. R. Tholfsen, *Working-Class Radicalism in Mid-Victorian England* (1976), pp. 288–305.

53 H. Perkin, *Origins of Modern English Society* (1969), pp. 45–9.

54 I owe this point to J. S. Bratton.

55 C. MacInnes, *Sweet Saturday Night* (1969), p. 150.

56 V. Turner, *The Ritual Process: Structure and Anti-Structure* (1969), chapter 3.

57 The story is told in H. G. Hibbert, *Fifty Years of a Londoner's Life* (1916), p. 230. For the commercially promoted sociability of Leybourne's career see below, Chapter 6.

58 *Era*, 14 July 1872.

59 *Ibid.*, 15 July 1882.

60 R. Dennis, *English Industrial Cities of the Nineteenth Century: A Social Geography* (Cambridge, 1984), p. 9.

5 CHAMPAGNE CHARLIE AND THE MUSIC-HALL SWELL SONG

1 *London, a Pilgrimage* (New York, 1970), p. 166 (the drawings were done in 1869–71); *St. James Gazette*, 21 April 1892; correspondence on George Leybourne in *Era*, 24 June 1893. (Place of publication is London unless otherwise stated.)

2 For the history and historiography of music hall, see above, chapter 4, n. 2.

3 R. Williams, *The Long Revolution* (1965), p. 291; G. Stedman Jones, 'Working-Class Culture and Working-Class Politics in London, 1870–1900', *Journal of Social History*, 7, Summer 1974, p. 495, reprinted in his *Language of Class* (Cambridge, 1983).

4 For recent attention to Leybourne, see P. Honri, 'Leybourne! Lion Comique of the Halls', *Theatrephile*, September 1984, pp. 65–7, and the dramatisation of his life by Christopher Beeching and Glyn Jones to whom I am grateful for generously sharing their own research findings. See also H. G. Hibbert, *Fifty Years of a Londoner's Life* (1916), *passim*, and H. Chance Newton, *Idols of the Halls* (1928), pp. 57–63.

5 C. Coborn, *'The Man Who Broke the Bank': Memories of Stage and Music Hall*, (1928), pp. 56–7.

6 *Era*, 26 February 1865; 11 November 1866. Other durable Leybourne hits were *If I Ever Cease to Love* and *The Daring Young Man on the Flying Trapeze*.

7 For the extracts from the contract, see *Era*, 12 July 1868; for Holland, see above, chapter 5.

8 *Entr'acte*, 2 November 1872.

9 *Era*, 17 June 1893.

10 Jay Didcott interview, *Era*, 23 July 1882; *Evening Transcript*, 17 October 1884, quoted in L. Senelick, 'A Brief Life and Times of the Music Hall', *Harvard Library Bulletin*, October 1971, p. 387. A. Roberts, *Fifty Years of Spoof* (1927), pp. 99–100, retells the 'friends' and teashop stories.

11 There are many comparative references to Vance in the literature on Leybourne, see e.g., Hibbert, *Fifty Years of a Londoner's Life*, and Newton, *Idols of the Halls*. See also the obituary in *The Times* (a recognition significantly not conferred on Leybourne), 28 December 1888; *Era*, 5 January 1889.

12 *Era*, 6 April 1865.

13 H. Jennings, *Chestnuts and Small Beer* (Birmingham, 1920), p. 203.

14 For biography in general, see R. Busby, *British Music Hall: An Illustrated Who's Who* (1976), and L. Senelick, D. F. Cheshire and U. Schneider, *British Music Hall, 1840–1923: A Bibliography and Guide to Sources*, (Hamden, 1981).

15 See chapter 4.

16 Select Committee on Theatrical Licences, *Parliamentary Papers* (1866), vol. 16, qq. 460–4, 2792. For the graphics, see W. H. Morton and H. C. Newton, *Sixty Years Stage Service, The Life of Charles Morton* (1905).

17 For competitive tensions in the profession, see *Musician and Music Hall Times*, 4 June 1862 and L. Rutherford, '"Managers in a Small Way": The Professionalism of Variety Artistes, 1860–1914', in J.S. Bratton (ed.), *Music Hall: Performance and Style* (Milton Keynes, 1986), pp. 93–117.

18 See, e.g., *Entr'acte*, 14 May 1870.

19 *London Society*, April 1862.

20 M. Booth, *English Plays of the Nineteenth Century*, vol. 3 (1973), pp. 146–53; D. Mayer, *Harlequin in His Element: the English Pantomime, 1806–1836*, (Harvard, 1969), pp. 61, 165–8; 'How Dundreary was Created', *Era*, 4 January 1874.

21 M. Vicinus, *The Industrial Muse* (1974), p. 258.

22 Morton and Newton, *Sixty Years Stage Service*, p. 40.

23 M. W. Judd, 'Popular Culture and the London Fairs, 1800–1860', in J. K. Walton and J. Walvin (eds), *Leisure in Britain, 1780–1939* (Manchester, 1983), p. 23.

24 E. Moers, *The Dandy: Brummell to Beerbohm* (1960), p. 215; J. Laver, *Dandies* (1968).

25 C. Kent, 'The Whittington Club: a bohemian experiment in middle-class social reform', *Victorian Studies*, 8 (1957), pp. 31–55.

26 *Town*, 12 May 1838; Ritchie, *The Night Side of London*, (1857), pp. 146, 211–20.

27 'Taverns', in the John Johnson Collection at the Bodleian Library, Oxford. J. W. Sharpe was recalled as the lion comique of the 1840s, see F. W. Robinson, 'Our Comic Singers', *Home Chimes*, February 1866, p. 29.

28 The swell in all his variants – dandy, rake, pretender, silly ass, broken down – was to continue as a fruitful model in music hall and the wider popular culture through to the 1950s. There are obvious correspondences in Ally Sloper, see chapter 3 above.

29 *Era*, 18 May 1895 recalls the selling of the song to its original publisher Sheard. I have used the 1925 edition, reproduced in P. Davison, *Songs of the British Music Hall* (New York, 1971), p. 17, and have cavalierly treated this source as unproblematic. I have too left aside the role of the (mostly petit bourgeois) song writer – death of the author? – for which see Senelick, 'Politics as entertainment: Victorian music hall song', *Victorian Studies*, December 1975 pp. 149–80, and am ill-equipped to deal with the music, for which see R. Middleton, 'Popular Music of the Lower Classes', in N. Temperley (ed.), *Music in Britain: The Romantic Age, 1800–1914* (1981), pp. 63–91 and A. Bennett, 'Music in the Halls', in Bratton, *Music Hall*, pp. 1–22.

30 From among many ingenious (and obscene) suggestions, the most plausible so far is from John Stanton – co-author with J. Earl of *The Canterbury Hall* (Cambridge, 1983) – who recalls a contemporary engraving of Covent Garden with a notice in a window advertising Private Rooms For Gentlemen. . .

31 On method and some theoretical models, see V. Gammon, 'Problems of Method in the Historical Study of Popular Music' in P. Tagg and D. Horn (eds), *Popular Music Perspectives*, (Gotenburg, 1982), pp. 16–31 and D. Laing, *One Chord Wonders: Power and Meaning in Punk Rock*, (Milton Keynes, 1985). Most of the songs treated here were consulted in the British Library, though a number of references are from the trade press. There are helpful comments on the swell song as a type in C. Pulling, *They Were Singing* (1952), ch. 2; Senelick, 'Brief Life and Times', pp. 386–88; Vicinus, *The Industrial Muse*, ch. 6: Davison, *Songs of the British Music Hall*, pp. 15–18; R. Pearsall, *Victorian Popular Music*, (1973), pp. 43, 77; J. S. Bratton, *The Victorian Popular Ballad* (1975), p. 177.

32 *Birmingham Stage and Concert Hall Reporter*, 13 July 1867.

33 *Era*, 5 January 1862.

34 A. L. Simon, *History of the Champagne Trade in England* (1905).

35 *Era*, 10 January 1864, 24 December 1865; *Wine Trade Review*, 15 September 1867; *Canterbury Music Hall Advertiser* (Sheffield), 17 October 1864.

36 A. E. Dingle, 'Drink and Working-Class Living Standards in Britain, 1870–1914', *Economic History Review*, 4, November 1972, p. 616; *Saturday Review*, 17 June 1882.

37 *Era*, 18 September 1864; *Beehive*, 10 June 1871; B. Spiller, *Victorian Public Houses* (Newton Abbott, 1972), pp. 24, 71. For the importance of 'brightness', see S. Yeo, *Religion and Voluntary Organisations in Crisis*, (1976), *passim*.

38 W. Tomlinson, *Bye-ways of Manchester Life*, (Manchester, 1887), p. 71.

39 *Era*, 6 September 1868; 7 January 1866.

40 P. Fitzgerald, *Music Hall Land*, (1890); p. 4; *Era*, 23 February 1895.

41 J. Tozer and S. Levitt, *Fabric of Society: A Century of People and Their Clothes* (1983), pp. 113–114.

42 T. E. Pemberton, *A Memoir of E. A. Sothern* (1890).

43 *Era*, 6 June 1872. Weston's had been equipped with mirrored walls and stage early in its career; *Concert Room Reporter*, 17 March 1858.

44 'Our Music-Halls', *Tinsley's Magazine*, 4, April 1869, p. 216; *Entr'acte*, 15 November 1873; T. Hopkins, 'Music Halls', *Dublin University Magazine*, 2, August 1878, p. 195; Newton, *Idols of the Halls*.

45 *Era*, 15 October 1865; *Diprose's London Guide* (1872).

46 T. Kennick, *Comic Singing Made Easy* (1869), p. 26.

47 William Pett Ridge, *I Like to Remember* (1925), p. 272.

48 I owe this point to Jane Traies.

49 *Daily Telegraph*, 12 January 1869.

50 R. de V. Renwick, *English Folk Poetry: Structure and Meaning* (Pittsburg, 1980), p. 11, presumably echoing Barthes who contends that all interpretation should be extravagant.

51 *Era*, 19 August 1877, on Leybourne's 'magic bottle'.

52 See Bratton, 'Beating the bounds: gender play and role reversal in the Edwardian music hall', in M. R. Booth and J. H. Kaplan (eds), *The Edwardian Theatre: Essays on Performance and the Stage* (Cambridge, 1996), pp. 86–110.

53 The penny pick was a Pickwick, a cheap cigar. For Page's recollections, see *Era*, 10 June 1893; for the missile incident, *Daily News*, 28 December 1885. As with several other swell songs, including *Champagne Charlie*, Power's hit was taken up in the theatre, though the song was more conciliatory, suggesting that the swell would still come up trumps when his country needed him.

54 Wright, *Some Habits and Customs of the Working Classes* (1867), pp. 180–1.

55 *Era*, 5 September 1880; W. F. Fish, *The Autobiography of a Counter Jumper*, (1929), pp. 36–37, 70–72; T. Okey, *A Basketful of Memories* (1930), p. 54. For further discussion of songs for and about the clerks in the music hall, see Jane Traies, 'Jones and the working girl: class marginality in music hall song 1860–1900', in Bratton, *Music Hall*, pp. 23–48.

56 G. E., 'Music hall songs and singers', *Era Almanack* (1872), pp. 38–41.

57 P. J. Keating, *The Working Classes in Victorian Fiction* (1971), pp. 141, 154, 280 n.42; Tomlinson, *Bye-ways of Manchester Life*, pp. 196–206. See also Stedman Jones, 'The "Cockney" and the Nation, 1780–1988', in D. Feldman and Jones, *Metropolis London: Histories and Representations since 1800* (1989), pp. 272–324.

58 *Era*, 30 June 1883.

59 Gammon, 'Problems of Method', p. 29.

60 For various aspects of the language and practice of incorporation, see H. E. Meller, *Leisure and the Changing City* (1976); T. R. Tholfsen, *Working Class Radicalism in Mid-Victorian England* (1976); Bailey, *Leisure and Class in Victorian England* (1987).

61 G.E., 'Music Hall Songs'; C. Ginzburg, *The Cheese and the Worms: The Cosmos of a Sixteenth Century Miller* (1980), p. 84, notes that the songs of primitive utopianism carried a coda mocking those who would believe such fantasies, suggesting a long tradition of folk wariness.

62 A. J. MacKay, *Bohemian Days in Fleet Street* (1913), pp. 225–27.

63 J. K. Cook, 'The Labourer's Leisure', *Dublin University Magazine*, 40 (1871), pp. 174–92.

64 For the swell and gentility, see also Hopkins, and 'The Genesis of the Cad', *Tinsley's Magazine*, March 1869, pp. 178–181. Cf. P. N. Furbank, *Unholy Pleasure: The Idea of Social Class* (1985), pp. 94–106.

65 Williams, *Country and the City*; Stedman Jones, 'Working Class Culture'.

66 Hall, 'Deconstructing the Popular', in R. Samuel (ed.), *People's History and Socialist Theory*, (1981), pp. 227–40.

67 On the suit as hegemony, see J. Berger, *About Looking* (New York, 1980), pp. 34–35; on the cap as uniform, E. J. Hobsbawm, 'Mass-Producing Traditions: Europe, 1870–1914', in Hobsbawm and T. Ranger, *The Invention of Tradition* (1983), pp. 287–8.

68 Factory Inspector Reports, *Parliamentary Papers*, (1875), vol. 16, pp. 332–333.

69 *Entr'acte*, 23 September 1871; W. H. Fraser, *Trade Unions and Society: The Struggle for Acceptance* (1974), p. 41.

6 MUSIC HALL AND THE KNOWINGNESS OF POPULAR CULTURE

This piece was originally a more vulgar, performance-oriented exercise entitled 'Did Foucault and Althusser ever play the London Palladium?', but has been revised in the interests of academic probity.

1 Michel de Certeau, *The Practice of Everyday Life* (Berkeley, 1988), p. 41.

2 George Orwell, *The Lion and the Unicorn: Socialism and the English Genius* (1941; London, 1982), p. 37.

3 For music hall bibliography, see chapter 4, n. 2.

4 Christopher Pulling, *They Were Singing, and What They Sang About* (London, 1952). In similar though more perceptive vein, see Colin MacInnes, *Sweet Saturday Night* (London, 1967).

5 See variously Peter Davison, *Songs of the British Music Hall* (New York, 1971); Martha Vicinus, *The Industrial Muse: A Study of Nineteenth Century Working-Class Literature* (London, 1974), ch. 6; J. S. Bratton, *The Victorian Popular Ballad* (London, 1975), ch. 6; Richard Middleton, 'Popular music of the lower classes', in Nicholas Temperley (ed.), *Music in Britain: The Romantic Age, 1800–1914* (London, 1981), pp. 63–91; Bernard Waites, 'The music hall', in *The Historical Development of Popular Culture in Britain* (Open University course booklet, Milton Keynes, 1981), pp. 43–76; Penelope Summerfield, 'The Effingham Arms and the Empire: deliberate selection in the evolution of music hall in London', in Eileen and Stephen Yeo (eds.), *Popular Culture and Class Conflict, 1590–1914* (Hassocks, 1981), pp. 209–40; Ulrich Schneider, *Die Londoner Music Hall und ihre Songs, 1850–1920* (Tübingen, 1984); Michael J. Childs, *Labour's Apprentices: Working-Class Lads in Late Victorian and Edwardian England* (Montreal and Kingston, 1992), pp. 118–32. See also, for the café-concert and music-hall in Paris, Charles Rearick, 'Song and Society in Turn of the Century France', *Jl Social History*, 22 (1989), pp. 46–63.

6 T. S. Eliot, *Selected Essays* (London, 1951), pp. 456–9.

7 Dave Harker, 'Joe Wilson: "comic dialectical singer" or class traitor?', in Bratton (ed.), *Music Hall: Performance and Style* (Milton Keynes, 1986), pp. 111–30.

8 Such is the (unsubstantiated) contention of Ronald Pearsall, *Victorian Popular Music* (Newton Abbot, 1973), p. 24. On songs and politics, see Laurence Senelick, 'Politics as entertainment: Victorian music-hall songs', *Victorian Studies*, 19 (1975–6), pp. 149–60; Waites, 'Music Hall'; Ian Watson, *Song and Democratic Culture in Britain: An Approach to Popular Culture in Social Movements* (London, 1983), pp. 49–52; Penelope Summerfield, 'Patriotism and empire: music hall entertainment, 1870–1914', in John Mackenzie (ed.), *Imperialism and Popular Culture* (Manchester, 1986), pp. 17–48; Dave Russell, *Popular Music in England, 1840–1914: A Social History* (Manchester, 1987), chs. 6–7.

9 Gareth Stedman Jones, 'Working-class culture and working-class politics in London, 1870–1900: notes on the remaking of a working class', *Journal of Social History*, 7 (1974), pp. 460–508, reprinted in his *Languages of Class: Studies in English Working Class History, 1832–1982* (Cambridge, 1983). For the germ of this characterisation, see Richard Hoggart, *The Uses of Literacy* (Harmondsworth, 1958), p. 140; for Hoggart on popular song, see pp. 156–66.

10 On the pitfalls of authenticity in other contexts, see Simon Frith, 'Towards an aesthetic of popular music', in Richard Leppert and Susan McClary (eds), *Music and Society: The Politics of Composition, Performance and Reception* (Cambridge, 1987), pp. 133–49; Richard Middleton, *Studying Popular Music* (Milton Keynes, 1990), pp. 139–40. See also Stuart Hall, 'Notes on deconstructing "the popular"', in Raphael Samuel (ed.), *People's History and Socialist Theory* (London, 1981), p. 233; Morag Shiach, *Discourse on Popular Culture* (Cambridge, 1989).

11 See Raymond Williams's injunction 'to get right inside the form itself': Stephen Heath and Gillian Skirrow, 'An interview with Raymond Williams', in Tania Modleski (ed.), *Studies in Entertainment: Critical Approaches to Mass Culture* (Bloomington, 1986), p. xiii; on 'the problem of popularity, the pleasure or the use value of subjective forms', see Richard Johnson, 'The story so far: and further transformations?', in David Punter (ed.), *Introduction to Contemporary Cultural Studies* (London, 1986), p. 307.

12 There is no systematic history of performance styles in the halls. The editor's introduction and several contributions to Bratton (ed.), *Music Hall*, make the best point of departure. For treatments of the later stand-up comic and his continuities with the halls, see John Fisher, *Funny Way To Be A Hero* (London, 1973); Peter Davison, *Contemporary Drama and the Popular Dramatic Tradition in England* (London, 1982), chapter 2. The missing dimension is that of the music itself, a greatly under-developed field. But see Middleton, *Studying Popular Music*; Anthony Bennett, 'Music in the halls', in Bratton (ed.), *Music Hall*, pp. 1–22.

13 Hugh Shimmin, *Liverpool Life* (Liverpool, 1856), p. 37; Blanchard Jerrold, *London: A Pilgrimage* (1872; New York, 1970), p. 167.

14 The street ballad was despised in older scholarship, which privileged a less vulgarised folk tradition. For a reconstruction of the form, its context and performance, see Natascha Wurzbach, *The Rise of the English Street Ballad, 1550–1650* (Cambridge, 1990), especially pp. 39–104, 241. Wurzbach suggests that the street ballad was incorporated and/or displaced by the new commercialised entertainments and media of the eighteenth century. For street seller performers in the music-hall era, see Vicinus, *Industrial Muse*, pp. 20–1, and Philemon Eva, 'Popular song and social identity in Victorian Manchester', (University of Manchester Ph.D. thesis, 1996), an excellent account of urban song culture in the streets and pubs.

15 On theatre, see Raymond Williams, 'Social environment and theatrical environment: the case of English naturalism', in his *Problems in Materialism and Culture: Selected Essays* (London, 1980), pp. 125–47.

16 Most helpful here is Davison, *Contemporary Drama*, ch. 2. See also Wurzbach, *English Street Ballad*, chapter 3.

17 Though Foucault has made the concept an academic commonplace, he provides no single definition. His passing identification of ' "illicit" discourse, that is, discourses of infraction' comes closest to what I have in mind here: Michel Foucault, *The History of Sexuality: An Introduction* (New York, 1980), p. 18. I note, however, with others, that Foucault and his followers have been almost exclusively concerned with discourse in the practice of professional or specialist knowledges, neglecting those subjected to such practices and the potential of discourse theory for the study of popular culture and everyday life. Gareth Stedman Jones, 'The "Cockney" and the nation, 1780–1988', in David Feldman and Gareth Stedman Jones (eds), *Metropolis London: Histories and Representations since 1800* (London, 1989), pp. 272–324, is one turn in this latter direction, but the most important work of

this kind is Patrick Joyce, *Visions of the People: Industrial England and the Question of Class, 1840–1914* (Cambridge, 1991). Joyce's extensive analysis of the role of language and representation in popular identities coincides at points with the argument of this essay, though our different focus in terms of evidence and place throws up somewhat conflicting readings of urban mentality.

For historians' new attention to language, see Peter Burke and Roy Porter (eds), *The Social History of Language* (Cambridge, 1987), and its sequel, *Language, Self and Society* (Cambridge, 1991); P. J. Corfield, 'Introduction: historians and language', in P. J. Corfield (ed.), *Language, History and Class* (Oxford, 1991), pp. 1–29. For a critique of such work, especially historians' reliance on intuition more than systematic analysis and their continuing neglect of language as social action, see Lorna Weir, 'The wanderings of the linguistic turn in Anglophone historical writing', *Jl Historical Sociology*, 6 (1993), pp. 227–45.

18 Louis Althusser, 'Ideology and ideological state apparatuses (notes towards an investigation)', in his *Lenin and Other Essays* (London, 1971), pp. 170–7.

19 On audiences, see Dagmar Höher, 'The composition of music hall audiences, 1850–1900', in Peter Bailey (ed.), *Music Hall: The Business of Pleasure* (Milton Keynes, 1986), pp. 73–92 and, as Dagmar Kift, *The Victorian Music Hall: Culture, Class and Conflict* (Cambridge, 1996), pp. 62–74.

20 Suggestive here is reception and reader response theory, though this is mostly applied to literary texts with little regard for social context. For relevant applications, see Marco De Marinis, 'Dramaturgy of the spectator', *Drama Review*, 31 (1987), pp. 100–14; Marvin Carlson, 'Theatre audiences and the reading of performance', in Thomas Postlethwait and Bruce A. McConachie (eds), *Interpreting the Theatrical Past: Essays in the Historiography of Performance* (Iowa City, 1989), pp. 82–98. Susan Bennett, *Theatre Audiences: A Theory of Production and Reception* (London, 1990), is a useful general text.

21 Fred Willis, *London General* (London, 1953), pp. 141–2. Political meetings were also characterised by a good deal of active audience response: see, e.g., Paul A. Pickering, 'Class without words: symbolic communication in the Chartist movement', *Past and Present*, no. 112, August 1986, pp. 150–1. We are dealing with a still vigorously oral culture whose psychodynamics remain close to those of primary oral societies, particularly in its agonistic tone: see Walter J. Ong, *Orality and Literacy: The Technologizing of the Word* (London, 1982), pp. 43–5. On the persistent drama of the markets, see Andrew Davies, *Leisure, Gender and Poverty: Working-Class Culture in Salford and Manchester, 1900–1939* (Buckingham, 1992), pp. 130–8.

22 Charles Mackay, *Memoirs of Extraordinary Popular Delusions* (1841; New York, 1980), pp. 619–31.

23 *London Singer's Magazine*, (1838–9?), p. 161. There are no dates for the individual (monthly?) issues, but their continuous publication is some index to the growth of concert-room activity.

24 Cf. James Obelkevich, 'Proverbs', in Burke and Porter (eds), *Social History of Language*, pp. 43–72.

25 The image, both apposite and irresistible, is borrowed from Bennett, 'Music in the halls', p. 20, and his analysis of the propulsion imparted by the rhythmic interaction of words and music. Sir Richard Terry also noted the development of a more concentrated song-form, with a distinctive 'snap' that 'knocked the audience every verse', though he places this in the 1880s: R. Terry, 'Old music halls', *John O'London Weekly*, 6 December 1924. See also Vic Gammon's work on early music-hall repertoire, principally that of Sam Cowell: V. Gammon, ' "Not Appreciated in Worthing": Class Expression and Popular Song Texts in Mid-Nineteenth Century Britain', *Popular Music*, 4 (1984), pp. 5–24; Bratton, *Victorian Popular Ballad*, pp. 200–1.

26 Anon., 'Amusements of the mob', *Chambers' Journal of Popular Literature*, 11 October 1856, pp. 225–9.

27 For similarly proprietory sentiment in a theatre audience, see Douglas Reid, 'Popular theatre in Victorian Birmingham', in David Bradby, Louis James and Bernard Sharratt (eds), *Performance and Politics in Popular Drama* (Cambridge, 1980), pp. 87–8 n. 53. The feeling is also manifest in the audience response to Frank Randle, the great Northern favourite of the 1930s and beyond, celebrated as the carbuncular eponymous hero of Jeff Nuttall, *King Twist* (London, 1978). For a similar phenomenon among rock fans today, see Frith on 'owning' in 'Towards an aesthetic of popular music', p. 143.

28 Henry Mayhew, *London Labour and the London Poor*, 4 vols. (1851; New York, 1967), i, pp. 40–2.

29 More combustible analogies, this one from Molly Mahood, *Shakespeare's Wordplay* (London, 1979), cited in Walter Redfern, *Puns* (Oxford, 1984), p. 5.

30 While 'competence' is routinely used in semiotics and literary theory to denote the reader's knowledge of a particular genre and its conventions, what I have in mind here is the additional, more dynamic sense of the living out of this knowledge. John Fiske identifies both a cultural competence and a social competence – 'how people are likely to act, feel or react within such conventions' – which together make for what he terms the 'producerly' activity of the modern consumer: J. Fiske, *Understanding Popular Culture* (London, 1989), p. 148. See too the suggestive essay by Bernard Sharratt, 'The politics of the popular? From melodrama to television', in Bradby, James and Sharratt (eds), *Performance and Politics*, pp. 275–95. His identification of the 'expertise' of popular life has, I realise, been subterraneously prompting me to this reading of knowingness for several years; what he terms the 'intimacy' of popular response has strong affinities with what I describe above as 'claiming'.

31 *The Oxford English Dictionary*, 2nd edn, *s.v.* 'knowing (3)'.

32 Quoted in Jim Davis, *John Liston, Comedian* (London, 1985), pp. 25, 26.

33 Louis James, *Fiction for the Working Man, 1830–1850* (Harmondsworth, 1974), pp. 20–1. Such periodicals were most numerous in London, but there were equivalents in most big provincial cities of the period. For a new wariness towards the city and its representation in literature, see Deborah Epstein Nord, 'The city as theater: from Georgian to early Victorian London',

Victorian Studies, 31 (1987–8), pp. 159–88; and for Mayhew's treatment of street people as an imaginative metaphor for a new cosmopolitan sensibility of mobility and alertness, see Richard Maxwell, 'Henry Mayhew and the Life of the Streets', *Journal of British Studies*, 17, part 2 (Spring 1978), pp. 87–105.

While the population of London nearly doubled between 1821 and 1851, the rate of increase in cities in the North and Midlands was higher still. While I acknowledge the preponderance of London sources used here, this and other evidence supports the contention that knowingness was a general urban phenomenon of the period and not, as might be objected, specifically and only metropolitan or cockney, though undoubtedly there would have been different regional inflections. For a work that departs substantially from the metrocentric bias of most music-hall studies, see Kift, *Victorian Music Hall.*

34 As quoted in Davis, *John Liston*, p. 25.

35 Gammon, 'Not Appreciated', p. 23.

36 Mayhew, *London Labour*, iv, p. 209.

37 Keith Thomas, *Religion and the Decline of Magic* (Harmondsworth, 1973), ch. 8; Robert Malcolmson, *Life and Labour in England, 1700–1780* (London, 1981), pp. 88–92.

38 See, e.g., Robert Colls, *The Collier's Rant: Song and Culture in the Industrial Village* (London, 1977), especially p. 51.

39 Raymond Williams, *Drama in a Dramatised Society* (Cambridge, 1975). Also compare Benjamin, who famously locates the onset of modernity and its aestheticisation of everyday life in these decades: Walter Benjamin, 'Paris, the capital of the nineteenth century' (1935), reprinted in his *Reflections*, Peter Demetz (ed.) (New York, 1978), pp. 146–62.

40 Edwin M. Schur, 'A sociological analysis of confidence swindling', *Journal of Criminal Law, Criminology and Police Science*, 68 (1957), pp. 296–304. Dan Leno described London as a 'large village on the Thames where the principal industries are music halls and the confidence trick': quoted in Davison, *Songs of the British Music Hall*, p. 3.

41 Compare the burlesque legalism that flourished in traditional artisan culture: Robert Darnton, *The Great Cat Massacre* (New York, 1985), p. 85.

42 Published in 1835 and 1836, the *Singer's Penny Magazine* was an antecedent, via the *British Pocket Vocalist*, of the *London Singer's Magazine* (see n. 23 above).

43 In North America, where similar developments took place, usage was different, for it was 'variety' which signified the unimproved originals now superseded by a would-be more refined 'vaudeville' theatre: see Robert Snyder, *The Voice of the City: Vaudeville and Popular Culture in New York* (New York, 1989).

44 A review of the controversies of this climacteric from the London proprietors' perspective is given in *Regulation of the Music Halls* (London, 1883); for resistance to the new controls, see Bailey, 'Custom, capital and culture', in Robert Storch (ed.), *Popular Culture and Custom in Nineteenth Century England* (London, 1982), pp. 180–208.

45 For a strong element of interaction in a closely allied form, see Lois Rutherford, ' "Harmless Nonsense": The Comic Sketch and the Development of Music Hall Entertainment', in Bratton (ed.), *Music Hall*, pp. 131–51.

46 Arthur Roberts, *Fifty Years of Spoof* (London, 1927), p. 28.

47 *Era*, 31 January 1885.

48 G. H. Mair, 'The music hall', *English Review*, 9 (1911), pp. 122–9.

49 F. Freeman, *Weekly Despatch*, 4 February 1883.

50 *Glasgow Daily Herald*, 6 March 1875; *Era*, 7 March 1875. See also, Kift, *Victorian Music Hall*, pp. 115–20.

51 An anti-language is defined in terms of an invented vocabulary, often of a semi-technical and oppositional kind, that serves a particular minority group; see M. A. K. Halliday, *Language as Social Semiotic* (London, 1978), pp. 164–82. Though music-hall had its own trade talk ('parlary'), and a keen appetite for slang, in general it was a powerful agent in the standardisation of language that was accelerating everywhere in the late nineteenth century. This is not to ignore the considerable popularity of dialect acts in this period, but it can be argued that they were as much a corollary of the main trend as a resistance to it. In music hall, as in the onset of mass culture generally, standardisation intensified differentiation. On the continuing significance of dialect, see Joyce, *Visions of the People*, ch. 12; P. J. Waller, 'Democracy and dialect, speech and class', in P. J. Waller (ed.), *Politics and Social Change in Modern Britain* (Brighton, 1987), pp. 1–33.

52 G. A. Blackwell on the Oxford, 2 Oct. 1908: Greater London Record Office, Presented Papers, Theatre and Music Hall Committee, London County Council.

53 M. A. K. Halliday, 'Language in urban society', in Halliday, *Language as Social Semiotic*, pp. 154–63.

54 The plainest case is that of education: see David Vincent, *Literacy and Popular Culture: England, 1750–1914* (Cambridge, 1989), ch. 3. Another powerfully restrictive regime in this respect was, of course, domestic service.

55 Basil Bernstein's comparison was with a more explicit, intellectualised or 'elaborated' (middle-class) code, a controversial thesis most readily sampled in his essay 'Social class, language and socialisation', in P. O. Giglioli (ed.), *Language and Social Context* (Harmondsworth, 1972), pp. 211–34.

56 Cf. Ross McKibbin, 'Class and poverty in Edwardian England', in his *The Ideologies of Class: Social Relations in Britain, 1880–1950* (Oxford, 1991), pp. 182–3.

57 Sir Lewis Fergusson, *Old Time Music Hall Comedians* (Leicester, 1941), pp. 12–16; Roberts, *Fifty Years of Spoof*, pp. 54–6.

58 *Era*, 18 November 1877.

59 *Entr'acte*, 12 April 1879.

60 J. Humphreys to *The Times*, 16 October 1883.

61 Bennett, 'Music in the halls', p. 12; see also management complaints from twenty years later that the chorus seized on and amplified offensive phrases in Rutherford, 'Harmless nonsense', p. 144.

62 *Era*, 19 October 1879.

63 E. Lynn Linton, 'The girl of the period', in her *The Girl of the Period and Other Social Essays* (London, 1883), pp. 1–9 (first published in 1868 in the *Saturday Review*).

64 The title for Susan Pennybacker's essay on the London County Council and its long-running campaign to purify the halls, in Bailey (ed.), *Music Hall*, pp. 119–40. See also Chris Waters, 'Progressives, puritans and the cultural politics of the council, 1889–1914', in Andrew Saint (ed.), *Politics and the People of London: The London County Council, 1889–1965* (London, 1989), pp. 58–62. For the Oxford case, see *Morning Advertiser*, 15 October 1896, a copy of which is filed with the licensing proceedings: Greater London Record Office, Presented Papers, Theatre and Music Hall Committee, London County Council (Oxford Music Hall, 1896). The most controversial case of this kind, over the notorious promenades at the Empire, was three years earlier.

65 Frank Merry, 'Music Hall and its Music', *Music* (November 1896), pp. 385–6; I owe this reference to Kate McCrone. On the gleeful sexual literacy of middle-class males in reading cues that played off a *sub rosa* knowledge of pornography and prostitution in the West End, see the parallel findings of Tracy C. Davis, *Actresses as Working Women: Their Social Identity in Victorian Culture* (London, 1991), ch. 5.

66 For the changing pattern among the young, see John Gillis, *For Better, For Worse: British Marriages, 1600 to the Present* (Oxford, 1985), pp. 164, 268.

67 The cross-cutting engagement of singer and audience in this context is analysed above, Chapter 5.

68 Robert C. Allen, *Horrible Prettiness: Burlesque and American Culture* (Chapel Hill, 1991), p. 129.

69 *Era*, 30 April 1892.

70 *Glasgow Daily Herald*, 6 March 1875. See also the observations on female response by the critic William Archer in his account of the knowingness ('aposeopesis') of the allied genre of musical comedy in W. Archer, *The Theatrical 'World' for 1896* (London, 1897), pp. 298–305, and Chapter 8 below.

71 Jane Traies, 'Jones and the working girl: class marginality in music hall song, 1860–1900', in Bratton (ed.), *Music Hall*, pp. 23–48.

72 See Chapter 7 below; Judith Walkowitz, *City of Dreadful Delight: Narratives of Sexual Danger in Late-Victorian London* (Chicago, 1992), especially pp. 45–52. Hoggart, *Uses of Literacy*, treats knowingness very much as a male mode; see n. 85 below.

73 Anon, 'Our Music Halls', *Tinsley's Mag.* (Apr. 1869), pp. 216–23.

74 *Ibid.*; see also Anon, *Life, Career and Adventures of a Gent 'Or Any Other Man'* (London, 1862); Stedman Jones, '"Cockney" and the Nation', pp. 290–4, on the new ''Arry-stockracy'.

75 Talbot Baines Reed, *The Cock House at Fellsgarth* (London, n.d.), pp. 21–7, 34.

76 On examples of upper-class and other styles, see John Clive, *In a Manner of Speaking* (Kenneth B. Murdock Lecture, Harvard University, 1979); K. C. Phillips, *Language and Class in Victorian England* (London, 1984).

77 Ashby minor might have learned the formula from F. Anstey, *Mr. Punch's Model Music Hall* (London, 1890), though, for all its conventional manner-isms, this could be an elusive and highly nuanced mode.

78 P. N. Furbank, *E. M. Forster: A Life*, 2 vols. (London, 1977), i, p. 51.

79 George Orwell, 'The art of Donald McGill', in his *Collected Essays*, 3 vols. (London, 1968), ii, pp. 161–2. Nonetheless, music-hall humour of this period continued to evince considerable class tension: see Rutherford, 'Harmless Nonsense', p. 149. It would be interesting to plot the later course of knowingness and other comic modes in registering class distance even as they were shared with a middle-class audience, testing Hoggart's claim that 'the consensus of critical laughter is a great British tradition': Hoggart, 'The future of television', *Guardian*, 13 September 1982.

80 Anon, 'Our Popular Amusements', *Dublin University Magazine* (August 1874), p. 199.

81 See, e.g., John Fiske, 'British cultural studies and television', in Robert C. Allen (ed.), *Channels of Discourse: Television and Contemporary Criticism* (Chapel Hill, 1987), pp. 276–7 (on Madonna). For a critique of such positions, see John Clarke, 'Pessimism versus populism: the problematic politics of popu-lar culture', in Richard Butsch (ed.), *For Fun and Profit: The Transformation of Leisure into Consumption* (Philadelphia, 1990), pp. 28–44.

82 On the limits of comic forms generally, see Umberto Eco, 'The Frames of Comic "Freedom"', in T. A. Sebeok (ed.), *Carnival* (Berlin, 1984), pp. 1–9.

83 Cf. 'good sense': Sue Golding, *Gramsci's Democratic Theory* (London, 1992), pp. 110, 180–1 n. 78.

84 See Iain McCalman, *Radical Underworld: Prophets, Revolutionaries and Pornogra-phers in London, 1795–1840* (Cambridge, 1988), pp. 162–77; Anna Clark, 'Queen Caroline and the sexual politics of popular culture', *Representations*, no. 31 (1990), pp. 47–68; Christopher A. Kent, 'Victorian self-making, or self-unmaking? The Tichborne claimant Revisited', *Victorian Review*, 17, no. 1 (1991), pp. 18–34; Rohan McWilliam, 'Radicalism and popular culture: the Tichborne Case and the politics of "fair play"', in E. Biagini and A. Reid (eds), *Currents of Radicalism* (Cambridge, 1991), pp. 44–64.

85 Hoggart, *Uses of Literacy*, ch. 9; and on press 'ventriloquilism', Hall, 'Decon-structing "the popular"', p. 232. In keeping with his more wholesome values, Hoggart is informing but judgmental on the latter-day knowingness he observes flourishing – festering? – amid 'the doggy communion of the bars': Hoggart, *Uses of Literacy*, pp. 235–6. This does, however, suggest something of its specifically male properties. The ultimate pathology of knowingness is wincingly caught in the Monty Python sketch, 'Nudge, Nudge, Wink, Wink': Graham Chapman *et al.*, *Monty Python's Flying Circus: Just the Words*, 2 vols. (London, 1990), i, pp. 40–1.

86 See Richard Ohmann, 'History and literary history: the case of mass culture' in James Naremore and Patrick Brantlinger (eds), *Modernity and Mass Culture* (Bloomington, 1991), pp. 24–41.

87 One such strand that has received passing historical attention is 'camp', the argot of the homosexual subculture. Derived from parlary, the theatre and showbiz slang (see n. 51 above), camp has obvious affinities with knowingness, and its similarly ambiguous inflections heavily colour more recent comic wit. See Jeffery Weeks, *Sex, Politics and Society: The Regulation of Sexuality since 1800* (London, 1981), p. 111; Susan Sontag, 'Notes on "Camp"', in her *Against Interpretation* (New York, 1966), pp. 275–92. At present, however, pioneering work on popular discourse tends to privilege more formalised modes, notably melodrama.

88 Pierre Bourdieu, *Distinction: A Social Critique of the Judgement of Taste* (London, 1984), pp. 43, 52–4, 89, 499, quotes Proust: 'True distinction does not explain', and notes a 'knowing silence' as a particular bourgeois bluff employed in playing the culture game. Discussion of the present paper by North American audiences has been directed at national rather than class or gender variations, with suggestions that knowingness is absent from some modern cultures.

7 THE VICTORIAN BARMAID AS CULTURAL PROTOTYPE

1 Jeff Hearn and Wendy Parkin, *'Sex' at 'Work': The Power and Paradox of Organisation Sexuality* (Brighton, 1987), p. 3.

2 See R. A. Padgug, 'Sexual matters: on conceptualising sexuality in history', *Radical History Review*, 20 (1974), pp. 3–23; M. Vicinus, 'Sexuality and power: a review of current work in the history of sexuality', *Feminist Studies*, 8 (Spring 1982), pp. 133–56; Jeffrey Weeks, *Sex, Politics and Society: The Regulation of Sexuality since 1800* (London, 1981 and 1989) offers an admirable synthesis, and of more recent work I note P. Gay, *The Bourgeois Experience: Victoria to Freud*, vol. I, *Education of the Senses*; vol. II, *The Tender Passion* (Oxford University Press, New York, 1985, 1986) and Catherine Gallagher and Thomas Laqueur (eds), *The Making of the Modern Body: Sexuality and Society in the Nineteenth Century* (Berkeley, 1987); Michael Mason, *The Making of Victorian Sexuality* (Oxford, 1994).

3 On the complexities of this divide see Janet Wolff, 'The culture of separate spheres: the role of culture in nineteenth century public and private life', in Wolff and John Seed (eds), *The Culture of Capital: Art, Power and the Nineteenth Century Middle Class* (Manchester, 1988), pp. 117–34.

4 For critiques, see Carroll Smith-Rosenberg, 'The female world of love and ritual: relations between women in nineteenth century America', *Signs*, 1 (Autumn 1975), pp. 1–29; Vicinus, 'Sexuality and power', pp. 136–7.

5 Colin Mercer, 'A poverty of desire: pleasure and popular politics', in *Formations of Pleasure* (London, 1983), p. 97.

6 Bernice Martin, *A Sociology of Contemporary Cultural Change* (Oxford, 1981), p. 243; Victor Turner, 'Comment', in B. A. Babcock (ed.), *The Reversible World: Symbolic Inversion in Art and Society*, (Ithaca, N.Y., 1978), pp. 286–7.

7 Cf. M. Cleave, 'The greater British barmaid', in A. McGill (ed.), *The Pub: A Celebration* (London, 1969), pp. 131–48 and Valerie Hey, *Patriarchy and Pub*

Culture (London, 1986), pp. 43–4, who is valuable on contemporary pub sexuality.

8 Peter Clark, *The English Alehouse: A Social History, 1200–1830* (London, 1983), ch. 12; Brian Harrison, *Drink and the Victorians: The Temperance Question in England, 1815–1872* (London, 1975), pp. 45, 66; Mark Girouard, *Victorian Pubs* (New Haven, 1975), pp. 19–32.

9 For photographic illustrations of typical interiors which can also be compared with the graphic texts considered below, see Girouard, *Victorian Pubs*.

10 On women as proprietors and servants, see Clark, *English Alehouse*, pp. 83–6, 206; Leonore Davidoff and Catherine Hall, *Family Fortunes: Men and Women of the English Middle Class, 1780–1850* (London, 1987), pp. 299–301; *Notes and Queries*, 7, 21 March 1914.

11 Girouard, *Victorian Pubs*, p. 26; Clark, *English Alehouse*, pp. 275–6.

12 Observer, *The Gin Shop: History of Inherent Evils, Special Influences, Deceptive Allurements and Demoralising Nature of the Worship of the Ginshop* (London, 1837).

13 *Note and Queries*, 21 February 1914; Barbara Drake, 'The barmaid', *Women's Industrial News*, 65 (April 1914), pp. 221–38; Francis Bond Head, *Stokers and Pokers or the London North Western Railway* (1849) (Newton Abbott, 1968), pp. 86–7.

14 Emily Soldene, *My Theatrical and Musical Recollections* (London, 1897), pp. 41–2; M. Willson Disher, *The Pleasures of London* (London, 1950), pp. 296–7.

15 On Spiers and Pond, see Robert Thorne, 'Places of refreshment in the nineteenth-century city', in A. D. King (ed.), *Buildings and Society* (London, 1980), pp. 240–243. The quote is from Royal Commission on the employment of women, *Parliamentary Papers (PP)* (Victoria, Australia), 2 (1983), 1. 1382. For the Kaiser, see *The Barmaid*, 17 December 1891.

16 For Australia see also Royal Commission on the employment of women; report of Inquiry into intoxicating drink to New South Wales Legislative Council (1887); John Freeman, *Lights and Shadows of Melbourne Life* (London, 1888), pp. 46–53; (C.A. Wright), *Caddie: The Autobiography of a Sydney Barmaid* (London, 1953); Keith Dunstan, *Wowsers* (Australia, 1968), pp. 72–84. For New Zealand, see Jock Phillips, *A Man's Country? The Image of the Pakeha Male: A History* (Auckland, 1988), pp. 65–6. A cross-cultural study of the barmaid would be useful.

17 *Era*, 12 April 1867.

18 Joint Committee on the Employment of Barmaids, *The Barmaid Problem* (London, 1904).

19 Final report of Royal Commission on Liquor Licensing Laws, *PP*, 36 (1898), q. 31807.

20 Larry Carr, *Four Fabulous Faces* (New York, 1970), p. 3.

21 *Oxford English Dictionary*, 1933.

22 For historical distance in legitimising Victorian erotic art, see Gay, *Education of the Senses*, pp. 379–402; for the shop window as barrier and transparency, see Rachel Bowlby, *Just Looking: Consumer Culture in Dreiser, Gissing and Zola* (London, 1985), pp. 332–4.

23 T. J. Clark, 'The Bar at the Folies Bergères', in J. Beauroy, M. Bertrand and E. Gargan (eds), *Popular Culture in France*, (Saratoga, CA., 1997), pp. 233–52 and Clark, *The Painting of Modern Life: Paris in the Art of Manet and his Followers* (London, 1985), pp. 205–58. As noted above, the barmaid was exceptional for France.

24 Originally published by Bogue, the collection was reissued by Dean and Son in 1859.

25 H. A. Jones, *The Masqueraders: A New and Original Modern Play* (London, 1979), first performed 1894. I thank Joel Kaplan for this.

26 This reading is influenced by John Berger, *Ways of Seeing* (London, 1972).

27 'Bar and Saloon London' in George Sims, *Living London*, vol. 2 (London, 1901–3), pp. 286–92. Thanks to David Cheshire for this.

28 Michael A. Smith, 'Social usages of the public drinking house', *British Journal of Sociology*, 34 (September 1983), pp. 367–85.

29 Rosalind Coward, *Female Desire: Women's Sexuality Today*, (London, 1984), p. 76; see also, Hey, *Patriarchy and Pub Culture*, p. 43.

30 Antony Easthope, *What a Man's Gotta Do: The Masculine Myth in Popular Culture* (London, 1986), pp. 75–6.

31 *Barman and Barmaid*, 12 July 1879; Avril Lansdell, *Fashion à la Carte, 1860–1900: A Study of Fashion through Cartes de Visite* (Aylesbury, 1985).

32 The evidence for such considerations is sketchy and diffuse. The most authoritative and systematic source, including interview material, is that of Eliza Orme, 'Report on conditions of work of barmaids', to Royal Commission on Labour, *PP*, 37 (1893–4), pp. 197–229. For Orme, a prominent Liberal, feminist, and middle-class professional woman (who liked a good cigar), see Leslie Howsam, ' "Sound-minded women": Eliza Orme and the study and practice of law in late-Victorian England', *Atlantis*, 15 (Autumn 1989), pp. 44–55. Later pamphlet and periodical treatments drew heavily on Orme while often ignoring her judicious approach. For material on bar*men*, see Booth Mss. B135, London School of Economics; Dr. V. Padmavathy of Miami University, Oxford, Ohio has completed her thesis on the politics of the barmaid question, and Professor David Gutzke of Southwest Missouri State University, is working on a much-needed history of the licensed trade, 1840–1940. I am grateful to both for sharing references and ideas.

33 National British Women's Temperance Association, *Facts about Barmaids* (December 1907); Eva Gore-Booth, Sarah Dickenson and Esther Roper, *Barmaids Political Defence League* (Manchester, n.d.), for the higher counter estimate.

34 Barbara Drake, 'The barmaid', *Women's Industrial News*, April 1914, pp. 222–38; 'The girl workers of London, II. The barmaid', *The Young Woman: An Illustrated Monthly Magazine*, 6 (1897–8), pp. 52–4.

35 *Women and Work*, 19 December 1874; *Barmaid*, 17 December 1891; Orme, 'Report on conditions', pp. 205, 208–210; W. H. Wilkins, 'A plea for the barmaid', *Humanitarian* (June 1896), pp. 423–34; cutting, 5 February 1898 in the Philip Norman collection, London Inns and Taverns, Guildhall Library; Drake, 'The barmaid'.

36 Orme, 'Report on conditions', pp. 200, 204; Norman Collection cutting, 5 February 1898. For Birmingham, see 'Prisoners at the Bar', *Cassell's Saturday Journal*, 4 March 1911.

37 Orme, 'Report on conditions', pp. 198–203.

38 *Ibid.*, pp. 200, 204.

39 Report of Select Committee of House of Commons on the Shop Hours Bill, *PP*, 17 (1892), qq. 5453, 5375–82, 5485.

40 George Gissing, *The Nether World* (London, 1903), p. 23; M. Powell, *My Mother and I* (London, 1972), p. 107.

41 Orme, 'Report on conditions', p. 207.

42 *Entr'acte*, 27 October 1877.

43 Drake, 'The barmaid'.

44 Among many references, see F. Freeman, 'Barmaids', *Weekly Despatch*, 4 February 1883.

45 For an early note of the issue see Select Committee of the House of Lords on Intemperance, *PP*, (1878), qq. 118–19. See also *Toilers in London: An Enquiry Concerning Female Labour in the Metropolis* (London, 1889), pp. 205–14; *Barmaid*, 14 January 1892. Joint Committee, *The Barmaid Problem*, details the later, more concerted campaign and its legislative proposals.

46 On the campaign for prohibition, see *The Times*, 19, 21, 28 December 1903; correspondence with the Home Secretary, Herbert Gladstone, from the Countess Carlisle, President of the British Women's Temperance Association, and from Ramsay MacDonald, British Museum Additional Ms. 46065 f. 208, 1 April 1908 and Add. ms. 45986 f. 102, 8 April 1908 respectively. For the LCC, see also George Foster, *The Spice of Life: Sixty Five Years in the Glamour World* (London, 1939), pp. 172–7. For the defence, see below.

47 *Ally Sloper's Half-Holiday*, 11 May 1889, 24 October 1891.

48 See Gore-Booth *et al.*, *Barmaids Defence League;* Gifford Lewis, *Eva Gore-Booth and Esther Roper: A Biography* (London, 1988), pp. 103–6; *Licensing World*, 16 March 1907, 4 April 1908; *Brewing Trade Review*, 1 July 1908.

49 Orme, 'Report on conditions', pp. 207–8.

50 *Manchester Guardian*, 11 July 1906.

51 Joint Committee, *The Barmaid Problem*.

52 'The prisoner at the bar', *Cassell's Saturday Journal*, 7 January 1911; Carlisle to Gladstone, add. ms.

53 Drake, 'The barmaid'.

54 Norman Collection cutting, 5 February 1898; Orme, 'Report on conditions', p. 197.

55 *Barman and Barmaid*, 12 July 1879; A. B. Deane (ed.), *Licensed Victuallers Official Annual for the Year 1895*, (London, 1895), pp. 159–60.

56 A. Esquiros, *The English at Home* (London, 1861–3), vol. I, p. 272.

57 Representative evidence in *Toilers in London*, pp. 209–10; 'The girl workers of London', p. 54; *Young Girls in Drinking Bars: A Narrative of the Facts*, pamphlet reprinted from Church of England Temperance Chronicle (n.d.); *Licensed World*, 17 September 1904.

58 Leonore Davidoff, 'Class and gender in Victorian England: the diaries of
    Arthur J. Munby and Hannah Cullwick', *Feminist Studies*, 5 (1979), pp.
    89–141; Peter Stallybrass and Allon White, *The Politics and Poetics of Trans-
    gression* (London, 1986), pp. 149–70.

59 *Barman and Barmaid*, 12 July 1879; Frederick Willis, *101 Jubilee Road: A Book of
    London Yesterdays* (London, 1948), p. 57; Willis, *London General* (London, 1953),
    pp. 50–7; Hey, *Patriarchy and Pub Culture*, p. 44.

60 Select Committee on Shop Hours (1892), q. 3276; *Licensed World*, 16 March
    1907. Cf. Davidoff, *Family Fortunes*, p. 301.

61 *Manchester Guardian*, 13 July 1906.

62 Deane, *Licensed Victuallers Annual*, p. 159.

63 *Women and Work*, 19 December 1874. See also *Rosa Grey: The Life of a Barmaid*
    (London, n.d.), Lilly Collection, University of Indiana.

64 Diana Petre, *The Secret Orchard of Roger Ackerley* (London, 1985), pp. 38–9.

65 Report of Royal Commission on Liquor Licensing Laws, *PP*, 36 (1898),
    p. 308.

66 George Moore, *Spring Days: A Realistic Novel* (London, 1888), p. 308.

67 Orme, 'Report on Conditions', p. 209.

68 Tracy Davis, *Actresses as Working Women: Their Social Identity in Victorian Culture*
    (London, 1991). See also Juliet Blair, 'Private parts in public places: the case
    of actresses', in Shirley Ardener (ed.), *Woman and Space: Ground Rules and
    Social Maps* (New York, 1981), pp. 205–28.

69 Later commentators spoke of 'the eclipse of the barmaid' as a consequence
    of wartime when 'sex, as far as it concerned the public house, was abol-
    ished'. See M. Gorham, *The Local* (London, 1939), pp. 5–7; Disher, *Pleasures
    of London*, p. 297, but cf. *The Pub and the People by Mass Observation* (London,
    1987), pp. 56–7.

70 For this 'white blouse revolution' in general, see Jane Lewis, *Women in
    England, 1870–1950* (Brighton, 1984), pp. 145–58. For accounts from parallel
    societies of women's work and culture in this sector, see Michael B. Miller,
    The Bon Marché: Bourgeois Culture and the Department Store, 1869–1920 (Princeton,
    1981); Susan Porter Benson, *Counter Cultures: Saleswomen, Managers, and Cus-
    tomers in American Department Stores, 1890–1940* (Urbana, 1986); Kathy Peiss,
    Cheap Amusements: Working Women and Leisure in Turn of the Century New York
    (Philadelphia, 1986).

71 Jane Traies, 'Jones and the working girl: class marginality in music hall
    song, 1860–1900', in J. S. Bratton, *Music Hall: Performance and Style* (Milton
    Keynes, 1986), pp. 23–48.

72 William Archer, *The Theatrical World of 1896* (London, 1897), pp. 35–8. On
    musical comedy, see chapter 8 below.

73 *Saturday Review*, 30 October 1909.

74 For context and the sense of crisis, see Judith Walkowitz, 'Male vice and
    female virtue; feminism and the politics of prostitution in nineteenth-
    century Britain', *History Workshop Journal*, 13 (Spring 1982), pp. 79–83; Frank
    Mort, 'Purity, feminism and the state: sexuality and moral politics, 1880–

1914', in Mary Langan and Bill Schwarz (eds), *Crisis in the British State 1880–1930* (London, 1985), pp. 209–25; Rubinstein, *Before the Suffragettes: Women's Emancipation in the 1890s* (Brighton, 1986); Susan Kingsley Kent, *Sex and Suffrage in Britain, 1860–1914* (Princeton, 1987).

75 Moore, *Spring Days*, pp. 54–5; *Barman and Barmaid*, 29 May 1880. Problems of identification were noted from the 1860s, see Lynda Nead, *Myths of Sexuality: Representations of Women in Victorian Britain* (Oxford, 1988), pp. 180–1.

76 For a persuasive model of another overlapping cultural nexus, though it lacks people, see Tony Bennett, 'The exhibitionary complex', *New Formations*, 4 (Spring 1988), pp. 73–102, reprinted in his *The Birth of the Museum: History, Theory, Politics* (London, 1995).

77 For America see Peiss, *Cheap Amusements*; Lewis A. Erenberg, *Steppin' Out: New York Night Life and the Transformation of American Culture* (Westport, Conn., 1981). In a study of 'adult entertainment' in New York since 1900 Laurence Senelick identifies a phenomenon similar to parasexuality in what he terms 'spectation', see Private parts in public places', in William R. Taylor (ed.), *Inventing Times Square: Commerce and Culture at the Crossroads of the World*, (New York, 1991), p. 332.

78 Sims, 'London sweethearts', in *Living London*, Sims, II, pp. 15–21.

79 See above, Chapter 6.

80 E.g., the female flight attendant invites attention as a latterday bearer of parasexuality; for details of her occupational training in the US, see the sociological study by Arlie Hochschild, *The Managed Heart: The Commercialisation of Human Feelings*, (Berkeley, 1983).

8 MUSICAL COMEDY AND THE RHETORIC OF THE GIRL, 1892–1914

1 The quotation is from Jonathan Rose, *The Edwardian Temperament, 1895–1919* (Athens, Ohio, 1986), p. 165. There is no trace of musical comedy in the important work of John Stokes, *In the Nineties* (London, 1989), and Karl Beckson, *London in the Eighteen Nineties: A Cultural History* (New York, 1992).

2 Kathleen Tynan, *The Life of Kenneth Tynan* (New York, 1987), p. 227.

3 The musical was nonetheless a late addition to the agenda in film studies, but see Rick Altman (ed.), *Genre: The Musical* (Boston, Mass., 1981); Jane Feuer, *The Hollywood Musical* (1982; Bloomington, 1993); Bruce Babington and Peter W. Evans, *Blue Skies and Silver Linings: Aspects of the Hollywood Musical* (Manchester, 1985).

4 William Archer, *The Theatrical World of 1894* (London, 1895), p. 245. His statistical analysis over four years is reported in *The Theatrical World of 1897* (London, 1898), pp. 351–72.

5 I have, however, defaulted on a prime priority of the historian by treating the period indiscriminately as all of one piece. A fuller account would be more specific. There is, for example, the contention that the Wilde trial effectively marked the end of the nineties. Did this so register in musical comedy, however indirectly? The year 1914 is plainly a social watershed,

but in the history of the form the first major developmental break comes in the mid-1920s with the impact of film and a more pronounced Americanisation.

6 See George Rowell, *The Victorian Theatre, 1792 – 1914* (Cambridge, 1978), pp. 143–4; Hugh Hunt, Kenneth Richards, and John Russell Taylor, *The Revels History of Drama, VII, 1880 to the Present Day* (London, 1978), pp. 65–6; Andrew Lamb, 'Music of the Popular Theatre', in Nicholas Temperley (ed.), *Music in Britain: The Romantic Age, 1800–1914*, (London, 1981), pp. 97–104; Michael R. Booth, *Theatre in the Victorian Age* (Cambridge, 1991), pp. 196–8. For useful popular treatments, see Raymond Mander and Joe Mitchenson, *Musical Comedy: A Story in Pictures* (London, 1969); Ronald Pearsall, *Edwardian Popular Music* (Newton Abbott, 1975). See also Dave Russell, *Popular Music in England, 1840 -1914: A Social History* (Manchester, 1987), pp. 71–2, 193.

7 For a stimulating treatment of the American equivalent with its imported English female stars, see Robert C. Allen, *Horrible Prettiness: Burlesque and American Culture* (Chapel Hill, 1991). See also Peter G. Buckley, 'The Culture of "Leg-Work": The Transformation of Burlesque after the Civil War', in James Gilbert *et al.* (eds), *The Mythmaking Frame of Mind: Social Imagination and American Culture* (Belmont, Calif., 1993), pp. 113–34, and forthcoming work on the Ziegfeld Girl by Linda Mizejewski.

8 Phyllis Hartnoll (ed.), *Oxford Companion to the Theatre* (Oxford, 1983). See also Walter Macqueen-Pope, *The Gaiety: Theatre of Enchantment* (London, 1949); Ursula Bloom, *Curtain Call For the Guv'nor: A Biography of George Edwardes* (London, 1954); Alan Hyman, *The Gaiety Years* (London, 1975).

9 Tracy C. Davis, *Actresses as Working Women: Their Social Identity in Victorian Culture* (London, 1991), pp. 27, 29 and *passim*; James Jupp, *Gaiety Stage Door: Thirty Years Reminiscences of the Theatre* (London, 1923).

10 Arthur Roberts, *Fifty Years of Spoof* (London, 1927), pp. 189–90. Edwardes was represented on stage in the character of Carlton Smythe, impresario, in Sir Arthur Pinero's play about the musical comedy world, *The 'Mind the Paint' Girl* (1912).

11 'A Chat with George Edwardes', *Era*, 12 September 1894; Ada Reeve, *Take It for a Fact: A Record of My Seventy-five Years on the Stage* (London, 1954), pp. 77–84.

12 Doremy Vernon, *Tiller's Girls* (London, 1988); 'Tiller Training Schools', *Era*, 22 August 1903.

13 Musical comedy play scripts can be consulted at the British Library, Lord Chamberlain's Play Collection. The Lord Chamberlain's office was responsible for licensing and censorship.

14 The caption reports on a bill before the New York Legislature to suppress the nuisance of 'Stage Door Callers', noting that at big theatres 'every chorus girl, every stage hand and, indeed, all principals must register their arrival and departure, as employees in shops and factories are required to do', *Sketch*, 13 January 1909.

15 *Sketch*, 28 November 1894. Archer noted 'the close reproduction of the

external phases of everyday life' in musical comedy. By 'external', Archer may have been emphasising the public setting of much musical comedy action, which contrasted with the more private, domesticated realism of contemporary mainstream drama.

16 Compare the drudgery of shop life as exposed by Cicely Hamilton, the feminist activist, in her *Diana of Dobson's* (1908), reprinted in Linda Fitzsimmons and Viv Gardner (eds), *New Woman Plays* (London, 1991).

17 Theatrical agents prowled the West End stores for new recruits to the chorus line, Jupp, *Gaiety Stage Door*, p. 51. For the enhanced visibility of young women service workers and an expanded public zone of licit sexual exploit, see Chapter 7 above. The tensions between pleasure and danger implicit in this theme are developed in Judith Walkowitz, *City of Dreadful Delight: Narratives of Sexual Danger in Late-Victorian London* (Chicago, 1992), pp. 43–52.

18 On this theme and promotion of haute couture in particular, see Joel Kaplan and Sheila Stowell, *Theatre and Fashion: Oscar Wilde to the Suffragettes* (Cambridge, 1994). For other relevant scholarship, see Erika Rappaport, 'The West End and Women's Pleasure: Gender and Commercial Culture in London, 1860–1914' (Ph.D. dissertation, Rutgers, 1993), chapter 6, 'Acts of consumption: musical comedy and the desire of exchange'. I am grateful to the author for the opportunity to read this chapter ahead of publication.

19 Madeleine Bingham, *Earls and Girls: Dramas in High Society* (London, 1980).

20 *Saturday Review*, 30 October 1909.

21 *Sketch*, 22 April 1896.

22 *Stage*, 20 November 1902. For the new resonance of the seaside girl as male fetish and consumer icon, see Thomas Richards, *The Commodity Culture of Victorian England: Advertising and Spectacle* (London, 1991), chapter 5.

23 I owe this point to Joel Kaplan.

24 For further definition, and its deployment elsewhere, see chapter 7 above.

25 E. M. Forster, *Howard's End* (1910; Harmondsworth, 1989), p. 151.

26 Davis, *Actresses as Working Women*, pp. 78–86.

27 Edwardes of the Gaiety was also Edwardes of the Empire music hall, who was at the same time defending himself against charges that he encouraged high-class prostitution in the Empire's promenade. As part of his counter-attack, women with loose unbuttoned hair were being ostentatiously denied entrance to the Empire as likely prostitutes; *Evening News*, 13 October 1894. (The Empire scandal is returned to, yet again, in Beckson, *London in the 1890s*, pp. 118–28, with no acknowledgment of Edwardes's other role.) These associations were made plainer when the 'artless Flo' of the song loses her virginity to, or rather proves the seducer of 'a friend of Mrs. Chant', the leading reform critic of Edwardes. See also *The Theatrical World of 1894*, pp. 316–20, and, for Hicks, *Theatre in the Victorian Age*, p. 129. Victor Emeljanow informs me that Hicks was notorious in the business as a sexual predator.

28 *The Theatrical World of 1894*, pp. 59–61. For knowingness see chapter 6 above. There are significant continuities here between the early stage form and the later film musical, which combines a modernist reflexivity with a

cultural conservatism; see Feuer, 'The self-reflective musical and the myth of entertainment', in *Genre: The Musical*, pp. 159–74.

29 Davis, *Actresses as Working Women*, pp. 137–46.

30 Holbrook Jackson, *The Eighteen Nineties* (London, 1913; New York, 1966), p. 31.

31 Country youths had their own refrain: 'Lottie Collins has no drawers/Will you kindly lend her yours.' See Flora Thompson, *Lark Rise to Candleford* (London, 1973), p. 502.

32 *Era*, 8 October 1892.

33 Jose Collins, *The Maid of the Mountains: Her Story* (London, 1932), pp. 16–17.

34 See chapter 4 above.

35 See Joel Kaplan, 'Edwardian Pinero', *Nineteenth Century Theatre*, 17 (1989), pp. 20–41.

36 The nineties was the take-off point in the commercial production and sale of rubber contraceptives: see Angus McLaren, *Birth Control in Nineteenth Century England* (London, 1978), ch. 12.

37 Kaplan, 'Edwardian Pinero', p. 44. Edwardes's shiftiness is apparent in his evidence to the Select Committee on Stage Plays (Censorship), *Parliamentary Papers*, 1909 (303), viii, pp. 240–8.

38 On Hardy's 'sensuous suavity', see M. H. Spielmann, 'Posters and poster-designing in England', *Scribner's Magazine* (July 1895), pp. 42–3. I am grateful to Bridget Elliott for this and other material on Hardy.

39 Robert Roberts, *The Classic Slum* (London, 1973), p. 168. See also Fred Willis, *101 Jubilee Road* (London, 1948), and C. Stella Davies, *North Country Bred* (London, 1963), pp. 48–9.

40 Archer, 'The case for national theatres', *Monthly Review* (July 1902), pp. 140–55.

41 *Victorian Theatre*, p. 144. Edwardes was anxious to foster the same impression before the 1909 Select Committee when he spoke proprietorially and protectively of the 'great middle classes of the theatre', receiving some incidental confirmation from a committee member who recalled going to see *The Shop Girl* in 1896 as an Eton schoolboy.

42 William Archer, *The Theatrical World of 1896* (London, 1897), pp. 298–301.

43 *Gaiety Stage Door*, p. 21; D. N. Pigache, *Cafe Royal Days* (London, 1934), pp. 41–2.

44 *Gaiety Stage Door*, pp. 70–1; 'Chat with Ada Reeve', *Sketch*, 8 August 1894. See also Margaret Penn, *Manchester Fourteen Miles* (London, 1982), p. 213.

45 Significant here is the great appeal of the music. See Russell, *Popular Music*, pp. 72, 192, on the popularity of musical comedy selections with the brass bands of the industrial districts and their mostly lower-class audiences. Presumably the gramophone also gave the music increased currency among the middle class.

46 As an Oxford undergraduate he had been infatuated with the 15–year-old music hall star, Cissie Loftus; see David Cecil, *Max: A Biography* (London, 1964), pp. 80–8.

47 *The Theatrical World of 1896*, pp. 299–300. For an analysis of the meaning of musical comedy's consumerism for women and the question of female spectatorship, see Rappaport, 'The West End and Women's Pleasure'.

48 Meta Zimmeck, 'Jobs for the girls: the expansion of clerical work for women', in Angela John (ed.), *Unequal Opportunity: Women's Work and Employment in England, 1800–1918* (Oxford, 1986), pp. 165, 170. I owe this reference and other suggestions on this point to Arlene Young.

49 Kathy Peiss, *Cheap Amusements: Working Women and Leisure in Turn of the Century New York* (Philadelphia, 1986), pp. 107–14, 126. Allen, *Horrible Prettiness*, pp. 201–4, dates the popular characterisation of the working-class chorus girl as 'gold digger' – a strong motif in the later American musical – from this period. Though it has little to say on musical comedy, Taylor, (ed.), *Inventing Times Square* is richly suggestive on the turn of the century promotion of New York's equivalent of the West End, and the construction of new styles of pleasure, sexuality, and consumerism that exploited the higher visibility of women and an intensive nexus of theatres, night clubs, and restaurants.

50 Sally Alexander, 'Becoming a woman in London in the 1920s and 1930s', in David Feldman and Gareth Stedman Jones (eds), *Metropolis London: Histories and Representations since 1800* (London, 1989), pp. 245–71.

9 BREAKING THE SOUND BARRIER

1 A. Corbin, *The Foul and the Fragrant: Odour and Social Imagination* (London, 1994).

2 J. Attali, *Noise: The Political Economy of Music* (Manchester, 1985), p. 3.

3 R. Murray Schafer, *The Tuning of the World* (New York, 1977); D. Howes (ed.), *The Varieties of Sensory Experience: A Sourcebook in the Anthropology of the Senses* (Toronto, 1991).

4 M. Jay, *Downcast Eyes: The Denigration of Vision in Twentieth-Century French Thought* (Berkeley, 1993).

5 S. Levarie, 'Noise', *Critical Inquiry*, vol. 1, no. 4, 1977, pp. 21–31.

6 J. Fiske, *Introduction to Communication Studies* (London, 1982).

7 M. Bakhtin, *Rabelais and his World* (Bloomington, 1984), Chapter 1.

8 K. Thomas, 'The place of laughter in Tudor and Stuart England', *Times Literary Supplement*, 21 January 1977.

9 T. Staveacre, *Slapstick* (London, 1987), pp. 67–78.

10 E. Ladurie, *Carnival in Romans* (New York, 1980), p. 321.

11 E. Goffman, *Behaviour in Public Places* (New York, 1963), pp. 213–14.

12 E. Partridge, *A Dictionary of Historical Slang* (Harmondsworth, 1972).

13 J. Nohain and F. Carodoc, *Le Pétomane* (London, 1967).

14 J. B. Priestley, *Margin Released: A Writer's Reminiscences* (London, 1962), p. 100.

15 E. P. Thompson, *Customs in Common: Studies in Traditional Popular Culture* (New York, 1991), p. 467.

16 R. Darnton, *The Great Cat Massacre and Other Episodes in French Cultural History* (New York, 1985).

17 T. Wright, *Some Habits and Customs of the Working Classes* (1867; New York, 1967).

18 Schafer, *Tuning of the World*.

19 D. Macey, *The Lives of Michel Foucault* (London, 1993), p. 95.

20 C. Classen, *Worlds of Sense: Exploring the Senses in History and Across Cultures* (London, 1993).

21 F. Gonzalez-Crussi, *The Five Senses* (San Diego, 1989), pp. 28–9.

22 M. Dachy, *The Da-Da Movement* (New York, 1990); J. A. Cuddon, *The Penguin Dictionary of Literary Terms* (Harmondsworth, 1992), pp. 215–16.

23 S. Hall, 'Cultural Studies and its theoretical legacies', in L. Grossberg *et al.* (eds), *Cultural Studies* (London, 1992), p. 278.

24 M. Jay, *Downcast Eyes: The Denigration of Vision in Twentieth-Century Thought* (Berkeley, 1993).

25 A. Synott, 'Puzzling experiences from Plato to Marx', in D. Howes (ed.), *Varieties of Sensory Experience* (Toronto, 1991).

26 N. Elias, *The Civilising Process 1: The History of Manners* (Oxford, 1978), p. 130.

27 P. Stallybrass, 'Reading the body and the Jacobean theater of consumption', *Renaissance Drama*, no. 18, pp. 121–48.

28 W. Fitzgerald, 'The questionability of music', *Representations*, no. 46 (1994), pp. 121–47.

29 M. Girouard, *Life in the English Country House* (New Haven, CT, 1978), pp. 204–5, 233.

30 G. Duby, *Private Life in Medieval Europe* (Cambridge, 1987), p. 539.

31 B. I. Coleman, *The Idea of the City in Nineteenth-Century Britain* (London, 1973), pp. 33–5; Raymond Williams, *The Country and the City* (London, 1974), pp. 185, 196.

32 A. Brown-May, 'A blast from the past: towards a social heritage of the public space', *Historic Environment*, vol. 1, no. 11, pp. 19–23.

33 F. M. L. Thompson, 'Victorian England, the horse drawn society', An Inaugural Lecture (Bedford College, London, 1970).

34 W. Sharpe and L. Wallock (eds), *Visions of the Modern City* (Baltimore, 1987), p. 8.

35 R. Musil, *The Man Without Qualities* (1930; London, 1979), p. 3.

36 C. Prendergast, *Paris and the Nineteenth-Century* (Oxford, 1992), pp. 63–126.

37 S. Kern, *The Culture of Time and Space 1800–1918* (Cambridge, MA, 1983), p. 124; J. Godbolt, *A History of Jazz in Britain* (London, 1984), pp. 94–5.

38 C. Dickens, 'Noises', *All the Year Round*, no. 7, 16 December 1871.

39 C. Masterman (ed.), *The Heart of Empire: Problems of Modern City Life in England* (London, 1901), p. 137.

40 G. Gissing, *The Nether World* (1889; Cranbury, NJ, 1974), pp. 103–4.

41 A. Rifkin and A. Thomas (eds), *Voices of the People: The Social of 'la sociale' at the End of the Second Empire* (London, 1988).

42 G. Simmel, 'The metropolis and mental life', in R. Sennett (ed.), *Classic*

Essays on the Culture of Cities (1903; New York, 1969), p. 327.

43 J. Joyce, *Ulysses* (1922; Harmondsworth, 1972), p. 45.

44 W. Benjamin, 'The work of art in the age of mechanical reproduction', in J. Curran *et al.* (eds), *Mass Communications and Society* (London, 1992), pp. 141–8.

45 D. Olsen, *The City as Work of Art: London, Paris, Vienna* (New Haven, 1986), p. 189.

46 A. Helps, *Social Pressures* (London, 1875), pp. 45–6.

47 P. Bailey, *Leisure and Class in Victorian England* (London, 1987), pp. 114, 179.

48 C. Masterman, *The Condition of England* (London, 1909), p. 72.

49 C. Babbage, *Passages from the Life of a Philosopher* (London, 1864), chapter 26; J. Winter, *London's Teeming Streets* (London, 1993), pp. 70–9.

50 J. S. Mill, 'Civilisation', *London and Westminster Review*, April 1836, pp. 160–205.

51 E. Ross, *Love and Toil: Motherhood in Outcast London 1870–1918* (New York, 1993), p. 29.

52 D. Harker, 'The Making of the Tyneside Concert Hall', *Popular Music*, 1 (1), 1981.

53 D. Reid, 'Popular Theatre in Victorian Birmingham', in D. Bradby *et al.* (eds.), *Performance and Politics in Popular Drama* (Cambridge, 1980), pp. 74–76.

54 B. Buford, *Among the Thugs: The Experience and Seduction of Crowd Violence* (New York, 1992).

55 Bailey, 'Custom, Capital and Culture in the Victorian Music Hall', in R. Storch (ed.), *Popular Culture and Custom in Nineteenth Century England* (London, 1982).

56 R. Butsch, 'Bowery Boys and Matinee Ladies: Re-gendering American Theater Audiences', *American Quarterly*, 46 (3), 1994.

57 See chapter 5 above.

58 D. Ackerman, *A Natural History of the Senses* (New York, 1990).

59 J. F. Kasson, *Rudeness and Civility: Manners in Nineteenth Century America* (New York, 1990).

60 Ross, *Love and Toil*, pp. 14, 15.

61 J. Walkowitz, *Prostitution and Victorian Society* (Cambridge, 1980).

62 R. H. Gretton, *Modern History of the English People* (London, 1913).

63 A. Huyssen, 'Mass Culture as Woman: Modernism's Other', in T. Modleski (ed.), *Studies in Entertainment* (Bloomington, Ind., 1986).

64 J. Breckendridge, 'Sound Breeds Fury as Noise Pollution Grows', *Globe and Mail* (Toronto), 19 November 1994.

65 D. Hebdige, *Subculture: The Meaning of Style* (London, 1979).

66 Hall, 'Cultural Studies'.

67 J. Obelkevich, 'In Search of the Listener', *Journal of the Royal Musical Association*, 114, 1 (1989).

68 Schafer, *Tuning of the World*.

Index